ALEXANDER THE GREAT

'I should be glad, Onesicritus, to come back to life for a little while after my death to discover how men read these present events then. If now they praise and welcome them do not be surprised; they think, every one of them, that this is a fine bait to catch my goodwill.'

ALEXANDER THE GREAT, quoted by
Lucian in *How to Write History*

right: The reverse of a gold stater of Alexander, showing Nike (Victory), and the inscription 'Alexander'.

frontispiece: Alexander in the so-called 'Issus mosaic', which perhaps conflates details from the Granicus and Gaugamela as well. It was copied *c.* 100 BC for the owner of the House of the Faun in Pompeii from a famous painting by Philoxenus of Eretria, originally commissioned by Antipater's son Cassander, who in 317/16 became King of Macedon, some six years after Alexander's death.

Peter Green

ALEXANDER THE GREAT

BOOK CLUB ASSOCIATES

LONDON

—ποῦ εἶναι ὁ Μεγαλέξανδρος;

—ὁ Μεγαλέξανδρος ζεῖ καὶ βασιλεύει

For George and Ismene Phylactopoulos

This edition published 1973 by
Book Club Associates
By arrangement with Weidenfeld and Nicolson

Designed by Behram Kapadia

Photoset by BAS Printers Limited, Wallop, Hampshire, England
Printed by C. Tinling & Co. Ltd, Prescot and London

Contents

1 Philip of Macedon   19

Chaos and intrigue in early Macedonia – the Argead dynasty – Philip's predecessors – the Greek city states – Philip's military training – the Macedonian army – early victories – Olympias and the birth of Alexander – from primitive kingdom to most powerful state – a career of expansion and conquest

2 The Gardens of Midas   32

Enfant terrible – early lessons – father and son – the siege of Olynthus – the *Address to Philip* – the common foe – Aristotle and the 'Precinct of the Nymphs' – trouble with the Greek states – the anti-Macedonian league – Regent of Macedonia

3 From a view to a death   47

Alexander's first campaign – divide and rule – Philip invades central Greece – Demosthenes, champion of Athenian liberty – Athens and Thebes unite – the battle of Chaeronea – Alexander and Olympias in exile – the Hellenic League – war against Persia – Alexander recalled – the murder of Philip

4 The keys of the kingdom   71

King of Macedonia – revolt amongst the Greek city states – *Hegemon* of the League – whirlwind conquest of the Greeks – old-guard allegiances – the Danube campaign – victory over the Thracians and Illyrians – more revolts – the siege of Thebes

List of maps and battle plans

Preface and Acknowledgments

In a necessarily brief text much has had to be omitted, much more cut down. Above all, there is no room for documentation, especially of the many controversial episodes with which Alexander's life abounds; nor for an exhaustive bibliography. However, I have, I hope, taken account of all important work published on Alexander and his times within recent years, and I am very conscious of what I owe to scholars working in the same field. Since this book's format precludes footnotes, it has been impossible to acknowledge, in detail, the help of others. I hope they will accept this general expression of my indebtedness.

Two names, however, I cannot overlook. Dr J.R.Hamilton, with great generosity, allowed me to consult the proofs of his then unpublished *Commentary* on Plutarch's Life of Alexander, from which I benefited more than I can say; while Professor Ernst Badian not only sent me offprints of his articles, but also took time he could ill spare to correspond with me, at length and in detail, on various aspects of Alexander's career. To both these scholars I would like to express my sincere thanks for their more than generous help; it goes without saying that they are not to be held responsible for any of the views expressed here. Lastly, I must thank Miss Susan Phillpott of Weidenfeld and Nicolson for her devoted and meticulous editorial nursing of what proved a somewhat recalcitrant literary baby, and Mrs Jo Labanyi and Miss Veronica Franklyn for invaluable help with the illustrations.

The translation of Arrian used here is that by the late Aubrey de Selincourt (Penguin Classics); Diodorus is quoted in the Loeb version by Professor C. Bradford Welles (published by Heinemann); Plutarch's Life of Alexander is, again, the Loeb version, by Bernadotte Perrin (Heinemann). The quotation from Euripides' *Andromache* on p. 199 is translated by Mr John Frederick Nims, in the *Complete Greek Tragedies* series published by the University of Chicago Press.

P.G.

Sources of Illustrations

Alinari, 33, 37b, 45, 71, 161, 174; Archaeological Museum, Florence, 35, 44; Ashmolean Museum, Oxford, 249, 251; Bibliothèque Nationale, 260a; British Museum, 3, 23, 25, 26, 29, 37a, 41, 49, 54, 65a, 66, 69, 72, 79, 80, 86, 92a (Hamilton Collection), 99, 102, 109, 111, 138, 141, 152, 158, 159, 162, 169, 217, 218, 219a, 235, 246, 247, 255, 258; Camera Press, 119, 209; Dimitri, Athens, 52, 61, 83, 134, 150b; Egyptian State Tourist Organisation, 150a; Fosco Maraini, 206; Frances Mortimer, 207; Freer Gallery of Art, Washington, 236; Freya Stark, 103a, 117; German Archaeological Institute, Athens, 92b; Giraudon, 42, 43, 168, 260a; Greek Ministry, Athens, 63, 239; Halûk Köknar, 189; Hermitage, 190, 200a, 200b; Hirmer Photo Archives, 67, 88, 100, 135, 219b, 233a; Ian Graham, 158, 178, 179; Imperial Iranian Embassy Press and Information Centre, 175; Iraq Ministry of Guidance, 257; Istanbul Museum, 67, 189, 224, 245, 248, 254, 259a, 259b; J. Allan Cash, 112–13; John Freeman Ltd., 3, 41, 54, 69, 80, 86, 99, 102, 141, 152, 159, 217, 218, 246, 247; Josephine Powell, 192, 194b, 203, 226-7; Kabul Museum, 204a; Kunsthistorisches Museum, Vienna, 70; Louvre, 168, 174; Loyola University of Chicago, 34a, b, 143; Mansell Collection, 19, 33, 37b, 45, 55, 71, 161, 174, 239, 243; Metropolitan Museum of Art, New York, 85 (Rogers Fund), 90-1; Middle East Archives, 106-7, 120a, 146-7, 210-11; Museo Barracco, Rome, 243; Musée Condé de Chantilly, 42, 43; Museum of Fine Arts, Boston, 27; National Museum, Beirut, 30b; National Museum, Berlin, 77; National Museum, Naples, 4, 55, 125, 126-7, 128; National Museum, Taranto, 87; National Tourist Organisation of Greece, 20a, 39; Norman Davis, 75; Novosti Press Agency, 197; Ny Carlsberg Glyptothek, 46, 47, 233b; Oriental Institute, University of Chicago, 183, 240-1; Paul Popper, 31, 53, 58-9, 60, 163, 164, 172, 176, 194a, 204b, 205, 256; Peshawar Museum, 226-7; Peter Clayton, 18, 221, 229, 238, 260b; Picturepoint, 57, 105, 108; Radio Times Hulton Picture Library, 151; Roger Wood, 145, 180, 212; Roloff Beny, 17; Royal Geographical Society, 21a, 65b; Rugby School, 249; Scala, 4, 44, 125, 126-7, 128; Seattle Art Museum, 20b, 24, 30a, 75, 130, 184, 223, 225, 232, 253, 260c; Sonia Halliday, 120b, 157, 245, 248; Turkish Tourist Board, 103b; U.A.R. Tourist and Information Centre, 148, 149; University of Mississippi, 32; Victoria and Albert Museum, 199.

Table of Dates

The central pebble-mosaic from the dining room of the Villa of Good Fortune, Olynthus (fourth century BC), showing Dionysus' chariot drawn by panthers, and accompanied by Hermes, Nike (Victory) and other figures.

13

339	September: Philip occupies Elatea. Isocrates' *Panathenaicus*.
338	? 2 August: Battle of Chaeronea. Alexander among ambassadors to Athens. Philip marries Attalus' niece Cleopatra. Olympias and Alexander in exile.
337	Spring: Hellenic League convened at Corinth. Recall of Alexander to Pella. Autumn: League at Corinth ratifies crusade against Persia.
336	Spring: Parmenio and Attalus sent to Asia Minor for preliminary military operations. June: accession of Darius III Codomannus. Cleopatra bears Philip a son. Wedding of Alexander of Epirus to Olympias' daughter. Murder of Philip. Alexander accedes to the throne of Macedonia. Late summer: Alexander calls meeting of Hellenic League at Corinth, confirmed as Captain-General of anti-Persian crusade.
335	Early spring: Alexander goes north to deal with Thrace and Illyria. Revolt of Thebes.
334	Alexander and the attacking force cross into Asia Minor (March-April). May: Battle of the Granicus. General reorganisation of Greek cities in Asia Minor. Siege and capture of Miletus. Autumn: reduction of Halicarnassus.
334/3	Alexander advances through Lycia and Pamphylia.
333	Alexander's column moves north to Celaenae and Gordium. Death of Memnon (early spring). Mustering of Persian forces in Babylon. Episode of the Gordian Knot. Alexander marches to Ancyra and thence south to Cilician Gates. Darius moves westward from Babylon. September: Alexander reaches Tarsus: his illness there.
333	Darius crosses the Euphrates. ? Sept.-Oct.: Battle of Issus. Alexander advances southward through Phoenicia. Marathus: first peace-offer by Darius.
332	? January: submission of Byblos and Sidon. Siege of Tyre begun. ? June: second peace-offer by Darius refused. July 29: fall of Tyre. Sept.-Oct.: Gaza captured. 14 November (?): Alexander crowned as Pharaoh at Memphis.

The head of Alexander, in the 'Alexander sarcophagus'.

331	Early spring: visit to the Oracle of Ammon at Siwah.
	? 7-8 April: foundation of Alexandria.
	Alexander returns to Tyre.
	July-August: Alexander reaches Thapsacus on Euphrates; Darius moves his main forces from Babylon.
	18 September: Alexander crosses the Tigris.
	Darius' final peace-offer rejected.
	30 Sept. or 1 Oct.: Battle of Gaugamela.
	Macedonians advance from Arbela on Babylon, which falls in mid-October.
	Revolt of Agis defeated at Megalopolis.
	Early December: Alexander occupies Susa unopposed.
331/0	Alexander forces Susian Gates.
330	? January: Alexander reaches and sacks Persepolis.
	? May: burning of temples etc. in Persepolis.
	Early June: Alexander sets out for Ecbatana.
	Darius retreats towards Bactria.
	Greek allies dismissed at Ecbatana; Parmenio left behind there, with Harpalus as Treasurer.
	Pursuit of Darius renewed, via Caspian Gates.
	July (after 15th): Darius found murdered near Hecatompylus.
	Bessus establishes himself as 'Great King' in Bactria.
	March for Hyrcania begins (July-August).
	Late August: march to Drangiana (Lake Seistan).
	The 'conspiracy of Philotas'.
	March through Arachosia to Parapamisidae.
329	March-April: Alexander crosses Hindu Kush by Khawak Pass.
	April-May: Alexander advancing to Bactria; Bessus retreats across the Oxus.
	June: Alexander reaches and crosses the Oxus; veterans and Thessalian volunteers dismissed.
	Surrender of Bessus.
	Alexander advances to Maracanda (Samarkand).
	Revolt of Spitamenes, annihilation of Macedonian detachment.
329/8	Alexander takes up winter quarters at Zariaspa.
	Execution of Bessus.
328	Campaign against Spitamenes.
	Autumn: murder of Cleitus the Black.
328/7	Defeat and death of Spitamenes.
327	Spring: capture of the Soghdian Rock.
	Alexander's marriage to Roxane.
	Recruitment of 30,000 Persian 'Successors'.
	The 'Pages' Conspiracy' and Callisthenes' end.
	Early summer: Alexander recrosses Hindu Kush by Kushan Pass: the invasion of India begins.

Darius, with attendants, on the southern doorway of the Tripylon at Persepolis.

327/6	Alexander reaches Nysa (Jelalabad); the 'Dionysus episode'. Capture of Aornos (Pir-Sar).
326	Advance to Taxila. Battle of the Hydaspes (Jhelum) against the rajah Porus. Death of Bucephalas. ? July: Mutiny at the Hyphasis (Beas). Return to the Jhelum: reinforcements from Greece. Early November: fleet and army move down-river.
326/5	Campaign against Brahmin cities: Alexander seriously wounded
325	Revolt in Bactria: 3000 mercenaries loose in Asia. Alexander reaches Patala, builds harbour and dockyards. ? September: Alexander's march through Gedrosian Desert. Defection of Harpalus from Asia Minor to Greece. The satrapal purge begins (December). Nearchus and the fleet reach Harmozia, link up with Alexander at Salmous (Gulashkird). Arrival of Craterus from Drangiana.
324	January: Nearchus and fleet sent on to Susa. The episode of Cyrus' tomb. Alexander returns to Persepolis. Move to Susa, long halt there (February-March). Spring: arrival of 30,000 trained Persian 'Successors'. The Susa mass-marriages. March: the Exiles' Decree and the Deification Decree. Craterus appointed to succeed Antipater as Regent, and convoy troops home. Alexander moves from Susa to Ecbatana. Death of Hephaestion.
323	Assassination of Harpalus in Crete. Alexander's campaign against the Cossaeans and return to Babylon (spring). Alexander explores Pallacopas Canal; his boat-trip through the marshes. Arrival of Antipater's son Cassander to negotiate with Alexander. 29/30 May: Alexander falls ill after a party, and dies on 10/11th June.

right: Lion at bay: detail
from a late fourth-century
mosaic found at Pella, the
capital of Macedonia.

1 Philip of Macedon

Alexander as he appears in a medallion carved on the façade of the Charterhouse in Pavia.

left: Olympias, on a gold medallion found at Aboukir in Egypt. This portrait is stylistically parallel to other late Roman-Macedonian coin-representations which show the Queen seated on a throne, feeding a tame snake.

The story of Alexander the Great is inextricably bound up with that of his father, King Philip II, and with his country, Macedonia. Unless we understand this – and them – Alexander's career must remain for us no more than the progress of a comet, flaring in unparalleled majesty across the sky: a marvel, but incomprehensible. Genius Alexander had, and in full measure; but even genius remains to a surprising extent the product of its environment. What Alexander was, Philip and Macedonia in great part made him, and it is with them that we must begin.

On an early September day in the year 356 BC a courier rode out of Pella, Macedonia's new royal capital, bearing dispatches for the King. He travelled south-east, making for Potidaea, a city of the Chalcidic peninsula, where the Macedonian army now lay; and he did not waste any time on his journey. Philip, son of Amyntas, lately Regent and now King by right of acclamation, was not a man who took kindly to delay or inefficiency in his servants.

If the courier had not known Philip by sight, he might have been hard put to it to pick him out from among his fellow-nobles and staff officers. The King wore the same purple cloak and broad-brimmed hat that formed the regular attire of a Macedonian aristocrat.

He was now twenty-seven years old: a strong, sensual, heavily bearded man, much addicted to drink, women and (when the fancy took him) boys. Normally of a jovial disposition, he had even more reason for cheerfulness after studying the dispatches which the courier now handed over. His most reliable general, Parmenio, had won a decisive victory over a combined force of Illyrians and Paeonians – powerful tribes on the Macedonian marches, whose territory was roughly equivalent to that of modern Albania and Serbia. In the Olympic Games, which had just ended, his entry for the horse-race had carried off first prize. Best of all, on about 20 July, his wife Myrtale – better known to us by her adopted name of Olympias – had given birth to a son: his name was Alexander.

After he had finished reading, Philip is said to have begged Fortune to do him some small disservice, to offset such overwhelming favours. What was it, we well may ask, that gave these three particular events such extreme, almost symbolic significance for him? To understand the King's reaction

left: The lion-hunt motif, absent from Greek art for some three centuries, seems to have been brought into fashion again by Alexander. It has been suggested that the two hunters in this late fourth-century BC pebble mosaic from Pella represent Alexander and his contemporary, Craterus.

it is necessary to look back for a moment, at the chequered history and archaic customs of Macedonia prior to his accession.

First – and perhaps most important of all – the country was divided, both geographically and ethnically, into two quite distinct regions: lowlands and highlands. The case of Scotland provides close and illuminating parallels. Lower Macedonia comprised the flat, fertile plain round the Thermaic Gulf. This plain is watered by two great rivers, the Axius (Vardar) and the Haliacmon (Vistritza), and ringed by hills on all sides except towards the east, where the first natural frontier is provided by a third river, the Strymon (Struma).

This silver tetradrachm of Philip II shows a bearded Zeus, perhaps modelled on Philip himself.

Lower Macedonia was the old central kingdom, founded by semi-legendary cattle-barons who knew good pasturage when they saw it, and ruled over by the royal dynasty of the Argeads, to which Philip himself belonged. Their capital – until Philip transferred it to Pella, down in the marshy plain – was Aegae (Edessa), a commanding and picturesque fortress town on the north-west frontier: the district was so rich in orchards and vineyards that people called it the 'Gardens of Midas'.

Upper Macedonia and Paeonia formed a single geographical unit, backed – except, again, towards the Strymon – by mountain ranges. Passes across these mountains are few, the best-known being the Vale of Tempe and that followed by the Via Egnatia. Thus Macedonia as a whole tended to remain in isolation from the rest of Greece: like Sparta, it preserved institutions (such as kingship and baronial feudalism) which had lapsed elsewhere.

Upper Macedonia, lying mostly to the west and south-west of the central plain, was divided into three originally autonomous kingdoms: Elimiotis in the south, Orestis and Lyncestis in the west and north-west. Originally, the three cantons had been independent kingdoms, each with its own ambitious and well-connected royal house. The Molossian House of Epirus, on the borders of Orestis and Elimiotis, claimed descent from Achilles through his grandson Pyrrhus – a fact destined to have considerable influence on Alexander, whose mother Olympias was of Molossian stock.

The Argeads themselves headed their pedigree with Heracles, and could thus (since Heracles was the son of Zeus) style themselves 'Zeus-born' like

The River Strymon (Struma) formed a natural eastern frontier for Macedonia. This view was taken from Amphipolis, the vital port and communication-centre colonised by Athens in 437, and captured by Philip of Macedon in 357.

any Mycenaean dynast: both Zeus and Heracles appear regularly on Philip's coinage. At least as early as the fifth century BC the Argeads were claiming 'traditional' suzerainty over Upper Macedonia. The overlordship much resembled that of Agamemnon over his fellow kings: each canton gave just as much allegiance to the Argead throne as any individual monarch could exact. The out-kingdoms were quite liable to connive at Illyrian or Paeonian invasions, if not to give them active backing. Add to this the endless intrigue – often ending in bloody murder and usurpation – which took place at the Argead court, and we begin to see why Macedonia before Philip's time played so insignificant a part in Greek history.

The attitude of the city-state Greeks to this sub-Homeric enclave was one of genial and sophisticated contempt. They regarded Macedonians in general as semi-savages, uncouth of speech and dialect, retrograde in their political institutions, negligible as fighters, and habitual oath-breakers, who dressed in bear pelts and were much given to deep and swinish potations, tempered with regular bouts of assassination and incest.

Mount Olympus, on the borders of Macedonia and Thessaly, was the traditional home of the Greek gods, and a formidable obstacle for those attempting to invade Greece from the northeast. Their only direct route lay between Olympus and Ossa, through the Vale of Tempe.

Nor was Macedonia's record in the Persian and Peloponnesian Wars liable to improve her standing with patriotic city-state Greeks. Alexander I had collaborated shamelessly with the Persians, marrying his sister to a Persian satrap, and accompanying Xerxes' army as a kind of liaison officer – in which capacity he strongly advised the Athenians to surrender before Salamis, saying it was impossible for them to win. His son, Perdiccas II, switched his allegiance so many times during the Peloponnesian War that one modern scholar thoughtfully provides a tabulated chart to show which side he was on at any given point. What, Athenian democrats must have said, could you do with a man like *that*? Not to mention the unspeakable Archelaus, Perdiccas' illegitimate son, who reached the throne by murdering his uncle, cousin, and half-brother, proceeded to marry his father's widow, and was murdered himself as a result of his lurid homosexual intrigues?

Yet it is, precisely, the careers of Perdiccas and Archelaus which hint at Macedonia's true potential. Perdiccas' remarkable tergiversations were mostly due to his possessing, in abundance, a basic raw material which both sides needed desperately: good Macedonian fir for shipbuilding and oars. He kept Macedonia from any serious involvement during the Peloponnesian War, thus preventing that ruinous drainage of manpower which so weakened Athens and Sparta. It was surely Perdiccas' example that Philip had in mind when he said: 'Cheat boys with knucklebones, and men with oaths.'

But it was Archelaus who, with realistic insight, first formulated the basic problems that had to be dealt with before Macedonia could become any kind of force in Greek affairs, and who seriously applied himself to solving them. First, it was vital to safeguard the country against constant incursions by over-ambitious neighbours. This meant both strengthening the army and achieving some kind of permanent unification between Upper and Lower Macedonia. Secondly, a great deal more Hellenisation – a programme, in fact, of conscious cultural propaganda – was essential before democratically advanced Greek states would begin to treat Macedonia on equal terms. Archelaus set himself up (like so many tyrants in antiquity) as an enlightened patron of literature, science and the arts.

But after Archelaus was murdered the whole edifice he had laboured to build collapsed overnight, to be followed by forty years of the worst anarchy and intrigue Macedonia had ever experienced. His claim to the throne, dynastically, was weak at best; the out-kingdom princes saw their chance, and took it. In any case, most Macedonian nobles preferred the manly pleasures of hunting, carousing and casual fornication to literature and philosophy. Sodomy – with young boys or, at a pinch, with each other – they also much enjoyed; but they had no intention of letting it be contaminated by decadent Platonic notions of spiritual uplift.

It is significant that the 'guardian' of Archelaus' young son Orestes was a prince of Lyncestis, Aeropus. Until 396 they reigned conjointly. Then Aeropus, having secured his own position, made away with Orestes and ruled alone. Two years later he died. His son Pausanias succeeded him, but was promptly assassinated by the legitimate Argead claimant, Alexander I's grandson Amyntas.

Heracles, on a silver coin
of Amyntas II (392–370).
The reverse shows a
Macedonian stallion.

In 394 Amyntas was nearer sixty than fifty. He had already made one unsuccessful bid for the throne, some three decades earlier, against his wily old uncle Perdiccas. Even now he found it a hard business claiming his inheritance. The Lyncestian barons, led by Pausanias' son, called in an Illyrian army to help them, and drove Amyntas out of Macedonia again, but in 392, with Thessalian backing, he made his come-back – this time for good. As Amyntas II he reigned until 370; precariously enough, but the main wonder is that he survived so long. In his old age he sired three legitimate sons. The youngest of these late-born heirs was Philip, Alexander the Great's father, born in 383/2 when Amyntas was well over sixty-five. It is not hard to see how the rumour arose that all three of them had been supposititious.

Trimmers, traitors, drunks, assassins, vacillating money-grubbers, cowardly and inefficient despots, the Argead dynasty had not won much respect from Greek public opinion, and Amyntas did little to improve matters. He touted indiscriminately for alliances; in his efforts to please Athens (and to protect his crumbling authority) he had even gone so far as to adopt an Athenian general, Iphicrates, as his son. On top of all this, the usual palace intrigues continued to flourish. The King's wife, Eurydice, had taken a lover, a Macedonian named Ptolemy, from Alorus. With enviable *sang-froid* she married him off to her own daughter – in order, presumably, to have an unchallengeable reason for keeping him around the house. After a while she got careless, and Amyntas actually caught her in bed with his son-in-law. Unwisely, he did nothing – as usual. He was much attached to his daughter and anxious to avoid any scandal that might cause her distress.

The lovers now decided to murder Amyntas, and set Ptolemy up as King of Macedonia in his place. However, they reckoned without the Queen's daughter, whose Grizelda-like submissiveness clearly drew the line at parricide, and who lost no time in warning her father what was afoot. Any social embarrassment the situation might have caused at court was obviated by Amyntas promptly dying, perhaps of shock. After all, he was close on eighty.

The King's eldest legitimate son, Alexander II, at once established his claim to the succession. But Ptolemy, resourceful as ever, had the young King assassinated during a Macedonian folk-dancing exhibition, married Eurydice, and assumed the Regency on behalf of Perdiccas, Alexander's brother, who was next in line for the throne. Realising that such a move was open to misconstruction by political cynics abroad, he proceeded to negotiate an alliance with the Thebans, who were rapidly emerging as the most powerful state in Greece.

In token of his sincerity, he also dispatched to Thebes a group of highly distinguished hostages. Among them was Amyntas' only other legitimate son, the young Philip, at this time about fifteen years old. Ptolemy can hardly have foreseen the consequences of his action. For Philip, while in Thebes, stayed with Pammenes, who was not only an excellent general himself but a close friend of Epaminondas, who had broken the invincible Spartan army at Leuctra, and perhaps the finest strategist Greece produced before Alexander. Philip's whole military career – and that of Alexander after him – was incalculably influenced by the lessons the great Theban commander taught him.

He learnt the importance of professional training in drill and tactics, of close cooperation between cavalry and infantry, of meticulous staff planning combined with speed in attack. By watching the manoeuvres of the Sacred Band, Thebes' crack infantry regiment, he came to appreciate the potential of a permanent *corps d'élite* – so much so that thirty years later he and his formidable son destroyed this famous military unit almost to the last man. Above all, he learnt one cardinal principle: that 'the quickest and most economical way of winning a military decision is to defeat the enemy not at his weakest but at his strongest point'.

Philip's training for power was proceeding along useful if unorthodox lines. His experience as a member of the Macedonian royal household had given him an understandably cynical view of human nature. In this world murder, adultery, incest and usurpation were commonplaces, as liable to be practised by one's own mother as anyone else. In Thebes he saw, too, the besetting weaknesses of a democratic city-state: constant party intrigue, lack of a strong executive arm, the inability to force quick emergency decisions, the unpredictable vagaries of the Assembly at voting time, the system of annual elections which made any kind of serious long-term planning almost impossible, the amateur, seasonally conscripted military levies (though here Thebes was far better off than, say, Athen). For the first time he began to understand how Macedonia's outdated institutions of feudalism and autocratic monarchy, so despised by the rest of Greece, might prove a source of strength when dealing with such opponents. After all, the King of Macedonia was (with certain trifling caveats) the supreme authority over his people. The Macedonian army confirmed each King's succession and could, in theory, depose him by vote. Apart from this, and a vague requirement that he observe 'the traditional laws', the King's power was absolute.

Macedonian noblemen were the ancient equivalent of French or English feudal barons; as a general rule they held their land in fee from the King, and owed him personal service, together with their retainers, in return. It was from these tribal aristocrats that the King selected his *hetairoi*, or 'Companions', who acted both as a peacetime Council, and as a General Staff when Macedonia was at war. They also furnished Gentlemen of the Bodyguard (*somatophylakes*), who appear to have been eight in number, and who attended the King not only in battle, but on all public occasions.

Like that other feudally organised horse-breeding state Thessaly, Macedonia possessed a fine heavy cavalry arm. Their horses were small and unshod, little more than wiry ponies – though they had begun to breed heavier mounts from bloodstock captured during the Persian Wars. They used neither saddle nor stirrups, as we can see from the Sidon sarcophagus (see pages 245 and 259); and this meant that the lance charge of the Middle Ages was unknown to them. Instead, they carried a short stabbing spear, the *xyston*, some six feet long, with which they were adept at spiking their opponents through the face during close-quarters combat.

It was Philip's eldest brother Alexander, during his all too brief reign, who formally established a regular body of *pezetairoi*, or 'Foot Companions'.

Apollo wearing a laurel wreath, on a gold stater of Philip II. The reverse shows a furiously-driven two-horse chariot, which may be connected with Philip's famous victory at Olympia in 356. The issue would then have been designed to promote Philip as patron of both sport and the arts.

The name implies not merely organisation, but also (perhaps no less important) social acceptance. After Alexander's assassination the Foot Companions survived, to be transformed out of all recognition by Philip, and forged into one of the most formidable heavy infantry units the world has ever seen.

This was the Macedonian phalanx. Its members were as highly trained and drilled as Roman legionaries; they were armed with the terrible *sarissa*, a spear some 13–14 feet long, heavily tapered from butt to tip, and much resembling a mediaeval Swiss pike. Since a normal infantry thrusting spear was only half the length of the *sarissa*, the Macedonians could always rely on making their first strike before the enemy got to grips with them.

From Thebes the young Philip waited upon events at home, in the intervals of studying military tactics and being lectured by his tutor, a Pythagorean. Opposition to Ptolemy's rule was considerable; but most of it, once again, came from the House of Lyncestis. No one paid much attention to young Perdiccas, Philip's brother. This, as things turned out, was a mistake. Perdiccas might, like Archelaus, have a regrettable weakness for literature and philosophy, but he was not on that account a person to trifle with. He waited three years, until he attained his majority (there was to be no excuse for foisting another Regent on him), and then had Ptolemy arrested and put to death (365/4). After this he settled down to rule Macedonia in his own right, and one of his first acts was to arrange for Philip's release, or escape, from Thebes. On his return, Perdiccas very sensibly made him governor of a district, and let him recruit and train troops there.

Philip at once began to put the lessons of Epaminondas into practice. Discipline and organisation were completely overhauled. Macedonian troops, infantrymen of the levy, suddenly found themselves learning tactical manoeuvres and complex close-order drill. Aristocrat and peasant sweated side by side in joint exercises; it is a moot point which of them, to begin with, was the more disconcerted by the experience. Slowly but surely, Philip began to train a corps of professional soldiers who were still, at the same time, Macedonia's national levy. It was a momentous innovation.

Greeks fighting Amazons, from the Mausoleum at Halicarnassus. When Mausolus, ruler of Caria, died in 353, his widow Artemisia built him a fantastic tomb (subsequently reckoned one of the Seven Wonders of the World), of which this frieze formed part. She also took a pinch of his ashes in her wine at dinner every night until she had drunk him all: so the tomb was, in effect, a cenotaph.

By 359 Perdiccas felt strong enough to chance a show-down with Illyria. The situation on his western frontier was, obviously, intolerable. Lyncestis had more or less seceded from Macedonian control; despite the humiliating annual tribute which he paid, Perdiccas had no guarantee that at any time he would not be swept off the throne by an Illyrian-backed *coup*. He mustered a large army, left Philip behind as Regent for his infant son Amyntas, and marched westward. Days later a terrified messenger reached Pella bringing the news that Perdiccas had been defeated and killed in a great battle against the Illyrians, and 4000 Macedonians lay dead on the battlefield with him. Philip of Macedon had come into his inheritance at last.

Having stalled or eliminated all internal opposition between summer and autumn, Philip spent the winter of 358/9 putting through a crash military training programme. In the early spring came news that the King of Paeonia had just died. This was too good a chance to miss. Philip swept over the northern passes, defeated the Paeonians in a pitched battle, and forced them to acknowledge Macedonian overlordship. Attack is the best defence: Philip knew that at this psychological moment he had a unique chance to smash the Illyrian threat once and for all. But it was a tremendous gamble. When he marched, he had 600 horse and no less than 10,000 infantrymen behind him. King Bardylis of Illyria, in some alarm, offered terms, but only on the basis of the *status quo*: he refused to give up any of the territory he had won. Philip rejected his offer. The two armies finally met in the plain near Monastir, by Lake Okhrida.

Here, for the first time, we see Philip applying the tactical lessons of Epaminondas, as Alexander was to apply them after him. There was little to choose between the two sides numerically; what told was superior strategy and discipline. The Illyrians, seeing themselves in danger of being out-flanked by Philip's cavalry, formed up in a hollow square. Philip himself led the infantry, holding back his centre and left, deploying his line in the oblique echelon that was Epaminondas' speciality.

As he had anticipated, the Illyrian right wing stretched and spread as it tried to make contact with this oddly positioned line. Philip waited until the inevitable, fatal gap appeared in the left of the square, and then sent in his right-wing cavalry, flank and rear. They drove a great wedge through the gap, and the Macedonian phalanx followed close behind them. A long and desperate struggle now took place. But at last the square broke, and 7000 Illyrians were slaughtered before the fugitives reached the safety of the hills. Perdiccas' defeat and death had been amply avenged. These, allowing for variations of detail, were precisely the tactics which gave Alexander victory at the Granicus, at Issus, and at Gaugamela.

Now, at last, Philip was in a position to dictate terms, and did so with some relish. Bardylis, grumbling but knowing when he was beaten, abandoned all his territorial gains in western Macedonia: the Illyrian frontier was at last secure. Philip's own prestige had been enhanced out of all recognition by this battle; he found himself, for the moment at least, something of a national hero. The only remaining question was how long he would stay content with the office of Regent. For a young man of twenty-three it was no mean achievement.

A silver coin of Perdiccas III (365–59), with the head of the young Heracles (possibly modelled on Perdiccas himself) on the obverse and a Macedonian stallion on the reverse.

The young Alexander with lion-helmet, as Heracles. The portrait may be by Lysippus, and was found at Sparta.

26

Amongst other concessions which Philip obtained from Bardylis was the hand in marriage of his daughter Audata. Feudal societies such as Macedonia, Thrace and Illyria (in contrast to the politically more developed Greek city-states) operated on a tribal system of kinship and reciprocal obligations. For them dynastic marriage, as an instrument of political self-insurance, stood second only to dynastic murder. Those with whom one had acquired a formal family relationship were that degree less likely to conspire against one; and a chieftain's daughter could always, at a pinch, be used as a high-level hostage. Philip, of all people, was unlikely to ignore so promising a diplomatic weapon. During his comparatively short life he took no fewer than five wives.

All the same, Philip's liaison with this Illyrian princess brought him only temporary security abroad and did little to stabilise his position at home. Audata died, probably in childbirth (spring 357), leaving Philip with a daughter, Cynane, rather than the male heir for whom he must have hoped. He now married Phila, a princess from the House of Elimiotis. But Phila, too, seems to have died soon after her marriage. By the high summer of 357 Philip was once more looking for a wife.

His third and most famous choice was, once again, a foreigner, a scion of the royal Molossian House of Epirus. Illyria might be secure for the moment, but an alliance with her southern neighbour and rival offered decided advantages. The reigning prince, Arybbas, had two nieces. The elder, Troas, he had economically married himself; but her sister Myrtale (or Olympias, as we know her) was still available, and Arybbas promptly – almost too promptly – gave his consent to the match.

In the autumn of 357 the Regent of Macedonia married his Epirot princess. For the first time in his life he found that he had taken on rather more than he could handle. Olympias was not yet eighteen, but already, it is clear, a forceful, not to say eccentric, personality. She was, among other things, passionately devoted to the orgiastic rites of Dionysus, and her Maenadic frenzies can scarcely have been conducive to peaceful domestic life. One of her more *outré* habits was keeping an assortment of large tame snakes as pets. Our sources, while admitting Olympias' beauty, describe her variously as sullen, jealous, bloody-minded, arrogant, headstrong and meddlesome. To these attributes we may add towering political ambition and a quite literally murderous temper. She was determined to be Queen in something more than name: this did not endear her to the Macedonian barons and was later to involve Philip in the most serious crisis of his career. But for the moment his main concern was to sire an heir, and he lost no time in getting Olympias with child.

So far, both as strategist and diplomat, Philip had scarcely put a foot wrong. *Expansion and* But there was still one vital element lacking to his plans for expansion, and *conquest* that was a large and regular source of income. Philip, like his son, was no natural economist; both of them had the pirate's mentality when it came to finance. For them credit meant, quite simply, enough gold and silver in the vaults to stave off an immediate crisis: the Treasury was equated with treasure. Furthermore, they knew only two ways of acquiring these precious metals: to dig them out of the ground or to steal them from anyone weaker than themselves.

The nearest and best source of both gold and silver was the region round Mt Pangaeus, east of the Strymon. In spring 356 Philip occupied Crenides – a key stronghold in the area – renamed it Philippi, sent a large body of settlers there, and set his mining engineers to work. Before long precious metal, gold above all, began to pour into the Macedonian treasury. Philip's annual income rose to 1000 talents, or 300,000 gold pieces – as much as fifth-century Athens had extracted from her whole great maritime empire. He promptly began to coin on a large scale, issuing gold staters (which he called 'Philips', perhaps a deliberate challenge to their Persian equivalent, the 'Daric'), and silver *sigloi*, or shekels. This surplus was quickly mopped up by the needs of Philip's near-professional army, and – perhaps even more – by the lavish bribes which he was for ever handing out to foreign politicians.

So, on that late summer day in 356 BC, Philip of Macedon sat and read the dispatches from Pella, and called on Fate to grant him some small setback to offset so unbroken a line of successes. In less than four years he had transformed Macedonia from a backward and primitive kingdom to one of the most powerful states in Greece. The threat to his frontiers was removed. The country had a secure and indeed princely national income, not to mention a legitimate heir to the throne. A formidable new army was being trained, while the out-kingdoms were beginning to show grudging respect for Argead sovereignty. Lastly, his victory at Olympia was, Philip hoped, the prelude to social acceptance by the Greek city-states, above all by Athens.

Philip's relations with Athens were always somewhat ambivalent. He despised her chattering, venal demagogues, with their empty rhetoric and sordid petty intrigues. He found the whole ramshackle democratic system mildly ridiculous. 'The Athenians', he remarked once, 'manage to dig up ten generals every year; I only ever discovered one in my life – Parmenio.' Yet he did not underestimate his opponents. He knew that venality often goes hand in hand with genuine patriotism – as the example of Themistocles so strikingly demonstrates – and that even a democracy can, on occasion, act with speed and decision.

Zeus holding an eagle, the reverse of an Alexander tetradrachm of 333 BC from Amphipolis (which replaced Pella as Macedonia's premier royal mint after Alexander's accession).

He had, indeed, some very practical motives for avoiding a head-on clash, not least the powerful Athenian fleet: Macedonia had never been a maritime nation. But he was also impressed, despite himself, by Athens' near-legendary past. His contempt was always mingled with a kind of wide-eyed colonial admiration.

Now, at last, he was ready to embark on that astonishing career of expansion and conquest which only ended with his premature death. He sent congratulations to his wife on having given birth to a son, to the trainer and rider of his horse on their achievement at Olympia, and to Parmenio on his military success in the north-west. Then he returned home in triumph to Pella. It needed little persuasion to make Perdiccas' son Amyntas formally repudiate his claim on the throne. To the cheers of an enthusiastic crowd, the army, exercising its traditional prerogative, acclaimed Philip King of Macedonia. His Regency was over: a new era had begun.

left: A young rider carrying a palm-branch: the reverse of the silver tetradrachm of Philip II on p. 20.

right: The entrance to the stadium at Olympia.

below: Philip, Olympias and Alexander in a mosaic from Baalbek (Heliopolis) on the Damascus-Emesa caravan-route. Like all such mosaics, this one is almost certainly based on some well-known painting.

2 The Gardens of Midas

Bellerophon and the Chimaera in a pebble-mosaic from Olynthus. Just as Alexander's burning of Persepolis was largely responsible for its archaeological survival, so Philip's destruction of Olynthus in 348 preserved the city's ground-plan, together with almost as many domestic artifacts as were found in Pompeii.

opposite: Alexander on Bucephalas – a bronze statuette found at Herculaneum, probably of the late Hellenistic period, and adapted from Lysippus' group set up at Dium to commemorate the victory of the Granicus. The general's scarf and the symbolic rudder show that victory involved crossing the river.

We have surprisingly little direct evidence about Alexander's childhood from any source, and what does exist is of very limited historical value. He is generally represented as a precocious *enfant terrible*. When he was only seven, it is said, he entertained a group of Persian envoys, during Philip's absence at the siege of Olynthus. They brought the Great King's pardon and recall for three rebels who had found refuge with Philip: Menapis the Egyptian, the satrap Artabazus, and the Greek mercenary captain Memnon of Rhodes. After the usual exchange of courtesies, Alexander proceeded to grill his guests like any intelligence officer. Not for him wide-eyed questions about such marvels as the Hanging Gardens or the Persian royal regalia. What *he* wanted to know were such things as the size and morale of the Persian army, the length of the journey to Susa, the condition of the roads that led there.

This anecdote has obviously been touched up for propaganda purposes; but it may well contain a core of truth. The envoys, Plutarch says, were much impressed. Whether they told him what he wanted to know is another matter; but Artabazus and Memnon are unlikely to have forgotten the incident. By a curious quirk of fate, the first afterwards became one of Alexander's own Eastern satraps, while the second was his most formidable opponent in Asia Minor.

There could certainly be no doubts about the aggressive policy of the child's father. His career up to 349 is graphically described by Demosthenes:

Has any man amongst you watched Philip's progress, observed his rise from weakness to strength? First he seizes Amphipolis, next Pydna, then Potidaea. After that it is Methone's turn. Next he invades Thessaly . . . and then goes off to Thrace, deposing various chieftains there and appointing his own nominees in their place. A short interval while he is sick, and then, the minute he recovers, off he goes to invest Olynthus. All this quite apart from minor campaigns against Illyria and Paeonia and King Arybbas, to name but a few.

Alexander's relationship with Philip was complex, an ambivalent blend of genuine admiration and underlying competitiveness. If imitation be the sincerest form of flattery, then Alexander's attitude to his father was little short of hero-worship. But the rivalry was there too: *odi et amo*, the perennial

love-hate relationship. The son followed in his father's footsteps not only to emulate, but also to excel. As a boy he identified himself closely with Achilles, from whom, through the Aeacids, his mother's house claimed descent. On his father's side he could trace his ancestry back to Heracles. It is a great mistake to underestimate the seriousness with which such genealogies were regarded by the ancient world. Heroic myth was, for Greeks and Macedonians alike, a living reality, invoked time and again by politicians or pamphleteers. What they were exploiting was near-universal faith: otherwise no one would have listened to them.

History tells us something of Alexander's teachers, but remains almost wholly silent as to what they taught him. His nurse's name was Lanice; her brother Cleitus, known as 'the Black', saved Alexander's life at the battle of the Granicus, only to be murdered by him many years afterwards, during a drunken quarrel in Samarkand. His first tutor was a kinsman of Olympias,

top: Two griffins attacking a stag, in a pebble-mosaic from Olynthus.

below: Thetis and her Nereids bringing the armour forged by Hephaestus to Achilles: a mosaic found in the so-called Villa of Good Fortune.

a stern and crabbed old disciplinarian named Leonidas, who (like his Spartan namesake) placed great emphasis on feats of physical endurance. Alexander used to say that Leonidas' idea of breakfast was a long night-march – and of supper, a light breakfast. Though the boy chafed under this discipline at the time – Philip said that he was amenable to argument, but not to compulsion – Leonidas' training left its mark on him. His personal powers of endurance, his forced marches through deserts and over mountains, became legendary.

Alexander did not forget his old bear of a tutor. There is one anecdote about their relationship which has never had quite the attention it deserves. Once, when the young prince was offering sacrifice, with would-be royal lavishness he scooped up two whole fistfuls of incense to cast on the altar-fire. This brought down a stinging rebuke on his head from his tutor. 'When you've conquered the spice-bearing regions,' Leonidas said, with that elaborate sarcasm characteristic of schoolmasters the world over, 'you can throw away all the incense you like. Till then, don't waste it.'

Years later Alexander captured Gaza, the main spice entrepôt for the whole Middle East (see below, p. 143). As always, he sent presents home to his mother and sister. But this time there was one for Leonidas as well. A consignment of no less than *eighteen tons* of frankincense and myrrh was delivered to the old man, 'in remembrance of the hope with which that teacher had inspired his boyhood' – together with an admonition to cease being parsimonious towards the gods. There is something terrifying about this story: the minor slight that rankled for fifteen years, the elaborate and un-answerable *réplique*. But it affords us a most valuable insight into Alexander's character. Anyone who ever did him a disservice, however trivial, lived to regret it in the end. He never forgot, seldom forgave: 'Vengeance is mine, I will repay, saith the Lord.' His implacability was only equalled by his patience. He would nurse a grudge for a decade or more, waiting for the propitious moment; and when that moment came, he struck.

The young Alexander was taught music (he showed a remarkable aptitude for the lyre) and reading and writing. Experts instructed him in the arts of sword-play, archery and javelin-throwing. Like all well-born Macedonian children, he could ride a horse almost before he could walk. His precocious horsemanship, indeed, gave rise to one of the most famous surviving anecdotes about him. When he was not more than eight or nine – perhaps in 347, on the occasion of Philip's 'Olympian' Games at Dium – a Thessalian horse-breeder, Philonicus, brought the King a pedigree stallion which he offered to sell him for the vast sum of thirteen talents. The stallion was black, except for a white blaze on its forehead, and branded with an ox-head, the mark of Philonicus' ranch: hence his name, Bucephalas. To command such a price, Bucephalas must have been in his prime – that is, about seven years old. Philip, together with his friends and attendants, went down to the open plain to try the horse out. Alexander followed. The King's grooms soon found that Bucephalas was quite unmanageable. Philip lost patience, and told Philonicus to take his horse away. This was too much for Alexander. 'What a horse they're losing!' he exclaimed. 'And all because they haven't the skill or courage to master him!'

'Oh,' said Philip, eyeing his eight-year-old son, 'so you think you know more about managing horses than your elders, do you?'

'Well, I could certainly deal with *this* horse better than they've done.'

Philip's one eye twinkled in his seamed and bearded face. 'All right then. Suppose you try and fail, what forfeit will you pay for your presumption?'

'The price of the horse,' Alexander said boldly. A ripple of laughter ran through the group round the King.

'Done,' said his father.

Alexander ran across to Bucephalas, took his bridle, and turned him towards the sun. One thing he had noticed was that the horse started and shied at his own shadow fluttering in front of him. He stood there for a little, stroking and patting the great stallion, calming him down, taking the measure of his spirit. Then he threw off his cloak and vaulted lightly on to Bucephalas' back, with that dynamic agility which was so characteristic of him as a grown man. At first he held the stallion on a tight rein; then, at last, he gave him his head, and the powerful steed went thundering away over the plain.

Philip and those around him were 'speechless with anxiety', Plutarch tells us; but Alexander soon came cantering back to them. There was cheering from the crowd. Philip, half-proud, half-resentful, said jokingly: 'You'll have to find another kingdom; Macedonia isn't going to be big enough for you.' But it was Demaratus of Corinth who brought matters to a triumphant

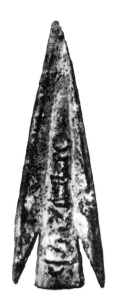

conclusion by buying Bucephalas himself and giving him to Alexander as a present. Boy and horse became inseparable. Bucephalas carried Alexander into almost every major battle he fought.

In August 348 Olynthus fell to Philip's siege engineers, and his two surviving half-brothers were captured and executed. The Athenians, who had dithered in the Assembly and sent reinforcements too late to save the city, made a great huff-and-puff about treachery. Aeschines denounced Philip's cruelty and ambition, but his attempt to make the Greek states combine against Macedonia proved a total fiasco. Athens salved her conscience by admitting Olynthian refugees, and after long negotiations finally sent a peace embassy to Pella in March 346. Macedonia was rapidly becoming the most powerful state in the Balkan peninsula.

It was now that the veteran Athenian pamphleteer Isocrates published his *Address to Philip*, calling for a Panhellenic crusade against Persia under Philip's leadership. Such a project was no new idea. Isocrates had originally formulated it in the *Panegyricus* (380), a high-minded monograph which envisaged Athens leading the crusade against barbarian Asia, with a penitent and regenerate Sparta at her side. This particular scheme misfired disastrously, but Isocrates never lost faith in what he termed 'the only war that is better than peace: more like a sacred mission than a military expedition'.

Isocrates (436–338 BC), the long-lived Athenian sophist and pamphleteer, who in old age came to believe that his life-long dream of Panhellenism might yet be achieved, under Macedonian leadership, through a joint crusade against Persia.

Despite the great difference in tone between the *Panegyricus* and the *Address to Philip* (the intervening years had rubbed Isocrates' idealism perilously thin) several of the main arguments are identical. There is the same emphasis on Persian cowardice, effeminacy, and military incompetence. Both pamphlets dilate on the fabulously rich pickings to be had, for little effort, by an invading army. Both, above all, recommend common action, against a common foe, as the best possible antidote to those interminable inter-state feuds which continued to tear Greece apart, and rendered her incapable of any concerted action. On the other hand the *Address to Philip*, being designed for a specific audience, contains certain new features. The glorification of free institutions is discreetly dropped; instead we get a set-piece on the advantages of one-man rule. There are extended parallels with the war conducted by Heracles against Troy, for the general benefit of mankind. Heracles, of course, was Philip's ancestor, and is described as such. 'It is your privilege,' Isocrates declares, working up for his peroration, 'as one who has been blessed with untrammelled freedom, to consider all Hellas your fatherland' – a piece of rhetorical hyperbole which Philip, in the event, took somewhat more literally than had been intended.

The King, though probably amused, was by no means ungrateful. It was pleasant – and advantageous – to have his Heraclid descent upheld by so venerable an Athenian pundit. Furthermore, the scheme the pundit advocated was eminently practical, and many of his detailed suggestions were subsequently carried out. Though Philip did not give a fig for Panhellenism as an idea, he at once saw how it could be turned into highly effective camouflage.

Artaxerxes III of Persia, known as Ochus, has been variously described as 'the last of the great rulers of the ancient Near East' and 'the most bloodthirsty of all Achaemenid monarchs' – not necessarily incompatible statements. The harsh regime he introduced had driven some of his subjects to rebellion, and many more into exile. Not a few of these banished malcontents already saw the powerful young King of Macedonia as their future leader in a crusade against the Achaemenid dynasty; and Philip, who had granted asylum to several of them at Pella, did nothing to discourage such a notion. He had also given private backing, for his own purposes, to various would-be independent local dynasts in Asia Minor. One of these was Hermeias a eunuch and ex-slave who ruled over Atarneus in the southern Troad, opposite Mytilene, and whose territory offered a most promising bridgehead for any future invasion. How long this link could be preserved, however, was another matter. Already Hermeias had come under some suspicion: sooner or later the Great King would surely close in on him. When that moment came, there was one member of his family whom Philip would much prefer to have safe at Pella – not only for his own sake, but because of the confidential information he possessed.

This was the son of old Amyntas' court physician, a boyhood friend some three years older than Philip himself, who had studied under Plato at the Academy and was now 'court philosopher' to Hermeias. Quite apart from his philosophical activities, he was also acting as a confidential political agent, a link-man between Hermeias and Philip. His personal appearance was foppish, not to say eccentric. He was balding, spindle-shanked, and had small eyes. Perhaps in an effort to compensate for these disadvantages, he wore dandified clothes, cut and curled his hair in an affected manner, and spoke with a lisp. Numerous rings sparkled on his fingers; the overall effect must have been rather like the young Disraeli at his worst.

His name was Aristotle.

In 345/4, with canny foresight, Aristotle left Atarneus and moved across the straits of Mytilene. It was here, during the winter of 343/2, that Philip's invitation reached him. Would he – in return for a suitably high fee – agree to come back to Macedonia and act as personal tutor to Alexander? The boy was thirteen now, and needed a first-class teacher to supervise his studies. He was, Philip indicated delicately, proving a trifle unmanageable. This was to be no ordinary tutorship; it would carry very special personal and political responsibilities.

The philosopher's decision was never in doubt.

Beroea (Verria), on the foothills of Mt Bermius, in Macedonia: traditionally the site of the Gardens of Midas, and still an extremely fertile and productive region.

Alexander's early years

Alexander had grown into a boy rather below average height, but very muscular and compact of body. He was already (like his hero Achilles) a remarkably fast runner. His hair, blond and tousled, is traditionally said to have resembled a lion's mane, and he had that high complexion which fair-skinned people so often display. His eyes were odd, one being grey-blue and the other dark brown. His teeth were sharply pointed – 'like little pegs', says the Alexander-Romance, an uncharacteristically realistic touch which carries instant conviction. He had a somewhat high-pitched voice, which tended to harshness when he was excited. His gait was fast and nervous, a trick he had picked up from old Leonidas; and he carried his head bent slightly upwards and to the left.

Philip decided, wisely, that what with political intrigues and the ubiquitous influence of Olympias, Pella was no place for the young prince at this stage in his career. Higher education demanded rural solitude. He therefore assigned to Aristotle the so-called 'Precinct of the Nymphs' at Mieza, a village in the eastern foothills of the Bermius range, north of Beroea (Verria). This precinct probably formed part of the famous 'Gardens of Midas', which occupied the modern Verria-Naoussa-Vodena region, a district of fine vineyards and orchards. As late as Plutarch's day visitors were still shown the stone benches and shady avenues where Aristotle conducted his lessons, and Naoussa still produces an excellent red wine.

Philip enjoined his son to study hard, and to pay close attention to all Aristotle taught him – 'so that,' he said, 'you may not do a great many things of the sort that I am sorry to have done'. At this point Alexander, somewhat pertly, took Philip to task 'because he was having children by other women beside his wife'. This does not mean that he was playing an adolescent Hamlet to Philip's Claudius; it merely indicates a natural anxiety about the succession. After all, Philip had had trouble enough with *his* illegitimate brothers; why should Alexander have to go through the whole weary business again?

The King's reply shows that he knew what was at the root of the matter. In answer to his son's criticisms he said: 'Well then, *if you have many competitors for the kingdom*' (my italics) 'prove yourself honourable and good, so that you may obtain the kingdom not because of me, but because of yourself.'

The story does much to discredit that quasi-Freudian element which modern scholars have professed to discover in the relationship between Alexander and Olympias. The truth is less romantic, but of considerable significance for future events. Even at this age Alexander's one over-riding obsession (and, indeed, his mother's) was with his future status as King. If he had any kind of Oedipus complex it came a very poor second to the burning dynastic ambition which Olympias so sedulously fostered in him.

As a good Greek philosopher, Aristotle must have found his pupil's royal status and ambitions somewhat embarrassing. The whole trend of current political theory, liberal and authoritarian alike, was towards some form of republicanism. But he managed (as we can see in the *Politics*) to get round this difficulty. While deploring monarchy in general as an institution, he nevertheless allowed one justification for it, and one alone: outstanding personal *areté* (excellence, glorious or meritorious achievement: the equivalent of Renaissance *virtù*). Monarchy was not morally justified except in a case where 'the *areté* of the King or of his family is so pre-eminent that it outclasses the *areté* of all the citizens put together'. It would have been tactless, to say the least, if Philip's employee had not made it clear that the Argead royal house fell squarely into this category.

On the Persian problem Aristotle was uncompromisingly ethnocentric. He believed slavery to be a natural institution, and equally that all 'barbarians' (i.e. non-Greeks) were slaves by nature. It was therefore right and fitting for Greeks to rule over barbarians, but not for barbarians to rule over Greeks. Like most intellectuals with a racialist axe to grind, Aristotle drew facts from geopolitics or 'natural law' in support of his thesis. In a celebrated fragment he counselled Alexander 'to be a *hegemon* [leader] to the Greeks and a despot to the barbarians, to look after the former as after friends and relatives, and to deal with the latter as with beasts or plants'. In this, he had the whole body of Greek civilised opinion behind him; and there is no reason to suppose that Alexander, to begin with, did not wholeheartedly share his racialist views. Barbarians, it is clear, were to be despised above all *because they lived exclusively through and for the senses*. This doctrine must have had a strong appeal for Alexander, who always placed a premium on self-control and self-denial.

Aristotle's advice on the treatment of Greeks and barbarians is, of course, capable of a more mundane interpretation: that in order to get the best out of those one intends to exploit, one must humour them far enough to win their cooperation. Greeks required to be treated as equals, to have their sense of independence – however illusory – fostered with the greatest care. Asiatics, on the other hand, only responded to, or respected, a show of rigorous authoritarianism – the Victorian District Officer's creed. Whether Aristotle intended this lesson or not, it was one that Alexander learnt all too well. As we shall see, he applied it to every individual or group with whom he subsequently came in contact.

He also absorbed a great deal of his tutor's omnivorous scientific curiosity, and the sharply empirical cast of mind that went with it. He developed an interest in medicine and biology, two of Aristotle's own favourite subjects. He read and discussed poetry, above all Homer: he was given a grounding in geometry, astronomy and rhetoric – particularly in that branch of rhetoric known as eristics, which means arguing a point from either side with equal facility. Alexander developed a great taste for eristics: this was one sphere in which Aristotle's training had disastrous consequences later.

right: The head of Apollo, on the obverse of one of the gold staters which Philip II began to issue after his capture of the mines around Crenides. These were the so-called 'Philips', later referred to by the Roman poet Horace as 'Philip's royal currency'.

Overleaf
left: The birth of Alexander, from a French manuscript of the second half of the fifteenth century, *Les Faits du grand Alexandre*.
right: Alexander on Bucephalas, from a Flemish manuscript of *c.* 1448, the *Liber Floridus de Lambert*.

40

Et tardant
les discors
et ses diesteurs
de seruer
ice et toy

aumes et vaillant mou
sterane en seure mal

bons toys et tous denosi
sa voulente de dieu ou desi
tine Je treuue que ladim
prouidence pourroit tous
et assortist tels toys de tel
peuples tels peuples de

Alexander Rex vultu et forma pulcrim[us]
sub crispa ¬ flauescente cesarie; coma leonina.
oculis egregii decoris: dextro nigro: leuo glauco:
philippo mortuo annos xx· habuit· et reg
nauit· xii· philippus rex responsu accepit
in hut modu· O philippe iste demu tu om-
q; orbi potietur Auicunq; equu bucefala
insiliens media pellem transiciet· Tunc
Alexander xiiii annos habebat
Equus bucefala.

Legati Cartaginesiu· hispanio;· Gallo;·
mouino;·et Sicilie atq; Saidinie· ad suppli-
candu alexandru babiloniam venerunt·
Tantus timor reges orbis teruui inuasit
ut inde peyrima cerneres toto mudo legatione
quo uix tederes puemisse rumore·

Alexander's sojourn in the Gardens of Midas lasted for three years, during which time relations between Macedonia and the Greek states, Athens in particular, grew steadily worse. Philip complained of Athenian privateering activities round the Dardanelles; Demosthenes was scared that Philip, by way of reprisal, might cut Athens' vital Black Sea grain route at the Bosporus. Behind all the complex political manoeuvres of the years between 342 and 338 loomed the ever-present – and highly effective – threat of economic blackmail.

Demosthenes kept hammering away at this danger in the Assembly with obsessional passion. Largely as a result of his recommendations, the Greek states formed a new anti-Macedonian league, Byzantium and Abydos joined the Athenian alliance, the naval programme was stepped up, and – most significant of all – an *entente* was at last reached with the Great King. Artaxerxes not only came out openly against Macedonia, but began to provide gold in large quantities for the express purpose of bribing neutral states to do likewise. Philip found himself facing perhaps the most serious crisis of his career.

He acted with characteristic promptness and vigour. As a test case, he called on Byzantium (still nominally his ally) to join him in a campaign against the Athenian privateers. Her government refused point-blank. Philip, without further argument, mobilised his new fleet. Since he intended to conduct operations himself, he summoned the sixteen-year-old Alexander home to Pella, where he formally appointed him Regent of Macedonia and Master of the Royal Seal, with the experienced Antipater as his adviser.

45

3 From a view to a death

above: Demosthenes (384–322 BC), the Athenian orator who kept warning his countrymen against the danger that Philip represented, and urging them to take firm action against him before it was too late. Probably a copy of the statue by Polyeuctus.
opposite: A marble portrait bust of the fourth century BC, thought to be of Philip II.

Alexander's schooldays were over. From now on the young Crown Prince was to be trained in a harder school, with greater responsibilities than even Isocrates would have dared to prescribe. This may well have been a deliberate 'hardening' policy on Philip's part: both he and Olympias were worried, among other things, by the boy's lack of heterosexual interests. But there was nothing effeminate about Alexander's conduct as Regent. No sooner had Philip left on his Byzantine campaign than rebellion broke out among the border tribes of Thrace and Paeonia. Alexander took a flying column up north, defeated the insurgents, captured their city, and turned it into a Macedonian military outpost. This new settlement he renamed Alexandropolis – a flamboyant gesture which Philip surely recognised for the danger signal it was. Alexander's appetite for royal power would not content itself for long with the Regency. Sooner or later there was bound to be trouble between father and son.

But for the moment they remained on close and friendly terms. During his absence Philip kept up a regular correspondence with the young Regent. Such extracts from his letters as have survived are as full of solid parental advice as those of Lord Chesterfield. 'He advised him,' says Plutarch, 'that, among the men of influence in the cities, he should make friends of both the good and the bad, and that later he should use the former and abuse the latter.' A report that Alexander had been trying to secure the cooperation of certain Macedonians by bribery caused his father intense annoyance. Since Philip himself was a past master at the art, his comment is worth noting. 'What on earth,' he enquired, 'gave you the deluded idea that you would ever make faithful friends out of those whose affections you had bought?' – an interesting comment on the King's attitude to Greek politicians.

By the summer of 339 Philip's position had become critical. For years he had successfully played the divide-and-rule game with the Greek states; now at last there was a real danger of their combining against him. He had looked forward to leading a Persian invasion under the specious banner of Panhellenism, with Athens, Thebes and Sparta, cowed or cooperative, marching at his side. Now the Greeks had done a deal with Artaxerxes, and if Philip did not act fast it would be they who invaded his territory, not he theirs.

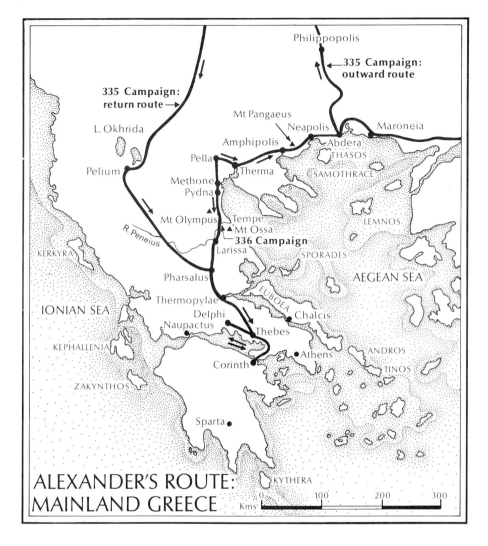

Philippopolis

**335 Campaign:
outward route**

**335 Campaign:
return route →**

L. Okhrida

Mt Pangaeus

Neapolis

Maroneia

Amphipolis

Abdera

THASOS

Pella

SAMOTHRACE

Pelium

Therma

Methone

Pydna

LEMNOS

Mt Olympus

Tempe

Mt Ossa

336 Campaign

R. Peneius

Larissa

SPORADES

KERKYRA

Pharsalus

AEGEAN SEA

Thermopylae

EUBOEA

IONIAN SEA

Delphi

Chalcis

Naupactus

Thebes

KEPHALLENIA

Corinth

Athens

ANDROS

TINOS

ZAKYNTHOS

Sparta

KYTHERA

ALEXANDER'S ROUTE:
MAINLAND GREECE

Kms   0   100   200   300

In the event, he moved faster than anyone could have predicted. The whole Macedonian army swept down into central Greece; on a quite legitimate excuse, to be sure, but once it was there, who could say in which direction it might turn next? All the time Philip kept up a smoke-screen of diplomatic blarney to lull Greek suspicions and camouflage his real objective. His ambassadors went ahead of him to Athens and Thebes: a last-minute pact between these two powerful states was something he intended to avoid if he possibly could.

Yet even now Philip still seems not to have given up all hope of a peaceful settlement, especially with Athens. An Athenian alliance would bring him great prestige. It might also swing a number of undecided states over to his side. Failing this, however, an Athenian army must be brought to battle and defeated, for all the world to see. By fair means or foul, Philip must provoke the Athenians and their allies into fighting on *his* terms – not at sea, where they had every advantage, but against the crack troops of the Macedonian phalanx.

A fourth-century lead
sling bullet from Athens.

Late one September afternoon, a horrified Athenian Assembly heard the
news that Philip, far from besieging Amphissa (his declared objective) had
turned east and occupied Elatea, a key point on the main road to Thebes
and Attica. Demosthenes now emerged as the patriotic hero of the hour,
the champion of Athenian liberty. By sheer force of conviction he brought
about precisely what Philip had feared – a defensive coalition between Athens
and Thebes. An Athenian army marched into Boeotia, and the two new
allies promptly set about fortifying the north-west passes into central Greece.
A force of 10,000 mercenaries was also dispatched westward to cover the
road from Amphissa. These dispositions blocked both his possible lines of
advance. Nevertheless, Athens' real strength and expertise lay in her still
formidable navy. At this period she had over 300 triremes available for
active service. Athenian operations in the Dardanelles and during the siege
of Byzantium (340) had shown just how vulnerable Philip was at sea. Yet
here was Demosthenes proposing to block his advance by land. Nothing
could have suited Philip better.

Now his only remaining task was to lure the Greek forces out of their
defensive positions and force an engagement. Macedonia's formidable
cavalry and the trained regiments of the phalanx would do the rest. In the
event everything proved absurdly easy. Philip arranged for a bogus dispatch
to be captured by the task-force guarding Amphissa. This informed them
that the King was withdrawing his army to deal with a rising in Thrace.
Thinking the enemy had gone, the Greek mercenaries became careless.
Philip launched a night-attack in strength and annihilated them.

The Greeks did the only thing possible in the circumstances: they abandoned the passes and established a shorter defence-line at Chaeronea, between
the Cephisus River and the citadel. This put them in a very strong position.
In cavalry the two sides were about equally matched, with 2000 on each
side. But the Greeks had mustered some 35,000 infantry to Philip's 30,000,
and the latter probably represented the full field strength of the Macedonian
army. Philip was sufficiently impressed to make one last attempt at negotiation. Phocion, back from the North Aegean, recommended accepting his
proposals, but Demosthenes, tireless and adamant, would have none of it.
The King, seeing that he would get nowhere by diplomacy, now prepared
for a final show-down. He captured Naupactus, as the Athenians had antici-

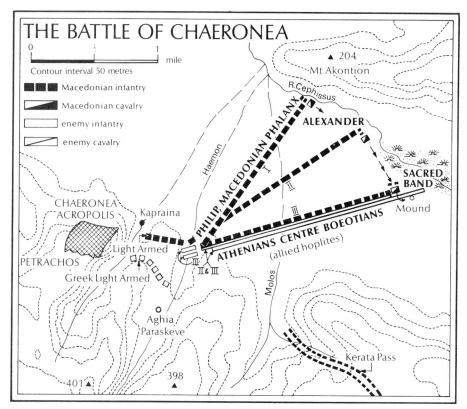

THE BATTLE OF CHAERONEA

0 — ½ — 1 mile

Contour interval 50 metres

- ▮▮▮ Macedonian infantry
- ◥ Macedonian cavalry
- ▭ enemy infantry
- ◹ enemy cavalry

▲ 204 Mt Akontion

R. Cephissus

ALEXANDER

Haemon

PHILIP, MACEDONIAN PHALANX

SACRED BAND

Mound

CHAERONEA ACROPOLIS

Kapraina

Light Armed

PETRACHOS

Greek Light Armed

ATHENIANS CENTRE BOEOTIANS (allied hoplites)

Molos

Aghia Paraskeve

Kerata Pass

401 ▲

398 ▲

Phase I
Macedonians advance; Greeks stationary

Phase II
Philip retreats, his centre and left advancing; Athenians, Centre and Boeotians advance to left front, but Sacred Band stands firm.

Phase III
Alexander charges, the centres engage, and Philip drives the Athenian wing up the Haemon valley.

pated, left a small holding force at Delphi, and deployed the rest of his troops across the plain north of Chaeronea. It was there, on 4 August 338, that the two armies met, in what proved one of the most decisive encounters of all Greek history.

The battle took place at dawn (see plan above). On the allied right wing were the Boeotians, some 12,000 strong, led by the famous Theban band. On the left were stationed Athens' 10,000 hastily mustered hoplites [heavy armed infantrymen]. The centre consisted of the remaining allied contingents reinforced with 5000 mercenaries. On the extreme left, a screen of light-armed troops linked the main force with the acropolis defences. The cavalry was held in reserve.

Philip knew that any serious opposition he got would come from the Thebans. Since they had been technically allied to him when they threw in their lot with Athens, they had the most to fear at his hands in the event of a defeat. Furthermore, their troops were experienced veterans, as well trained as his own: Philip knew, better than anyone, how much Macedonian discipline owed to Theban methods. His tactical dispositions were made accordingly. He himself would command the right wing. In the centre he placed the regiments of the phalanx. The command of the heavy cavalry on the extreme left wing, opposite the Sacred Band, went to Alexander – an extraordinarily responsible appointment for a boy of eighteen, since it was he who had to deliver the knock-out blow that would win or lose the battle.

Philip's strategy was, in essence, the same as that which he had employed against the Illyrians at Lake Okhrida (see above, p. 26). His right wing slightly outflanked the Athenian left, while his own centre and left were echeloned back at an angle from the Greek line. Thus when he and the guards brigade engaged the Athenians, the rest of the Macedonian army was still advancing. More important still, these tactics produced an inevitable – and probably unconscious – drift to the left among the Athenians, which was followed by the allied and mercenary troops of the Greek centre.

The Athenians, as Philip had anticipated, launched a wildly enthusiastic charge at the first onset. Their general, Stratocles, seeing the guards brigade give way, completely lost his head, and began shouting: 'Come on, let's drive them back to Macedonia!' But Philip's withdrawal, as Stratocles should have seen, was anything but disorderly. Step by well-drilled step the guards brigade moved back, still facing to their front, a hedgehog bristle of *sarissas* holding the pursuit at bay. On rushed the Athenians, yelling and cheering, the Greek centre stretching ever more perilously as they pressed forward. Presently two things happened for which Philip had been waiting. The Macedonians backed up on to rising ground by the banks of a small stream, the Haemus (Blood River), and that fatal gap at last opened between the Greek centre and the Theban brigade on their right.

Into that gap, at the head of Macedonia's finest cavalry division, thundered the young Crown Prince, driving a wedge to the very heart of the Theban ranks, while a second mounted brigade attacked the Sacred Band from the flank. Very soon the Thebans were entirely surrounded. At the same time Philip, away on the right, halted his retreat, and launched a downhill counter-charge. What the cavalry had begun, the phalanx completed. They poured through the broken lines in Alexander's wake and engaged the Greek centre front and flank simultaneously. After a severe struggle the entire allied army broke and fled – with the exception of the Sacred Band. Like Leonidas' Spartans at Thermopylae, these three hundred Thebans fought and died where they stood, as though on parade, amid piles of corpses. Only 46 of them were taken alive. The remaining 254 were buried on the site of their last stand. There they lie to this day, in seven soldierly rows, as the excavator's spade revealed them; and close by their common grave the Lion of Chaeronea still stands guard, weathered and brooding, over that melancholy plain.

When the battle was over, Philip called off his cavalry pursuit, raised a victory trophy, made sacrifice to the gods, and decorated a number of his officers and men for conspicuous gallantry. The future of Greece lay, at long last, in his strong and capable hands. But he knew well enough how close-run a fight Chaeronea had been. Furthermore, Athens could still cause him a great deal of trouble. Indeed, the day after the battle news reached Chaeronea that the Athenians were arming their slaves and resident aliens, and making ready to defend their city to the death. We are told – and there is no reason to disbelieve it – that Philip was thoroughly alarmed by this reaction. The Athenian fleet remained intact; so did the harbour and arsenals of Piraeus. If the city's inhabitants decided to stick it out, they could maintain supplies and communications by sea more or less indefinitely. In the circumstances, however complete his triumph at Chaeronea, there was every reason for the King to be conciliatory.

The terms which Philip now offered Athens were better than anyone had

The great stone lion which marks the site of Chaeronea undoubtedly commemorates the battle; it is generally held to be a memorial to the Thebans, though at least one scholar has suggested that it was a Macedonian monument, in honour of 254 Macedonians who fell under Philip's command.

dared to hope. The Athenian dead – or rather their ashes, it still being the hot season – would, after all, be given up. All 2000 prisoners would be released without ransom. Philip guaranteed not to send Macedonian troops across the frontiers of Attica, or Macedonian warships into Piraeus. Athens was to keep a nucleus of Aegean islands, including Delos and Samos. In return for these favours, however, she was required to abandon all other territorial claims, to dissolve the Athenian Maritime League, and to become Macedonia's ally. Her leaders accepted Philip's terms *en bloc*, without argument. They were in no position to object. Any privileges which Athens might henceforth be granted were an arbitrary favour from the Macedonian King, reversible at will.

All the same, the Athenians could at least take comfort from the fact that they had received incomparably better treatment than Thebes. If Philip was to hold central Greece, Thebes' very considerable power must be systematically broken up. He therefore abolished the Boeotian League, which was, in effect, an embryo Theban empire. Its member-cities, including Plataea, were given back their independence – a very shrewd piece of diplomacy. The Thebans themselves were forced to recall all political exiles, and a puppet government was set up, with a Macedonian garrison to watch over it from the Cadmea. Theban prisoners, unlike Athenians, had to be ransomed and at a good price; otherwise they were sold as slaves.

Philip could be magnanimous enough when it suited him. He had no objection to the Thebans raising a great monument at Chaeronea in memory of the Sacred Band: a soldier himself, he appreciated truly valorous opponents. He refrained from imposing garrisons on most – though not all – of the leading Greek cities, but despite his fits of jovial generosity, there could be little doubt now where the real power lay. The Greek states retained no more than a pale shadow of their former freedom.

To commemorate his great victory, Philip built and dedicated at Olympia a circular edifice known as the Philippeum, somewhat akin to the Delphic *tholos*. This contained several gold and ivory portrait-statues, specially executed by the sculptor Leochares, of Philip himself, of Olympias, of Alexander, of Philip's parents Amyntas and Eurydice. In general appearance it must have rather resembled a Shinto shrine.

What was Philip's purpose in creating so odd a monument? The conclusion seems inescapable: he hoped to establish a quasi-divine cult of himself and his family. Such a device undoubtedly had great advantages: its subsequent use throughout Hellenistic and Roman times offers clear

below: Ruins of the Philippeum at Olympia: its circular *tholos*-type base is clearly visible, and seems to have been a skilful imitation of the one at Epidaurus. The notion of using a shrine to house statues of mortals marked the introduction of a new factor into Greek life: what began here came to full fruition with Caligula, Nero, and Elagabalus.

proof of this. Philip's fast-expanding power was creating as many problems as it solved, not least as regards his personal status. Like Augustus after him, he was much preoccupied with the problem of converting *imperium* into *auctoritas*, and the policy embodied in the Philippeum was an initial step towards this goal.

One thing, however, the statue group of the Philippeum makes abundantly clear. At the time of its dedication – that is, towards the end of September 338 – Philip's dynastic plans, now of nearly twenty years' standing, remained firm and unaltered. Olympias was still his wife, and Alexander his legitimate successor. No one doubted that Alexander would, in due course, succeed to the throne.

After Chaeronea

About the same time as Philip's victory, Artaxerxes Ochus was assassinated by his Grand Vizier, Bagoas – 'a eunuch in fact but a militant rogue in disposition', as Diodorus pleasantly puts it. Persia remained in a state of near-anarchy until November, while Susa boiled with cut-throat palace intrigue. After all rival claimants had been successfully eliminated, Bagoas placed Ochus' youngest son Arses on the throne, and settled back into his favourite role of puppet-master.

These developments are unlikely to have escaped Philip's vigilant eye. With Greece effectively brought to heel, and Persian leadership seriously weakened, the prospects for an invasion of Asia had improved considerably. Panhellenism therefore now became his watch-word and the war was projected as a religious crusade, to avenge Greece for Xerxes' invasion a century and a half before. All that remained was to work out the logistics, and see how far each individual state was willing to cooperate. Philip's first concern, as always, was with Athens. Immediately after the armistice he sent an official embassy to escort the ashes of the Athenian dead home to their last resting-place. In the atmosphere of good-will which such a gesture would generate, profitable diplomatic exchanges might be expected. As ambassadors-extraordinary Philip appointed Antipater, Alcimachus, and Alexander. This, we may note, was the last occasion on which the Crown Prince was entrusted with any responsible task befitting his rank, a state of affairs which continued until Philip's death two years later. Alexander's

Greeks fighting Persians, in a frieze from the Temple of Athena Nike, Athens (built 427–4 BC), designed to commemorate the Persian Wars.

Darius the Great in the 'Darius Vase', a fourth century BC painted amphora from Canossa.

visit to Athens – the only time, so far as we know, that he ever set foot within its gates – seems to have coincided in some way with his fall from official grace.

One of the ambassadors' most important duties was to discuss Philip's future plans, informally, with leading statesmen such as Phocion and Lycurgus, and assess their reactions. The main points they stressed were the establishment of a 'general peace' (*koiné eirêné*) between all Greek states; the formation of a new Hellenic League; and the vigorous promotion, under Macedonian leadership, of a Panhellenic campaign against Persia. With each state Philip made a separate treaty: the maxim of 'divide and rule' had by now become second nature to him. Only Sparta, with defiant stubbornness, refused to negotiate, and here Philip did not force the issue. When the King announced a general peace conference, to be held at Corinth, Sparta alone abstained.

The delegates assembled about the first week of October; Philip was at great pains to charm them and to soothe their wounded susceptibilities. He needed the Greeks' support for his Persian venture, and was determined to get it. To begin with, he read out a draft manifesto (*diagramma*) of his proposals. This manifesto formed the basis for all subsequent discussion, and was adopted more or less unchanged. In essence, it boiled down to the following points. The Greek states were to make a common peace and alliance with one another, and constitute themselves into a federal Hellenic League. This League would take joint decisions by means of a council (*synhedrion*) on which each state would be represented according to its size and military importance. A permanent steering committee of five presidents (*prohedroi*) would sit at Corinth, while the Council itself would hold general meetings

55

during the four Panhellenic festivals – at Olympia, Nemea, Delphi and the Isthmus – in rotation.

Simultaneously, the League was to form a separate alliance with Macedonia, though Macedonia itself would not be a League member. This treaty was to be made with 'Philip and his descendants' in perpetuity. The King would act as 'leader' (*Hegemon*) of the League's joint forces, a combined civil and military post designed to provide for the general security of Greece. It was, technically at least, the Council that would pass resolutions, which the *Hegemon* then executed. If the Greeks were involved in a war, they could call on Macedonia to support them. Equally, if Philip needed military aid, he was entitled to requisition contingents from the League. In such a case he acquired a second, more purely military role. As well as *Hegemon* he became *strategos autokrator*, that is, General Plenipotentiary or supreme commander-in-chief of all Macedonian and League forces in the field, for as long as a state of hostilities might last.

Despite Philip's careful dressing-up of his authority in this elaborate quasi-federal disguise, there could be no doubt as to who took the real decisions. The King's *de facto* executive powers were virtually unlimited; he could, at will, dictate the whole future course of Greek foreign policy. Most Greek statesmen recognised this only too well. To them, their self-styled *Hegemon* was still a semi-barbarian autocrat, whose wishes had been imposed on them by right of conquest; and when Alexander succeeded Philip, he inherited the same bitter legacy of hatred and resentment. The Greeks, for the most part, knuckled under because, after Chaeronea, they had no alternative. The moment they saw the slightest chance of throwing off the Macedonian yoke, they would take it.

Having thus set the stage for the peace conference, Philip returned to Pella. At this critical point in his career, it might reasonably be assumed, the one thing he had to avoid, at all costs, was any kind of internal or dynastic upheaval. Yet it was now – and with every appearance of deliberation – that he embarked on a course of action which split the Macedonian royal house into two bitterly hostile camps, stirred up a whole wasps'-nest of aristocratic intrigue, and drove the hitherto highly favoured Crown Prince into exile at a time when his talents could ill be spared.

Philip – unpredictable as always – announced his intention of marrying Cleopatra, a young girl whose family was among the noblest in Macedonia. Alexander, nevertheless, was Philip's first-born son, and the acknowledged heir-apparent. His claim to the succession remained beyond challenge – until, that is, Philip suddenly put away Olympias on the grounds of suspected adultery, and began to encourage rumours that Alexander himself was illegitimate. At this point his latest marital adventure took on a new and ominous complexion.

The wedding-feast, as might be expected, was a tense affair. When Alexander walked in and took the place of honour which was his by right (opposite his father) he said to Philip: 'When my mother gets married again I'll invite *you* to *her* wedding' – not a remark calculated to improve anyone's temper. During the evening, as usual, a great deal of wine was drunk. At last Attalus, the bridegroom's uncle, arose, swaying, and pro-

right: A view of the Peloponnese from Acrocorinth (1,857 feet), which from early times was the fortress controlling the Isthmus. The visible ruins are medieval, not classical.

overleaf: The Temple of Apollo, Delphi.

Excavations at Pella have been going on since 1958. Philip's and Alexander's capital is an impressive site covering three and a half square kilometres, with streets up to thirty feet in width, and large, luxurious private houses. The most remarkable finds have been the superb pebble-mosaics (see pages 17 and 20).

left: The ruined temples and courtyard at Olympia.

posed a toast. He called upon the Macedonians to ask of the gods that from Philip and Cleopatra there might be born a legitimate successor to the kingdom'. At last the truth was out, and made public in a way which no one – least of all Alexander – could ignore. Infuriated, the Crown Prince sprang to his feet. 'Are you calling me a bastard?' he shouted, and flung his goblet in Attalus' face. Attalus retaliated in kind. Philip, more drunk than either of them, drew his sword and lurched forward, bent on cutting down, not Attalus (who after all had insulted his son and heir), but Alexander himself.

However, the drink he had taken, combined with his lame leg – skewered by a javelin while fighting Thracian tribesmen – made Philip trip over a stool and crash headlong to the floor. '*That*, gentlemen,' said Alexander, with icy contempt, 'is the man who's been preparing to cross from Europe into Asia – and he can't even make it from one couch to the next!' Each in that moment of crisis had revealed what lay uppermost in his mind.

61

Alexander thereupon flung out into the night, and by next morning he and Olympias were over the frontier. There can be little doubt that from now on both the Crown Prince and his mother were actively plotting against Philip, and doing their level best to stir up trouble for Macedonia from all the tribes along the western marches.

Philip's behaviour is, at first sight, very hard to explain in rational terms. Our ancient authorities, realising this, assume that he fell so wildly in love with Cleopatra as to more or less take leave of his senses. But Philip, as we have seen, never confused marriage with mere casual amours. Even if Cleopatra, like Anne Boleyn, held out for marriage or nothing, there was still no conceivable reason why Philip should repudiate Olympias – much less Alexander, whom he had spent nearly twenty years in training as his chosen successor. There is one motive, and one only, which could have driven Philip to act as he did: the belief – whether justified or not – that Alexander and Olympias were engaged in a treasonable plot to bring about his overthrow. He could not possibly set out against the Great King leaving Macedonia in the hands of a potential usurper. Equally, he could not entrust his élite cavalry corps to the command of a man whose loyalty had been called in question. Alexander would have to be sacrificed, and Olympias with him.

So much seems clear. But the crucial point for a modern reader is whether or not Philip's suspicions were in fact justified, and here the only possible verdict is 'non-proven'. At the same time, it is not hard to see how such suspicions could have been aroused. From the very beginning, Olympias had encouraged Alexander to think of himself as King in his own right, rather than as Philip's eventual successor. This, we need not doubt, was the main source of those 'great quarrels' between father and son, which the Queen's jealous temper actively encouraged, and in which she invariably took Alexander's side.

The natural rivalry between Alexander and his father was still further exacerbated by Chaeronea. It could well be argued that it was Alexander who had won Philip's victory for him – a claim which we find Philip going out of his way to deny. Olympias had taught the boy since childhood to regard kingship as his destiny. Aristotle had implanted in his mind the conviction that only through pre-eminent *areté* could that kingship be justified – and by his emphasis on a legitimate war of revenge against Persia, had shown him how such *areté* might be achieved.

But between Alexander and the throne which he held to be his by divine right there stood one seemingly insurmountable obstacle: his father. Philip was still only in his mid-forties, full of rude and jovial energy, no less ambitious than his son, and far more experienced. It was Philip, not Alexander, who was now preparing to launch the great Panhellenic crusade against Persia. It was Philip, not Alexander, who would reap the immortal renown that such an enterprise, if successful, must surely confer upon its victor. Unless some chance blow struck the King down, Alexander could expect no more than his father's reflected glory. No one could deny that he had powerful and urgent motives for wishing Philip out of the way.

The truth of the matter can never be known for certain. If we apply the

cui bono principle, Alexander undoubtedly had everything to gain by staging a *coup* before the expedition was launched. On the other hand, there was a powerful faction at court – including Attalus and, probably, Parmenio – which detested this haughty-mannered prince and his domineering mother, and would probably stick at nothing to secure their downfall.

At all events, by the late autumn of 338 Alexander's hitherto ascendant star seemed in total eclipse. While he and Olympias fumed and plotted in exile, their enemies at home established themselves ever more securely. Preparations for the invasion went ahead; and soon it became public knowledge that Philip's new wife Cleopatra was with child. The future now looked clear: few can have foreseen, at the time, the unsuspected turn events would take.

Hegemon of the League Throughout the winter of 338–7 the Peace Conference continued its deliberations at Corinth. In the spring the delegates finally ratified their 'common peace', and formed a Hellenic League along the lines that Philip had suggested in his manifesto. At their first official plenary session, an alliance with 'Philip and his descendants' was voted, and Philip himself was unanimously elected *Hegemon* – which made him, among other things, *ex officio* chairman of the Federal Council. In this capacity he moved a formal motion that the League declare war on Persia to exact vengeance for those sacrilegious crimes which Xerxes had committed against the temples of the Greek gods.

This proposal too was carried; but then the League had little choice in the matter. Nor could it very well object to appointing Philip supreme field-commander, 'with unlimited powers', of the expedition itself. Another revealing (and very necessary) decree provided that any Greek who henceforth chose to serve the Great King would be treated as a traitor. Some 15,000 Greek mercenaries, not to mention numerous doctors, engineers, technicians, artists and professional diplomats were already on the Persian pay-roll – more than twice as many men, in fact, as the League ultimately contributed for the supposedly Panhellenic crusade against Darius.

Philip returned home from Corinth feeling very pleased with himself – all the more so since there were rumours of a new revolt brewing in Egypt. Anything calculated to keep the Great King's hands full at this point was doubly welcome. His satisfaction, however, was due for a setback. About midsummer Cleopatra's child was born, and proved to be, not the male heir on which Philip had been counting, but a girl.

Philip was a fundamentally realistic statesman; he knew, better than anyone, just what this meant. He could not afford to leave Macedonia, during his absence, without a recognised heir to the throne. Nor could he sail for Asia while a dangerous and discontented claimant was stirring up trouble among the Illyrians, and his own discarded wife was similarly employed at her brother's court in Epirus. There was nothing for it; Alexander would have to be brought back and reinstated.

Somehow, by skilful diplomacy, this seemingly impossible task was accomplished. The least Philip can have offered was the reassurance that, appearances to the contrary, Alexander remained his chosen successor. On the other hand, the King was determined not to let the boy fall under his mother's pernicious influence again. He therefore left Olympias in Epirus. Nor, in fact, did he restore Alexander to anything like his old position of trust. As though to emphasise the fact, he lost not a moment after Cleopatra's *accouchement* in getting her pregnant for the second time. Alexander could by no means yet count on the succession.

In the early spring of 336 an advance force of 10,000 men, including a thousand cavalry, crossed over to Asia Minor. Its task was to secure the Dardanelles, to stockpile supplies, and – in Philip's pleasantly cynical phrase – to 'liberate the Greek cities'. This force was led by Parmenio, his son-in-law Attalus, and Amyntas son of Antiochus. At first Parmenio's campaign went from one success to another. After crossing the Dardanelles, his army struck south along the Ionian seaboard. Chios came over to him, and so did Erythrae. When Parmenio approached Ephesus, the people rose spontaneously, threw out their pro-Persian tyrant, and welcomed the Macedonians. They also set up Philip's statue in the temple of Artemis, side by side with the goddess's own image.

Whether so curious a tribute was their own idea, or carried out in accordance with Philip's known wishes, must remain problematical. One can only say that it fits in uncommonly well with his known ruler-cult propaganda. At the same time he was genuinely anxious to get divine approval for his undertaking. He therefore sent to Delphi (where he was honoured

The 'liberation of the Greek cities'

as a benefactor) and asked the Pythia, with uncompromising directness, whether or not he would conquer the Great King. The priestess took this blunt approach in her stride. The answer Philip got was as outrageously ambiguous as usual. 'The bull is garlanded', he read. 'All is done. The sacrificer is ready.' Philip interpreted this to mean that the Great King would be slaughtered like a victim at the altar, and 'was very happy to think that Asia would be made captive under the hands of the Macedonians'.

The month of June 336 could hardly, on the face of it, have opened more auspiciously for Philip. First, there came encouraging news from Persia, where a fresh outbreak of palace intrigue had culminated, once again, in the Great King's assassination. As usual, the Grand Vizier, Bagoas, was responsible, and this latest murder finally extinguished the direct Achaemenid line. It looked as though Persia was in for yet another period of anarchy and civil war, with no strong central government, and little will to resist a determined attack.

Such a view, as events turned out, was a little optimistic. Bagoas, looking round for some suitably pliable successor, settled on Codomannus, a collateral member of the royal house, who now ascended the throne as Darius III – and inaugurated his reign by making Bagoas himself drink the poison he had administered to so many others. This disconcerting gambit put paid to any further court intrigue for the time being. Darius III, despite the harsh verdict of posterity, was not an opponent to be underestimated.

Meanwhile in Aegae, the old Macedonian capital, preparations were going ahead for the wedding of Alexander's sister Cleopatra and her uncle the King of Epirus. Philip planned to use this State occasion as the excuse for much lavish – not to say ostentatious – display and propaganda. Above all, he wanted to impress the Greeks. He had to make it clear that he was no mere military despot, but a civilised and generous statesman. Once the company was assembled, Philip felt, his munificent entertainment would do the rest. He had organised a non-stop round of rich banquets, public games, musical festivals, and 'gorgeous sacrifices to the gods'.

In the midst of these preparations, with impeccable timing, the King's young wife gave birth to a son. As though deliberately emphasising the child's future status as his successor, Philip named him Caranus, after the mythical founder of the Argead dynasty. Alexander's isolation at court was now almost complete. Among the Old Guard barons, only Antipater could still be regarded as a potential ally. However, with the arrival of the bridegroom's party from Epirus, Alexander gained one supporter who, in his eyes, was worth all the rest put together. Philip could hardly prevent Olympias returning to Macedonia as a guest at her own brother's wedding. Alexander, Antipater and the ex-Queen must have found a good deal to discuss when they finally met again.

The second day of the celebrations had been set aside for the Games. Before dawn every seat in the theatre was taken, and as the sun rose a magnificent ceremonial procession formed up and came marching slowly in. It was headed by 'statues of the twelve gods wrought with great artistry and adorned with a dazzling show of wealth to strike awe in the beholder'. These were accompanied by Philip's own image, 'suitable for a god', an intrusive and unlucky thirteenth. The King's Greek guests began to see that his propaganda had other purposes besides flattery. Whose, it might well be asked, was the *hubris* now? Finally Philip appeared in person, draped with a white ceremonial cloak, and walking alone between the two Alexanders – his son and his new son-in-law. He had ordered the Gentlemen of the Bodyguard to follow at a distance, 'since he wanted to show publicly that he was protected by the goodwill of all the Greeks, and had no need of a guard of spearmen'.

The King paused by the entrance to the arena. At that moment a young man, a member of the Bodyguard itself, drew a short broad-bladed Celtic sword from beneath his cloak, darted forward, and thrust it through Philip's ribs up to the hilt, killing him instantly. He then made off in the direction of the city gate, where he had horses waiting. There was a second's stunned silence. Then a group of young Macedonian noblemen hurried after the assassin. He caught his foot in a vine-root, tripped and fell. As he was scrambling up, his pursuers overtook him, and ran him through with their javelins.

Philip's murderer was one of the King's Bodyguard called Pausanias, from the out-kingdom of Orestis. A year or two before, Philip, attracted by his remarkable youthful beauty, had taken him as a lover. When the King transferred his homosexual attentions elsewhere, Pausanias made a great jealous scene with the new favourite, calling him, among other things, a hermaphrodite and a promiscuous little tart. Stung to the quick, the boy proved his manhood by saving Philip's life in battle at the expense of his own, during a campaign against the Illyrians. Now this boy was also, as it happened, a friend of Attalus, whose niece Philip had married; and Attalus decided to revenge himself on Pausanias. He invited Pausanias to dinner, and got him dead drunk. Then he himself, and all his guests, took

The head of Zeus, perhaps adapted from the famous statue of Olympian Zeus by Pheidias, on a silver stater of Philip II; the reverse shows a boy (probably a jockey) on a horse, carrying a palm branch, to symbolise victory at Olympia.

This head of Alexander from Pergamum, in marble, was probably executed during the reign of Eumenes II (197–159), and based on an original made during Alexander's lifetime. The expression has been described as 'full of pathos and pothos': there are certainly signs of premature ageing and fleshiness.

turns to rape the wretched youth, who was afterwards beaten up. When Pausanias recovered, he went straight to the King and laid charges against Attalus. This placed Philip in a very awkward position: he kept putting Pausanias off, making one excuse after another, until finally he dismissed the charges altogether. The incident, he hoped, would soon be forgotten. It was not.

A sordid tale of homosexual intrigue and revenge does not, at first sight, provide sufficient motive in itself for Pausanias' murderous attack on Philip – nor, indeed, do our ancient sources think so. The grudge he bore the King was legitimate, but secondary. His real enemy was Attalus; but Attalus, luckily for himself, was out of the country. Philip, after all, had merely failed to see justice done. Though Pausanias did, in the event, kill him for personal motives, he is unlikely to have done so without active help and encouragement from others.

His burning and notorious sense of grievance would at once suggest him as the perfect instrument for a political assassination – nor can there be any doubt as to who had the strongest motive. 'Most of the blame,' says Plutarch, 'devolved upon Olympias, on the ground that she had added her exhortations to the young man's anger and incited him to the deed.' Her subsequent behaviour, indeed, suggests that she not only planned her husband's death, but openly gloried in it – perhaps as a means of diverting suspicion from Alexander himself, who, after all, benefited more by Pausanias' action than anyone. The murderer's corpse was nailed to a public gibbet: that very same night Olympias placed a gold crown on its head. A few days later she had the body taken down, burnt it over Philip's ashes, and buried it in a nearby grave. Every year she poured libations there on the anniversary of the murder. Like mother, like son; Olympias, too, never forgave an insult, and when she exacted vengeance it was with a ferocity seldom equalled except in the gorier pages of the Old Testament.

Alexander himself inevitably incurred wide suspicion at the time. Cleopatra's new-born son, as everyone knew, represented a dire threat to his succession. Pausanias, after failing to obtain satisfaction from Philip, had taken his tale of outrage to the Crown Prince. Alexander heard him out, and then quoted an enigmatic line from Euripides – 'The giver of the bride, the bridegroom, and the bride' – which could be construed as incitement to the murder of Attalus, Philip, and Cleopatra. Furthermore, the three young noblemen who pursued and killed Pausanias – Perdiccas, Leonnatus, and Attalus son of Andromenes – were all close and trusted friends of Alexander. Pausanias, then, still hot with resentment at the abominable way he had been treated, will have been approached, probably by Olympias, and promised high rewards and honours if he would join with his three kinsmen from Orestis in assassinating the King. Olympias undertook to have horses ready for all four of them. But what Pausanias did *not* know was the true role assigned to his fellow-conspirators. Their business was not the murder of Philip; it was to silence *him*. He knew too much; once he had served his purpose he was expendable.

Circumstantial evidence does not (I repeat) amount to proof positive; but men have been hanged on weaker cumulative evidence than that assembled here. The motive was overwhelming, the opportunity ideal. Once Alexander was established on the throne, of course, all speculation as to his guilt quickly faded away: nothing, as they say, succeeds like success. Most people preferred to keep quiet about what they knew, or suspected, and cast their lot in with the new regime. *The King is dead; long live the King.*

right: Hellenistic jewellery of the fourth and third centuries BC.

4 The keys of the kingdom

above: A Roman portrait bust of Alexander, probably copied from a Hellenistic model.

left: A Hellenistic Greek onyx cameo of the third century BC, thought to represent Alexander and Olympias.

As soon as Philip's body had been removed from the arena, and some degree of order restored, Antipater, with admirable dispatch, presented Alexander before the Macedonian army, which at once acclaimed him King. There were, of course, at least two other candidates for the throne: Amyntas, recently married to Philip's daughter Cynane, and Cleopatra's baby son Caranus. But these did not constitute an immediate threat. Amyntas was no usurper, and to place a child on the throne would mean another Regency – something everyone was anxious to avoid. In any case, it would have made the worst possible impression, both at home and abroad, if Alexander had inaugurated his reign with a dynastic purge. For the moment, therefore, he left both Amyntas and Caranus untouched.

His next move was to address the Macedonian people. He assured them that 'the King was changed only in name and that the state would be run on principles no less effective than those of his father's administration' – a somewhat ambiguous promise. He also announced the abolition of all public duties for the individual except that of military service. In other words, Macedonian citizens were to be exempt from direct taxation – a clear bid for popular backing. By way of strengthening his position still further, he now recalled all his close friends from exile, and appointed them to key posts in the new administration.

The news of Philip's death triggered off a general wave of insurrection, not only among the Greek states, but also in tribal frontier areas such as Thrace. Some cities (including Argos and Sparta) saw this as an ideal opportunity to recover their lost freedom. In Ambracia and Thebes Philip's garrisons were driven out. The Thebans and Arcadians (who presumably had not sent representatives to Aegae) refused to recognise Alexander's overlordship. But the most active hostility (despite those flowery protestations of allegiance) came from Athens. When the news of Philip's death reached them, the Athenians reacted with almost hysterical enthusiasm. Having just voted Philip a statue, and sworn to surrender any man who plotted against him, they now decreed a day of public thanksgiving, and emulated Olympias by awarding a gold crown to the King's assassin.

If Athens wanted to topple the new Macedonian King, her best hope lay in an alliance with the aristocratic junta that had backed Cleopatra. The

71

above: A gold myrtle-wreath clasp from Cyme in Aeolis. Fourth century BC.

Assembly, persuaded by Demosthenes' arguments, gave him permission to communicate privately with Parmenio and Attalus in Asia. He at once wrote urging them to declare war on Alexander ('a stripling', he declared airily, 'a mere booby') and promising full Athenian support if they did so. But Alexander, as Demosthenes and others found to their cost, was a sharper operator than any of them when it came to political in-fighting. He had seen at once that his greatest potential opposition must inevitably come from the High Command in Asia, above all from his implacable enemy Attalus. He therefore chose a trusted friend named Hecataeus, and sent him, with a small detachment, to Parmenio's headquarters – ostensibly as a liaison officer, in fact with secret orders 'to bring back Attalus alive if he could, but if not, to assassinate him as quickly as possible'.

Alexander's Macedonian counsellors, led by Antipater, were all urging him to tread warily. Their advice was that he should leave the Greek states severely alone and make an effort to conciliate the barbarian tribes by concessions and diplomacy. To this Alexander replied that if he showed the least sign of weakness or compromise his enemies would all fall on him at once. He intended, he told them, to deal with the situation by a display of 'courage and audacity'. It was not a suggestion; it was a flat statement, and a highly characteristic one.

At the head of a picked corps, the young King rode south from Pella, taking the coast road through Methone and Pydna into Thessaly. When he reached the Vale of Tempe, between Olympus and Ossa, he found the pass strongly defended. The Thessalians told him to halt his army while they made up their minds whether or not they should admit him. Alexander, with dangerous politeness, agreed – and at once set his field-engineers cutting steps up the steep seaward side of Mt Ossa.

Before the Thessalians realised what was happening, Alexander had crossed the mountains and was down in the plain behind them. With their flank thus neatly turned, they decided to negotiate. The King – having made his point – was all charm and friendliness. 'By kindly words and by rich promises as well' – his father's reliable formula – he persuaded the Thessalian

League to elect him *archon*, or president, of their federation for life, as Philip had been before him. They also placed a strong contingent of cavalry at his command.

Alexander never wasted time. Before Greece learnt of his out-flanking stratagem at Tempe he had already reached the Hot Gates (Thermopylae). Here, relying on his father's ancient privileges, he convened a meeting of the Amphictyonic Council, which at once endorsed his status as *Hegemon* of the League. The Council, like the Vatican, had no big battalions behind it; but it enjoyed considerable religious and moral prestige.

Thebes, not surprisingly, was Alexander's next concern. As the most powerful and important city in central Greece, its reliability was of paramount importance; and the Thebans' stubborn opposition to Macedonia could hardly be called encouraging. Startled Theban citizens woke up one

below: An aerial view of the Vale of Tempe, with the Olympus massif on the left and Mount Ossa to the right, looking eastwards towards the sea. Besides being an obvious defensive position, Tempe was also a famous beauty spot, in antiquity as today. The Athens-Salonika railway now runs beside the Peneus River, on the Olympus side of the gorge.

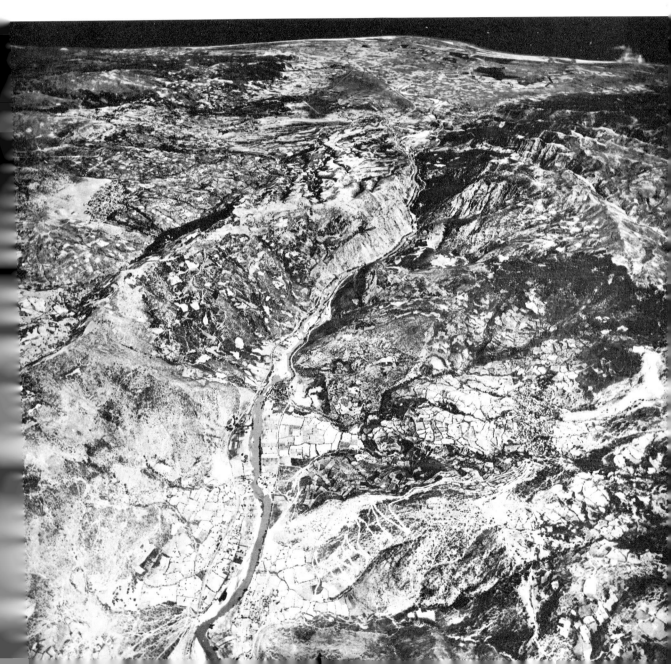

morning to find a Macedonian army in full battle array encamped outside the Cadmea. Alexander's ultimatum was simple enough: all he demanded was recognition as *Hegemon* of the League. If he got it, no more would be said about the expulsion of his father's troops, though they would, of course, be reinstated. Otherwise... The Thebans looked down at those grim Macedonian veterans and capitulated without further argument.

This caused something of a panic in Athens, which lay a bare forty miles beyond Thebes. The Athenians, anticipating a siege, brought in their property from the surrounding countryside and began to repair the city-walls. When Alexander offered them the same ultimatum as he had presented to Thebes, they accepted his terms with alacrity. An Athenian embassy was at once sent north, bearing profuse apologies for so regrettable a delay in acknowledging the King's official status.

The news of the King's whirlwind advance through Greece, followed by Athens' craven capitulation, made Attalus change his mind about a *coup d'état* with some speed. A neat *volte-face*, he calculated, might yet save him. He had kept all Demosthenes' correspondence, and this he now dispatched to Alexander, with many protestations of loyalty. He could have spared himself the trouble. Quite a few people did, in fact, change sides during those early months, and got away with it; but Attalus, the man who had publicly insulted Alexander's birth, could expect no mercy now or ever. That he did not realise this himself was a fatal error of judgment. Besides, by now Hecataeus – in accordance with Alexander's instruction – had reached a private understanding with Parmenio, who decided to cut his losses and go over to the winning side. It was this that finally sealed Attalus' fate.

What Parmenio had to offer was, in effect, nothing less than the removal of all organised Macedonian opposition to Alexander. If he swung his supporters over *en bloc* behind the new King, no one else would dare to challenge his position. Alexander was hard-pressed for time, and did not haggle over Parmenio's terms. This cause him a good deal of trouble later. When the army at last crossed into Asia, almost every key command was held by one of Parmenio's sons, brothers, or other nominees. It took Alexander six long years to break the stranglehold of this formidable clique. In return for such major concessions, Parmenio had to make one sacrifice: Attalus. Here Alexander proved adamant. Perhaps the sacrifice was not so great: a son-in-law could, after all, be replaced. A few days later Attalus was quietly liquidated.

In two brief months Alexander had achieved more than anyone would have dreamed possible at the time of Philip's death. Without a blow being struck he had won recognition from Thessaly, the Amphictyonic Council, Thebes, and Athens. The murder of Attalus and the transference of Parmenio's allegiance had insured him against any attempt at a counter-revolution by the Macedonian nobility. Now the time had come to have his position endorsed in more general terms. He therefore summoned a meeting of the Hellenic League at Corinth. To this were invited (if 'invited' is the right word) not only the existing delegates, but also representatives from such states as had so far refused to acknowledge his overlordship. The response was

A silver tetradrachm of Lysimachus (360–281 BC); on the obverse, the head of the deified Alexander, wearing the diadem and the ram's horn of Zeus Ammon; on the reverse, Athena with Nike (Victory) standing on her outstretched hand. Lysimachus was a Bodyguard of Alexander's, who once saved him from being mauled by a lion; after Alexander's death he became King of Thrace, but his kingdom did not outlast him.

all that he could have wished. His recent actions had thoroughly frightened the Greeks, and their envoys came flocking into Corinth with more haste than dignity.

So the League duly met, and elected Alexander *Hegemon* in his father's place. The treaty with Macedonia was also renewed: once again in perpetuity, so that it applied to the King's descendants as well as to himself. There were no substantial alterations. The Greek states were still to be 'free and independent'; it is not hard to imagine the delegates' feeling as they ratified *that* clause. But they had little choice in the matter. Nor could they very well avoid electing Alexander Captain-General and Plenipotentiary of the League's forces for the invasion of Persia. Moreover, if the Greeks imagined that this last honour was a mere empty formality, they very soon learnt better. The new Captain-General at once presented for their ratification a complex schedule 'defining the obligations of the contracting parties in the event of a joint campaign', and covering everything from military pay scales to the regulation of grain allowances.

When the congress was over, 'many statesmen and philosophers came to [Alexander] with their congratulations': we can imagine the scene all too clearly. But one famous character was conspicuous by his absence: Diogenes the Cynic. Piqued and curious, Alexander eventually went out to the suburb where Diogenes lived, in his large clay tub, and approached him personally. He found the philosopher sunning himself, naked except for a loin-cloth. Diogenes, his meditations disturbed by the noise and laughter of the numerous courtiers who came flocking at the Captain-General's heels, looked up at Alexander with a direct, uncomfortable gaze, but said nothing. For once in his life, Alexander was somewhat embarrassed. He greeted Diogenes with elaborate formality, and waited. Diogenes remained silent.

At last, in desperation, Alexander asked if there was anything the philosopher wanted, anything he, Alexander, could do for him? 'Yes,' came the famous answer, 'stand aside; you're keeping the sun off me.' That was the end of the interview. As they trooped back into Corinth, Alexander's followers tried to turn the episode into a joke, jeering at Diogenes and belittling his pretensions. But the Captain-General silenced them with one enigmatic remark. 'If I were not Alexander,' he said, 'I would be Diogenes.'

Having obtained a full mandate from the League, Alexander wound up the congress and set out, at the head of his army, for Macedonia, making a special detour to Delphi to consult the oracle. The priestess, under a certain amount of pressure, told him he was 'invincible'. He spent the winter of

336–5 giving his army an intensive training course in mountain warfare, to prepare them for the campaign he intended to undertake as soon as the snow was off the passes.

This campaign was intended to serve a threefold purpose. It would stabilise the frontiers, and thus leave Antipater – whom Alexander had earmarked for the onerous post of Regent during his absence – free to concentrate on Macedonia's rebarbative Greek allies if they made trouble. It would force the Thracians and Illyrians to admit that Alexander was no less formidable an opponent than his father. Finally, it would serve as a full-scale tactical exercise and dress rehearsal for the main assault on Persia.

With superb but calculated optimism, Alexander ordered a squadron of warships to sail from Byzantium into the Black Sea, and thence up the Danube, where they were to wait for the army at a prearranged rendezvous – probably near modern Ruschuk, south of Bucharest. Then he himself set out from Amphipolis by the overland route: eastward first past Neapolis (Kavalla), across the River Nestus (Mesta) and the Rhodope Mountains, then north to his father's military settlement Philippopolis (Plovdiv, in Bulgaria).

Up to this point he had been marching through friendly territory; but now came the first opposition. To reach the Danube he had to cross the main Haemus (Balkan) range, probably by the Shipka Pass. The Thracian tribes who remained independent of Macedonian rule decided to hold this pass against him. One of the qualities which most clearly marks Alexander off from the common run of competent field-commanders is his almost un-canny ability to divine enemy tactics in advance. He knew that the Thracians' favourite battle-manoeuvre was a wild broadsword charge, and instantly deduced what they planned to do. As soon as he and his men were into the narrow section of the gorge, their waggons would be sent rolling down the steep slope, shattering the Macedonian phalanx; and before its demoralised ranks could close again, the Thracians would charge through the broken spear-line, slashing and stabbing at close quarters, where the unwieldy *sarissa* was worse than useless.

Half the danger from such a manoeuvre lay in the element of surprise; and because of Alexander's inspired foreknowledge this advantage was now lost. According to Arrian (whose sources are, on the whole, sober about such details) when the waggons came hurtling down as predicted, not a man was lost: the front-rank troops crouched down with their shields above their heads so that the waggons bounced harmlessly over them. After the failure of the Thracians' initial stratagem, the battle itself proved an anticlimax. While Alexander's archers gave covering fire from the rocks above the right wing of the phalanx, and he himself led his *corps d'élite* up the western ridge, the main infantry divisions – doubtless delighted to find themselves still alive – stormed cheering to the head of the pass. The Thracians broke and ran, leaving 1500 dead behind them, together with many women and children. The road to the Danube lay open.

A good deal of plunder was taken: this Alexander sent back to the coast under escort. Then he and his men descended the far side of the Shipka Pass and pressed on across the Danube plain. There was no opposition.

A Thracian helmet, of the
fifth century BC.

When the Macedonians camped on the wooded banks of the Lyginus River
(probably the Yantra) the Danube itself was only three days' march away.
Crossing it was an exceedingly difficult task in the face of determined opposition from two local tribes, the Triballians and the Getae. Yet Alexander
seems to have been moved by an 'irresistible urge' (the Greek word is
to cross the river; *pothos*, geared to his tactical cunning and genius for
improvisation, took the Macedonian army over the Danube and back.

From the Danube the Macedonians marched back over the Shipka Pass,
then turned west instead of south, following the line of the Balkan range
the route which today links Lenskigrad with Sofia. This brought them out of
Triballian country and into the domains of Alexander's old friend Langarus,
king of the Agrianians. Langarus himself, together with his finest household
troops, had accompanied Alexander to the Danube. They did not operate
as an independent auxiliary unit, but were brigaded with the Guards
Division (Hypaspists) – the earliest instance of that military integration
policy which Alexander afterwards developed more fully in Asia and India.

At this point the most alarming reports began to come in. Alexander's
old enemy, Cleitus, King of Illyria – the son of Bardylis, whom Philip had
long ago defeated so crushingly at Lake Okhrida (see above, p. 26) – was
up in arms: Alexander's Danubian expedition had given him just the chance
he was waiting for. To make matters worse, he had formed an alliance
with another chieftain named Glaucias, the leader of the Taulantians –
an uncouth and mead-swilling tribe from the Durazzo area, the ancestors
of the modern Albanians. Yet a third Illyrian tribe, the Autaratians, had
agreed to attack Alexander on his line of march. The entire western frontier
of Macedonia was in grave danger.

Glaucias and his highlanders had not yet joined up with Cleitus, and Alexander's best hope was to reach the latter's fortress of Pelium before they did. This he managed to do, and Cleitus' reconnaissance patrols, after some brief skirmishing, retreated within the walls. Accordingly Alexander decided to blockade the fortress, and brought up his siege equipment – a curious tactical error. He had no time to waste, starving Cleitus out, and his chances of taking Pelium by assault were minimal. It was an almost impregnable stronghold, surrounded on three sides by thickly wooded mountains, and approached by way of a ford, and a pass so narrow that only four men with shields could walk abreast through it. The small plain between the fortress and river could all too easily become a death-trap.

For Alexander and his Macedonians it very nearly did. They were cut off. But the ruse by which Alexander extricated himself must stand as one of the most eccentrically brilliant stratagems in the whole history of warfare. Early next morning he formed up his entire army in the plain – apparently oblivious of the presence of the enemy – and proceeded to give an exhibition of close-order drill. The phalanx was paraded in files 120 men deep, with a squadron of 200 cavalry on each flank. By Alexander's express command, these drill-manoeuvres were carried out in total silence. The barbarians had never seen anything like it. From their positions in the surrounding hills they stared down at this weird ritual, half-terrified, half-curious. Then, little by little, one straggling group after another began to edge closer. Alexander watched them, waiting for the psychological moment. At last, he gave his final prearranged signal. The left wing of the cavalry swung into wedge formation, and charged. At the same moment, every man of the phalanx beat his spear on his shield, and from thousands of throats there went up the terrible ululating Macedonian war-cry – '*Alalalalai!*'

This sudden and shattering explosion of sound – especially after the dead stillness which had preceded it – utterly unnerved Glaucias' tribesmen. In headlong confusion, they fled for the fortress. Alexander and his Companion Cavalry flushed the last of them from a knoll overlooking the ford. The tribesmen, their first panic wearing off, suddenly realised that the Macedonians were breaking out of the trap so carefully laid for them. They rallied, and counter-attacked. Alexander, with the cavalry and light-armed troops, held them off from the knoll long enough for his siege-catapults to be carried through the ford and set up on the further bank. The archers, meanwhile, again on the King's instructions, had taken up a defensive position in mid-stream. While the final units struggled across, a covering fire of arrows and heavy stones (the catapults had a range of several hundred yards) kept Cleitus' men from engaging. Once again Alexander had concluded a complex and hazardous operation without losing a single man.

There was still no news from Langarus, who was dealing with the Auta-ratians; for all Alexander knew, his lines of communication with Macedonia might already have been cut. In the circumstances he showed quite in-credible *sang-froid*. Calculating, quite rightly, that the barbarians would assume the Macedonian army had gone for good, he withdrew for a few miles, and gave them three days in which to regain their confidence. Then he sent out a reconnaissance party. The news they brought back was just

A bronze statuette of
Alexander wearing the
goatskin aegis, traditionally associated with Zeus
and Athena, and adopted
by the Macedonian
Argead dynasty as an
emblem of royalty.

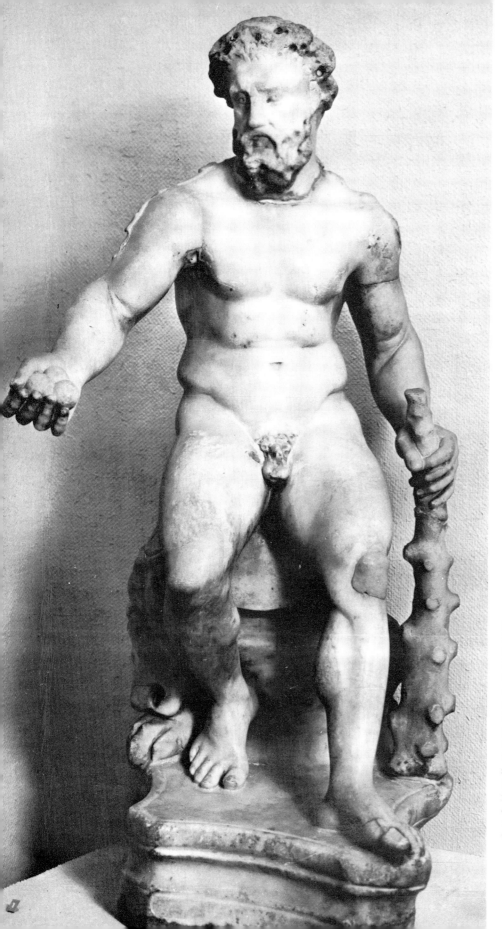

Lysippus, from whose Heracles Epitrapezius this statue was copied, was the famous fourth-century sculptor who was given a monopoly of Alexander's official portraiture by the King himself 'because he preserved his lion-like and manly looks as well as the turn of the neck and the softness in his eyes'. Lysippus was perhaps the first sculptor to break completely free of the relief concept and compose three-dimensionally.

what he had expected. The barbarian camp lay wide open. Over-confidence and lack of discipline in the enemy make powerful allies for any competent general. Besides – as these early campaigns amply demonstrate – the psychological exploitation of tribal indiscipline was one of Alexander's best weapons.

He at once marched back, at the head of a picked force, leaving the rest of the army to follow. Then, under cover of darkness, he sent in his archers and the Agrianians – aptly described as the Gurkhas of antiquity – to finish the job for him. It was a massacre pure and simple. Most of the tribesmen were still asleep, and Alexander's troops slaughtered them where they lay. Others were cut down as they tried to escape. The panic and chaos were indescribable. Cleitus, in desperation, set fire to Pelium, and fled with Glaucias to the latter's mountain stronghold near Durazzo.

The Illyrian threat had finally been destroyed.

A false report   It would, of course, have been very remarkable if the Greeks had not tried to capitalise on Alexander's absence during these crucial months. The question was, how to cause him maximum annoyance at the least risk to themselves? It was Demosthenes who hit on the obvious solution, and proceeded to stage-manage it with some skill. He announced in the Assembly that Alexander, *together with his whole expeditionary force*, had been massacred by the Triballians. To make this fabrication more plausible, he produced the 'messenger', bandaged and bloody, who swore he had received his 'wounds' in the same battle, and had actually been an eyewitness to Alexander's death.

The effect of such an announcement can well be imagined. If any citizens had doubts about the report, he patriotically suppressed them. This, after all, was just what every Greek had hoped and prayed might happen. Throughout the peninsula cities flared up in revolt. By far the most potentially dangerous uprising was that of Thebes, where the insurgents, having laid their plans with some care, were spectacularly successful. Had Thebes revolted spontaneously, without external aid, the situation – from Alexander's point of view – would have been bad enough. But in fact the success of the *coup* was due in no small measure to arms and gold supplied by Demosthenes, with the open connivance of the Athenian government.

The Athenians decided they would wait a while 'to see how the war would go' before committing troops to the defence of Thebes against the Macedonians. Despite this diplomatic fence-sitting, it was all too obvious where their real sympathies lay – and no one could doubt that the same was true, *a fortiori*, of Sparta and the Peloponnesian states. At any moment the whole of Greece might go up in flames. On top of this, the rumour of Alexander's death had had inevitable repercussions in Macedonia itself. Already Pella was humming with intrigue as various rival factions manoeuvred for a favourable opening. Clearly, the sooner the King came home the better. Yet nothing, it is safe to say, caused Alexander more alarm than the part which Persia was playing in this affair. The Great King had, at long last, reversed his earlier policy of non-interference, and was now channelling gold into Greece wherever he thought it would do most good. The mere thought of a possible Graeco-Persian coalition must have turned Alexander's blood cold.

Having digested the news from Greece and from Asia Minor, he saw that the first and most urgent task facing him was to scotch the rumour of his death. His first move was to dispatch a fast courier to Pella, to spread the news of his return. Besides dispatches for Antipater, this agent also carried a private, and probably coded, letter to Olympias – the one person in the world on whom Alexander could still rely absolutely. What he asked her to arrange was the immediate liquidation of Amyntas and of Cleopatra's baby son Caranus. Olympias carried out Alexander's instructions to the letter, as he knew she would.

One urgent piece of business being thus settled, Alexander struck camp and marched, at a cracking pace which shook even Philip's veterans, by way of Kastoria and Grevena, finally debouching on the Thessalian plain near Trikkala. Within seven days he had brought his army safely down to Pelinna. From here he swept on to Lamia, was through the Hot Gates before the rumour of his coming had reached the south, and – less than a fortnight after setting out – bivouacked at Onchestus in Boeotia. Twenty miles beyond Onchestus lay his ultimate destination: Thebes.

The leaders of the revolt – who only learnt that a Macedonian army had passed Thermopylae by the time it lay one day's march from Thebes – could not accept the fact that it was Alexander they had to deal with. Alexander, they insisted, was dead. This must be a force under Antipater. But twenty-four hours later, when the Macedonian phalanx lay entrenched outside the city-walls, no further wishful thinking was possible. Alexander lived and reigned indeed. The only decision, a vital one, left for the rebels was whether to hold out or sue for terms.

As Alexander himself no doubt reminded them, the Thebans could offer a perfectly acceptable diplomatic excuse for their actions. If he *had* in fact been dead, as they believed, the League treaty would at once have become null and void (since he left no issue), and their bid for independence would have been quite legitimate. They had acted in good faith; if they now returned to their allegiance, the whole episode could be forgotten, without loss of face on either side. The Thebans, however, proved unexpectedly stubborn. Their reaction to this overture was not a flag of truce, but a lightning raid on Alexander's outposts, during which quite a few Macedonians lost their lives. Next day the King moved his forces round to the south side of the city, and took up a position outside the Electra Gate, on the road to Athens.

When Alexander's approach was first confirmed, the Theban government had prepared a draft resolution – unanimously approved by the Assembly – that they should 'fight it out for their political freedom'. But when the Assembly met once more, there was a strong movement to abandon further resistance, and seek terms. However, those most directly responsible for the rising, in particular the returned exiles, held out against any compromise. They had breathed the heady air of freedom, and did not intend to give it up without a struggle. There was, too, always the chance that they might not have to give it up at all.

Alexander saw now what his course must be. It was at this point, Diodorus tells us, that he 'decided to destroy the city utterly and by this act of terror take the heart out of anyone else who might venture to rise against him'.

Recent excavations at the
Electra Gate, Thebes.

But first, to clarify his own position, and in hope of sowing dissension among the Thebans, he issued a final proclamation. Any individual who so wished might still come over to him, and participate in the 'common peace' of the Hellenic League. If the two main ringleaders of the revolt were surrendered, he would offer a general amnesty to the rest.

The Thebans' response deliberately blew Alexander's polite diplomatic fiction sky-high, in the most public possible manner. By so doing they sealed their own fate. From the highest tower of Thebes, their herald made a counter-demand and a counter-offer. They would, he announced, be willing to negotiate with Alexander – if the Macedonians first surrendered Antipater and Philotas. After this little pleasantry, he went on to proclaim 'that anyone who wished to join the Great King and Thebes in freeing the Greeks and destroying the tyrant of Greece should come over to them'. The venomous concision of this indictment was calculated to flick Alexander on the raw; and the reference to a Persian *entente*, which might just conceivably be true, could hardly help striking home. Alexander flew into one of his famous rages. From now on, he swore, he would 'pursue the Thebans with the extremity of punishment'.

He was as good as his word. The siege-engines were brought up, and the palisades breached. The Theban army fought a magnificent action outside the walls, and came within an ace of putting Alexander's phalanx to flight, even after the King threw in his reserves. But at the crucial moment Alexander saw that one postern-gate had been deserted by its guards, and sent a brigade under Perdiccas to get inside the city and make contact with the beleaguered garrison. This task Perdiccas successfully accomplished, though he himself sustained a severe wound during the action.

The moment the Thebans heard that their city-walls had been penetrated, they lost heart. Alexander counter-attacked: they wavered, broke, and fled in a wild stampede. There followed a period of savage street-fighting, which finally degenerated into wholesale butchery. Some of the Theban cavalry broke back and escaped across the plain; but for the most part Thebes' defenders fought and died where they stood, using broken spearshafts or their bare hands, asking no quarter and certainly getting none. Women and old men were dragged unceremoniously from sanctuary and 'subjected to outrage without limit'.

Next morning Alexander rapidly restored order. He issued a decree banning any further indiscriminate butchery of Theban citizens; they were worth more as slaves, and the Macedonian Treasury badly needed an infusion of hard cash. Both sides recovered and buried their dead, the Theban hoplites being placed together in a great common tomb by the Electra Gate. Then Alexander summoned a special meeting of the League Council – or such amenable delegates as he could lay hands on at short notice – in order to determine the city's ultimate fate.

The delegates' decision was 'to raze the city, to sell the captives, to outlaw the Theban exiles from all Greece, and to allow no Greek to offer shelter to a Theban'. The seven-gated city of history and legend, where Oedipus had ruled and Teiresias prophesied, was now, on the authority of a puppet commission, to be blotted from the face of the earth. There was a general rush by the Greek states to exculpate themselves and beg forgiveness for their 'errors'. The Athenian Assembly passed a resolution to pick ten men of known Macedonian sympathies, and send them as ambassadors 'to assure [Alexander], somewhat unseasonably, that the Athenian people rejoiced to see him safely returned from Illyria and the Triballians, and thoroughly approved his punishment of the Thebans for their revolt'.

This, though it may have amused the King, certainly did not impress him. He was polite enough to the envoys, but what they brought back to Athens was a curt letter requesting the surrender of ten Athenian generals and politicians 'who had opposed his interest'. Most prominent among these were Lycurgus, the freebooting *condottiere* Charidemus, and Demosthenes: no one doubted what their fate would be if they went. A stormy debate took place in the Assembly. In the end Demades – primed, it is said, with five talents from Demosthenes and his fellow-victims – volunteered to lead a second embassy to Pella, with the object of begging them off.

By now Alexander's temper had cooled somewhat, and his long-term strategic sense reasserted itself. He made it quite clear to Demades that he held Athens no less responsible than Thebes for the latter's rebellion. He also reminded him that welcoming Theban refugees was in itself a flagrant violation of the League's decree. Then he declared himself, with great magnanimity, willing to forgive and forget.

He removed all the names from his black-list except that of Charidemus, a licensed privateer whom Demosthenes, for one, was not sorry to see go; and even in this one case he merely required that the Athenians should banish him. Like his father, the King had no intention of embarking on a long and dangerous siege when there were more important things to be done. The concessions he made, moreover, were very real ones.

If Alexander expected any gratitude for such clemency, he was badly mistaken. His treatment of Thebes proved one of the worst psychological errors of his entire career. Had he spared the city he might, eventually, have reached some genuine accommodation with the Greek states. Now that was out of the question. After their first shocked terror had worn off, the Greeks' attitude towards Alexander hardened into a bitter and implacable hatred. Outwardly they collaborated, with cynical obsequiousness. But they never forgave him.

A Greek helmet in bronze (500–300 BC), found at Piraeus.

5 The Captain-General

A bronze statuette of Alexander on Bucephalas. Roman, of the Imperial period.

opposite: A Greek hoplite in combat against a Persian cavalryman.

Having thus summarily dealt with the Greek revolt, Alexander left the smoking ruins of Thebes behind him and hurried back north to Pella. There was much to be done, and little time in which to do it. First, Parmenio was recalled from Asia Minor: as Philip's best and most experienced general, he was to become Alexander's second-in-command. If the King could have found anyone else for the job he almost certainly would have done so; but the old marshal was indispensable, and knew it. Alexander next summoned a council to discuss that most burning of issues, the crusade against Persia. When was the campaign to be launched, and what strategy should be followed? Antipater and Parmenio both (as usual) advised him to proceed cautiously. In particular, with the grim struggle for the succession still fresh in their minds, they urged – very reasonably – that before leaving Macedonia he should marry and beget an heir. The King rejected this notion out of hand, a decision which was to cause untold bloodshed and political chaos after his death.

At the same time he undoubtedly had one very practical reason for his impatience. Philip had let the pay of his troops fall badly into arrears, and when he died he was 500 talents in debt. Even the 1000 talents a year which he milked from the Pangaeus mines was only about one-third of what it would cost to maintain the Macedonian field army on a standing basis. To make matters worse, Alexander had abolished direct taxation: this may have won him considerable support, but it was also rapidly leading the country into bankruptcy. Alexander found himself facing a very modern dilemma. Retrenchment could only be achieved by dissolving the splendid army on which all his hopes hung. To his way of thinking, an empty treasury was best filled at someone else's expense – and the Great King's coffers were fabulously well stocked. There was never much doubt which course he would choose. The Persian invasion was set, with the reluctant agreement of the council, for the following spring (334).

The final muster-roll of the expeditionary force is a revealing document in more ways than one. Apart from the advance corps already operating round the Dardanelles, which numbered 10,000 foot-soldiers and perhaps 1000 horse, Alexander's Macedonian army consisted of over 30,000 front-line infantrymen, and some 3300 cavalry. Even this by no means exhausted

Macedonia's reserves of manpower. From time to time fresh reinforcements were sent out, while numerous agricultural workers remained at home to till the soil and keep the farms productive. Of these 30,000 troops, perhaps 5000–6000 were on garrison duty in occupied cities, leaving 24,000 at Alexander's disposal. Yet no less than half this total – a really staggering figure – was earmarked for home defence under Antipater, together with 1500 of the 3300 cavalry available. Nothing could show more clearly what Alexander thought of the situation in Greece and the Balkans – or, indeed, what Greece thought of Alexander.

Alexander's field-army in Asia mustered 43,000 infantry all told; the League's contribution to this total was 7000. Of cavalry he had over 6000; the Greek states provided a beggarly 600. The League was responsible for Alexander's fleet, such as it was: 160 ships, of which Athens – with well over 300 triremes in commission – reluctantly supplied twenty. (These, together with 200 cavalrymen, were all Alexander ever got out of her.) Indeed, despite the League's official veto, far more Greeks fought for the Great King – and remained loyal to the very end – than were ever conscripted by Alexander.

The overall composition of the expeditionary force can perhaps be most easily understood if set out in tabulated form:

INFANTRY		CAVALRY	
12,000	Macedonians (phalanx and Guards Brigade)	1,800	Macedonians
		1,800	Thessalians
7,000	League troops	900	Thracian and Paeonian scouts
7,000	Odrysian, Triballian, and other tribal levies	600	League troops
1,000	light-armed troops (archers and Agrianians)	?1,000	advance expedition
5,000	mercenaries		
?11,000	advance expedition	6,100	total
43,000	total		

Overall total: 49,100

We should note the special status of the Thessalian cavalry, which stood in a category of its own among the other allied contingents. Philip had been elected *archon* of Thessaly for life, an office which Alexander had inherited. Thessaly was far more akin, ethnically speaking, to Macedonia than it was to the Greek city-states, being governed by a very similar type of feudal aristocracy. The Thessalian cavalry was, therefore, more or less indistinguishable from its Macedonian counterpart; its members were identically armed, and organised in the same way – that is, by territorial squadrons.

Another vital distinction between this unit and other League forces was the degree of trust which Alexander placed in it – though here his hand may have been forced to some extent. The Thessalians' permanent battle-station was on the left wing, which meant that they came under the direct command of Parmenio. This interesting alignment has considerable significance in the light of later events; it fits in very well with what we know of the quiet but deadly struggle that went on between Parmenio and Alexander, right

This gold stater of Philip II (probably posthumous issue) shows Apollo laureate, clearly modelled on the young Alexander.

The relief decoration on this gold plate, forming part of a scabbard for a Scythian sword, shows Greeks fighting Barbarians. Greek, late fifth or early fourth century BC, from Southern Russia.

from the beginning, to secure effective control of the army. Every key command must have been fought over tooth and nail. But Parmenio at this point was negotiating from strength. He was indispensable in the field, and he had secured Alexander's succession. His bill for these invaluable services proved a costly one.

In addition to front-line troops, the invasion force could call on large numbers of technicians and specialists, including a surveying section, the *bematistae*, who 'collected information about routes and camping-grounds and recorded the distances marched'. Staff administration and the secretariat were run by Eumenes of Cardia, Philip's former Head of Chancery. One unusual feature about this expedition – and here Aristotle's influence shows out most clearly – was the surprising number of scholars and scientists who accompanied it. Alexander had always known the value of good intelligence reports: this military principle he now applied on a far wider scale. His team included architects and geographers, botanists, astronomers, mathematicians and zoologists. All knowledge of the East for centuries to come depended, ultimately, on the accumulated information they brought back with them.

Alexander was also, so far as we know, the first field-commander in antiquity to organise an official publicity and propaganda section. Achilles had had Homer to immortalise him, and Achilles' descendant was determined that his own achievements should not go unsung. Besides the day-to-day record of the expedition, which Eumenes would keep, something a little more literary and grandiloquent was called for. To supply it, Alexander appointed Aristotle's nephew Callisthenes as the expedition's official historian. His task was to chronicle the King's achievements, in a way that would favourably impress Greek opinion. Though Alexander reserved the right to check Callisthenes' final draft, and sometimes (as we shall see) suggested a particular slanting of events, it should not be assumed that he virtually dictated all his chronicler wrote. There would be no need to stop Callisthenes setting down the truth as he saw it: it was for his all-too-predictable intellectual opinions that the historian had been hired in the first place.

He was, moreover, by no means an isolated phenomenon. Once it became known that Alexander not only wanted his exploits written up, but would hand out good money for the privilege, a whole rabble of third-rate poets,

historians and rhetoricians attached themselves to his train. Their numbers swelled as time went on, since Alexander's unbroken run of successes not only gave them more material, but increased the rewards they could command.

The campaign begins In early spring 334 King Alexander of Macedon set out at last from Pella at the head of his expeditionary force, and marched for the Dardanelles. Ever since childhood he had dreamed of this moment: now the dream had been fulfilled, and he was entering on his destiny of conquest. He was the young Achilles, sailing once more for the windy plains of Troy; but he was also Captain-General of the Hellenes, whose task it was to exact just vengeance for Xerxes' invasion of Greece. The two roles merged in his mind, as the two events had merged in history. 'Xerxes had made it clear that his expedition was the Trojan War in reverse; Alexander therefore in turn reversed the details of this most famous of all Oriental attacks.' To begin with, he crossed the Narrows at the same point. He brought his host the three hundred miles to Sestos in twenty days, which was good going. The advance corps had held the bridgehead, and his crossing took place without Persian opposition. This, however we look at it, was the most extraordinary piece of good luck for Alexander. His one great weakness lay in his fleet. Darius' Phoenician navy was almost three times as large, and far more efficient. A determined attack by sea during the actual crossing might well have scotched the invasion before it was well launched. But no such attack took place; not one enemy ship was sighted. Coordinated strategy could not

be called the Persian High Command's strongest point.

Accompanied by some six thousand men, Alexander made his way overland to Elaeum, at the southern tip of the Gallipoli peninsula. Here he sacrificed before the tomb of Protesilaus, traditionally the first Greek in Agamemnon's army who stepped ashore at Troy. Alexander prayed that his own landing on Asiatic soil might be luckier – an understandable request, since he intended to be first ashore himself, and Protesilaus had been killed almost immediately. He then set up an altar at the point where he was about to leave Europe, made sacrifice, and invoked the gods for victory in his war of vengeance. This done, he and his party crossed the Dardanelles in the sixty vessels which Parmenio had sent down from Sestos. Alexander steered the admiral's flagship in person. When the squadron was half-way across, he sacrificed a bull to Poseidon, and made libation with a golden vessel, just as Xerxes had done: the emphasis could hardly have been clearer.

The King's first act on landing at 'the Achaean harbour' – this, I suspect, was Rhoeteum – was to set up another altar, to Athena, Heracles, and Zeus of Safe Landings (throughout his life he showed himself genuinely scrupulous in religious matters) and to pray that 'these territories might accept him as King of their own free will, without constraint'. Then he set off on his pilgrimage to Ilium. He was welcomed by a committee of local Greeks who presented him with ceremonial gold wreaths. Alexander then offered sacrifice at the tombs of Ajax and Achilles, or what local tradition presented as such. To be on the safe side, the King also made a placatory offering at the sacred hearth of Zeus of Enclosures, where, according to legend, his own ancestor Neoptolemus had slain Priam. During a sightseeing trip round the town he was asked if he would care to inspect a lyre which had belonged to Paris. He refused curtly, saying that all Paris had ever played on this instrument were 'adulterous ditties such as captivate and bewitch the hearts of women'. 'But', he added, 'I would gladly see that of Achilles, to which he used to sing the glorious deeds of brave men.'

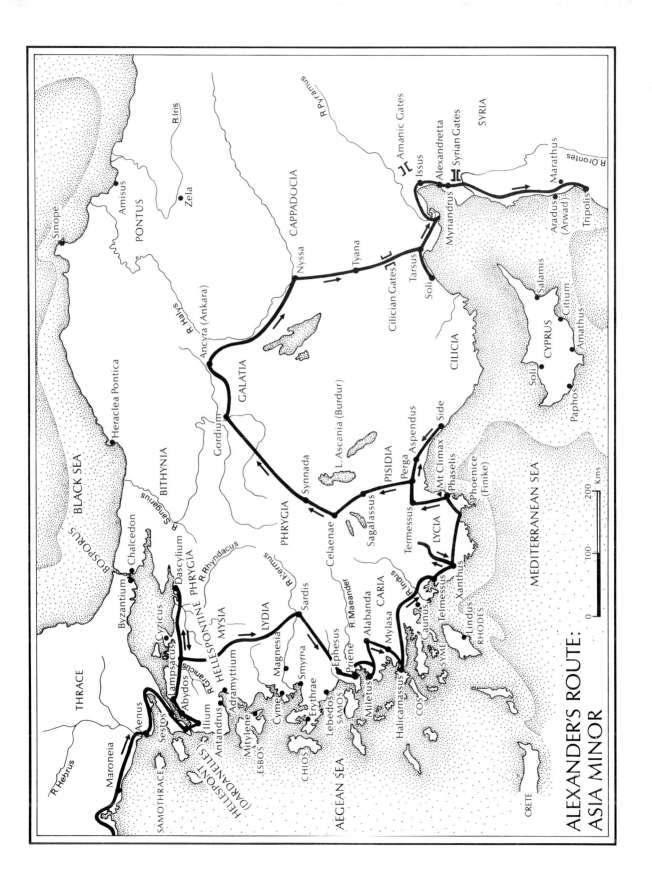

ALEXANDER'S ROUTE:
ASIA MINOR

From Ilium Alexander moved north again, and rejoined the main army at Arisbe, a little way outside Abydos. From here the invasion force marched north-east, following the road to Dascylium, where the Phrygian satrap had his seat of government. The first town they came to was Percote, still safely in Macedonian hands. But the next major city on their route, Lampsacus, was now controlled by Memnon – and to judge from our scanty evidence, quite a number of other Greek towns in Asia Minor were in the same position. The philosopher Anaximenes, acting as his city's official envoy, persuaded Alexander to by-pass Lampsacus, probably with a massive bribe; the King's shortage of money was already public knowledge.

With only a month's supplies – apart from what he could commandeer locally – and enough pay to last a fortnight, Alexander's one hope was to tempt the Persians into a set battle, and inflict a crushing defeat on them. Thus he had neither the time nor the reserves to invest a city: if it did not surrender on his approach, he left it severely alone. By now the Persians, who had been too late to stop him at the Dardanelles, saw clearly enough what his intentions were. Arsites, the satrap of Hellespontine Phrygia, sent out an appeal for help to his fellow-governors in Asia Minor: Arsamenes, on the Cilician seaboard, and Spithridates, who ruled over Lydia and Ionia. The three of them established a base-camp at Zeleia [Sari-Keia], east of the River Granicus, and summoned their commanders to a council of war.

The most sensible plan of campaign was that put forward by Memnon of Rhodes. What he proposed was a scorched-earth policy: destroy all crops, strip the countryside, if need be burn down towns and villages. Such a policy, as he made clear, would very soon force the Macedonian army to withdraw for lack of provisions. Meanwhile, the Persians should themselves assemble a large fleet and army, and carry the war across into Macedonia while Alexander's forces were still divided. This was first-class advice; unfortunately it came from a Greek mercenary, whose brilliance and plain speaking did not endear him to his Persian colleagues. A little tact might have got Memnon all he wanted; but he went on to say that they should at all costs avoid fighting a pitched battle, since the Macedonian infantry was so far superior to their own. The Persians were hurt in their dignity; Memnon's plan was therefore rejected, and the Persians decided to fight it out. Nothing could have pleased Alexander more. Nevertheless, his opponents still enjoyed one very considerable advantage: choice of terrain. Once they realised how badly Alexander needed a fight – and Memnon must surely have rubbed this point in – they could, without much difficulty, bring him to battle where and when they pleased.

In the event, they chose a defensive strategy: once Memnon's scheme had been discarded, this was probably the most sensible alternative. If Alexander could be lured into attacking a strongly held position, over dangerous ground, where his cavalry would find difficulty in charging and the phalanx could not hold formation, then that might well be the end of the invasion.

Having collected all available reinforcements, the satraps advanced from Zeleia to the River Granicus (now the Koçabas), which Alexander would have to cross if he wanted to reach Dascylium – or, indeed, to force an engagement. They chose a position on its eastern bank which offered the

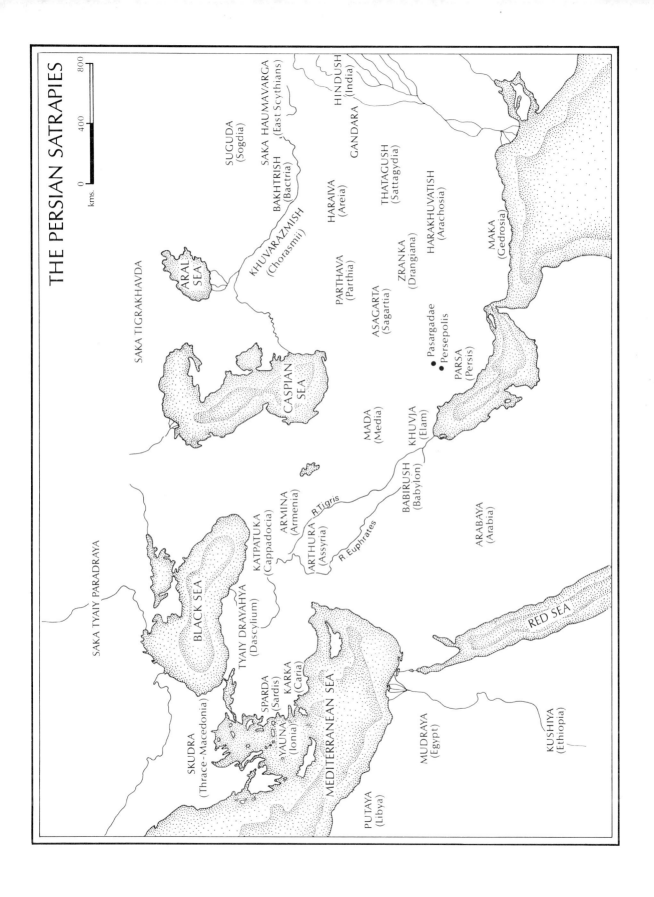

THE PERSIAN SATRAPIES

800

400

0

kms.

SUGUDA
(Sogdia)

SAKA HAUMAVARGA
(East Scythians)

HINDUSH
(India)

BAKHTRISH
(Bactria)

GANDARA
(India)

SAKA TIGRAKHAVDA

HARAIVA
(Areia)

THATAGUSH
(Sattagydia)

KHUVARAZMISH
(Chorasmii)

ARAL
SEA

HARAKHUVATISH
(Arachosia)

PARTHAVA
(Parthia)

ZRANKA
(Drangiana)

MAKA
(Gedrosia)

ASAGARTA
(Sagartia)

CASPIAN
SEA

Pasargadae
Persepolis

PARSA
(Persis)

MADA
(Media)

KHUVJA
(Elam)

SAKA TYAIY PARADRAYA

ARMINA
(Armenia)

R.Tigris

BABIRUSH
(Babylon)

KATPATUKA
(Cappadocia)

ARTHURA
(Assyria)

R.Euphrates

ARABAYA
(Arabia)

BLACK SEA

TYAIY DRAYAHYA
(Dascylium)

RED SEA

SPARDA
(Sardis)

KARKA
(Caria)

SKUDRA
(Thrace-Macedonia)

YAUNA
(Ionia)

MEDITERRANEAN SEA

MUDRAYA
(Egypt)

KUSHIYA
(Ethiopia)

PUTAYA
(Libya)

best possible conditions for the strategy they had in mind. Then they drew up their forces in depth, and waited. The overall force available to Arsites was not much over 30,000 men, whereas Alexander had 43,000 infantry alone. But in cavalry the satrap could count on a vast superiority of numbers: 15,000–16,000 to Alexander's 6000+. This factor dictated much of his subsequent tactics. Whatever he did, he must avoid exposing his inferior infantry to the Macedonian phalanx on open ground. If he was to defeat Alexander, it would be through the skilful use of his cavalry and mercenaries in combination.

When the Macedonians reached the river and saw the conditions under which they would have to attack, there was something of a panic among Alexander's officers, and small wonder. They were veterans with years of hard campaigning behind them, and they knew a death-trap when they saw one. Parmenio did his best to reason with the King. The Persians could not be tempted out of their entrenched position: they had every advantage, and knew it. The depth and speed of the river meant that the Macedonians would have to cross in column, and while they were struggling up that slippery bank on the far side, in general disorder, they would be fatally vulnerable. 'A failure at the outset,' Parmenio concluded – perhaps his most telling argument – 'would be a serious thing now, and highly detrimental to our success in the long run.'

Reluctantly, the King was forced to agree. The account of the battle composed afterwards by his official propagandists made it, nevertheless, take place that same afternoon, after a direct – and quite incredible – frontal assault across the river [see Arrian 1.13–15.5; Plutarch *Alexander* 16.1–3. The sequence of events leading up to the engagement, as given here, follows Diodorus, 17.19.1–3]. Under cover of darkness – probably leaving all campfires ablaze to deceive the Persians – the army marched downstream till a suitable ford was found. Here they bivouacked for a few hours. The crossing began at dawn. While it was still in progress, Arsites' scouts gave the alarm. Several regiments of cavalry hastily galloped down to the ford, hoping to catch Alexander's troops at a disadvantage – as they had done the previous afternoon. This time, however, they were too late. The bulk of the army was already on the eastern bank, and Macedonian discipline had no difficulty in coping with a surprise attack of this sort. While the phalanx formed up to cover their comrades in the river, Alexander led his own cavalry in a swift outflanking charge. The Persians wisely retreated. Alexander got the rest of his columns across at leisure, and then deployed in battle-formation (see plan opposite). It was rich, rolling, plainland, ideal for a cavalry engagement.

There was only one plan that Arsites and his fellow commanders could adopt. They put all their cavalry regiments into the front line, on as wide a front as possible, while the infantry was held in reserve. Then they advanced towards Alexander's position.

If they were also determined to kill the King himself, they certainly can have had no trouble in identifying him. He was arrayed in the magnificent armour he had taken from Athena's temple at Ilium; his shield was emblazoned as splendidly as that of Achilles, and on his head he wore an extraordinary helmet with two great white wings or plumes adorning it. All

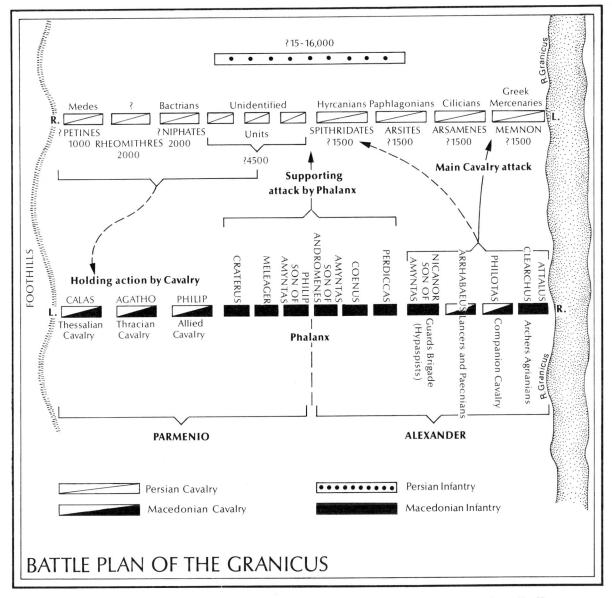

BATTLE PLAN OF THE GRANICUS

around him thronged an obsequious crowd of pages and staff officers.

Having observed that Alexander was taking up his battle-station on the right wing, the Persians transferred some of their best regiments from the centre to meet his assault. This was precisely what Alexander had hoped they would do. Then, with trumpets blaring, while hills and river re-echoed to the terrible '*Alalalalai!*' of the phalanx, the King charged, leading his cavalry in wedge formation. He feinted at the enemy left, where Memnon and Arsamenes were waiting for him; then he abruptly swung his wedge inwards, driving at the now weakened Persian centre. Meanwhile Parmenio, away on the left flank, was fighting a holding action against the Medes and Bactrians. Alexander was making a classic 'pivot' attack, with his left wing, as usual, forming the axis.

A desperate and truly Homeric struggle now ensued. Mithridates, Darius' son-in-law, counter-charged at the head of his own Iranian cavalry division, accompanied by forty high-ranking Persian nobles, and began to drive a similar wedge into the Macedonian centre. Alexander's spear had been broken in the first onslaught, and old Demaratus of Corinth gave him his own. The King wheeled round and rode straight for Mithridates. The Persian hurled a javelin at him with such force that it not only transfixed his shield, but pierced the cuirass behind it. Alexander plucked out the javelin, set spurs to his horse, and drove his own spear fair and square into Mithridates' breastplate. At this, says Diodorus, 'adjacent ranks in both armies cried out at the superlative display of prowess'. It is all remarkably like a battle-scene from the *Iliad*.

However, the breastplate held, the King's spear-point snapped off short, and Mithridates, shaken, but still game, drew his sword in readiness for a close-quarters mounted duel. Alexander, with considerable presence of mind, jabbed the broken spear into his opponent's face, hurling him to the ground. But he was so preoccupied with Mithridates that he had no eyes for anything else. Another Persian nobleman, Rhosaces, now rode at him from the flank, with drawn sabre, and dealt him such a blow on the head that it sheared through his winged helmet and laid the scalp open to the bone.

Alexander, swaying and dizzy, nevertheless managed to dispatch this fresh assailant; but while he was doing so, Rhosaces' brother, Spithridates, the satrap of Ionia, moved in behind him, sword upraised, ready to deliver the *coup de grâce*. In the very nick of time 'Black' Cleitus, the brother of Alexander's nurse, severed Spithridates' arm at the shoulder with one tremendous blow. It was none too soon; the King collapsed half-fainting to the ground, and a battle-royal raged over his prostrate body.

Meanwhile the phalanx was pouring through the gap in the Persian centre, and had begun to make short work of Arsites' native infantry. Somehow the King struggled on to his horse again, and the Companions rallied round him. The enemy centre began to cave in, leaving their flanks exposed. Parmenio's Thessalian cavalry charged on the left, and in a moment the entire Persian line broke and fled. Their infantry divisions, except for the mercenaries, put up little resistance. But Memnon and his men retreated in good order to a high knoll above the battle-field, and there made a last stand. They sent a herald to Alexander asking for quarter, but the King was in no mood to grant it. He now concentrated his entire attention on destroying them. While the phalanx delivered a frontal assault, his cavalry hemmed them in from all sides to prevent a mass break-out. Memnon himself somehow contrived to get away: Alexander had not yet seen the last of him.

The battle of the Granicus was over, and the Captain-General had won a famous victory. His personal conduct during the battle was heroic to a degree: seldom can the palm for valour, awarded him 'by common consent', have found a more deserving recipient. Casualties among the Persian cavalry units numbered some 2500, of which 1000 were native Iranians. The highest number of casualties said to have been suffered by Alexander's infantry is thirty: two sources reduce this figure to nine. Similarly with the cavalry: the maximum loss recorded is one hundred and twenty, but the same two authorities (Ptolemy and Aristobulus) admit no more than sixty, of which twenty-five were Companions who fell 'in the first charge'. Alexander subsequently had statues of these twenty-five erected at Dium in Macedonia: a unique gesture, never to be repeated. He also, characteristically, included his own statue in the group.

Memnon's 2000 surviving mercenaries were chained like felons and sent back to forced labour in Macedonia, probably down the mines. (Common sense would have suggested acquiring their valuable services for the Macedonian army, at cheap rates.) This was pure vindictiveness. Alexander's ostensible reason – still widely believed – was that 'they had violated Greek public opinion by fighting with Orientals against Greeks'. In other words, he was making a placatory gesture as Captain-General of the League.

A little good publicity in Greece never came amiss; but we may doubt whether propaganda was his primary motive. Aristobulus says he was 'influenced more by anger than by reason', and this, surely, is the plain truth. Once more, under cover of executing the League's decrees, Alexander had made it very clear what would happen to any Greeks – Athenians included – who might be rash enough to oppose him.

After this defeat Darius could no longer fail to take the Macedonian threat seriously. From the very jaws of defeat Alexander had snatched an overwhelming victory. The whole of western Asia Minor now lay open before him: the Persian crusade had begun in grim earnest.

Greeks fighting Orientals, in the Nereid Monument from Xanthus in Lycia. Fourth-century BC.

6 The road to Issus

Alexander wearing the royal diadem and the ram's horn of Zeus Ammon, on a silver tetradrachm of Lysimachus, issued by the Pergamum mint.

When news came in that the shattered remnants of the Persian army, Memnon among them, had retreated down the coast to Miletus, Alexander at once moved south in pursuit of them. He did not take the coast road himself, but went through Mysia. His initial destination was Sardis, capital of the Lydian satrapy and a city of great strategic importance, standing as it did at the head of the Royal Road to Susa. When he was still some nine miles off, the Persian governor of Sardis, Mithrines, accompanied by a group of leading citizens, came out to meet him. Mithrines offered to surrender not only Sardis itself, but also its acropolis and the treasure stored there. Alexander's victory at the Granicus was beginning to pay off in a gratifyingly literal way. From Sardis Alexander advanced to Ephesus – another key communication centre between Persia and the West – covering the seventy-mile journey in just under four days. At the news of his approach its mercenary garrison fled, taking with them the Macedonian renegade Amyntas, son of Antiochus. Clearly the way Alexander treated Memnon's troops at the Granicus had received wide publicity.

Ephesus, almost by accident, marked a turning-point in Alexander's policy towards the Greeks of Asia. On the mainland he had tended to back oligarchies. But at Ephesus it had been the oligarchs who ruled in Darius' name, and the democrats who welcomed Parmenio. Consequently a *democratic* puppet government was now installed. Until the King put an end to it (not too soon, one suspects), the democrats carried out a joyous purge of their political opponents. After a while, however, Alexander decided enough blood had been shed. This, we are told, earned him great popularity in the city. While he was still in Ephesus, ambassadors came from Magnesia and Tralles, offering their submission. Word had gone round that here at least – whatever he might do at home – the Macedonian invader looked kindly on democracies. Popular factions in the Greek cities, ever on the look-out for a promising *point d'appui*, were not slow to take the hint.

Hitherto Alexander may have been feeling his way as regards the administration of conquered territories: now the solution stared him in the face. Two large divisions, under Parmenio and Alcimachus, were sent off to accept the surrender of cities in Ionia, Lydia and the Aeolid. Before they left Sardis, both commanders were carefully briefed. Oligarchic juntas were to

be removed from office, and 'democratic' governments set up in their place. Local laws and customs were to be left untouched. Lastly, the tribute which each city had paid the Persians was to be remitted. These terms sound generous enough; but all they really meant was that one lot of puppet rulers was replaced by another. Moreover, despite the acquisition of Sardis' treasure (most of which, in all likelihood, had at once been dissipated on making arrears of pay) Alexander was still very short of ready cash. To forgo

above: A carved relief on a column-drum, from the later Temple of Artemis at Ephesus. This temple was under construction at the time of Alexander's visit to Ephesus, and he offered to finance its completion.

right: The Greek theatre
at Ephesus.

below: The amphitheatre
at Miletus. This colossal
construction, of late
Hellenistic or Roman
date, could seat 30,000
spectators.

tribute at this stage was a quixotic gesture he could ill afford. But to call it something else cost nothing. What it seems he did, in fact, was to insist on all 'liberated' Greek cities joining the Hellenic League. Once they had done this they became liable, under the League charter, to make cash 'contributions' (*syntaxeis*) to the Panhellenic war effort in lieu of providing men and ships. The sums involved, we may be sure, differed very little from what they had previously paid the Persians by way of tribute.

Another item on Parmenio's brief was to strengthen Ionian coastal defences against possible attacks by the Persian fleet. Such precautions, as events now showed, were by no means idle. The Great King's squadrons had been sighted off Caria, sailing north towards Miletus. Earlier, the commandant of the Milesian garrison, thinking his position hopeless, had sent Alexander a letter offering to surrender the city. Now he abruptly changed his mind. The King had to act fast. The League fleet was at once dispatched from Ephesus; if it reached Miletus before the Persians, the harbour could be held and the town saved. Parmenio and Alcimachus were recalled. Even so Alexander seems to have marched with what troops he had – over 15,000 were already on garrison duties or detachment, not counting casualties – before his second-in-command got back.

Nicanor, the commander of the Greek fleet, brought his squadrons to anchor by the off-shore island of Lade three days before the Persians arrived. He had only 160 ships to their 400, but his defensive position was superb. Alexander himself also reached Miletus in good time, and fortified Lade with a strong garrison. The Persians were forced to anchor offshore under Mt Mycale. This left them in an exposed position, and cut off from supplies of fresh water, since Alexander posted Philotas at the Maeander estuary to prevent their forage parties landing. He had already captured the outer city, and was now preparing to assault the acropolis.

The governor of Miletus sent a representative to Alexander's headquarters, offering to 'grant free use of their harbours, and free entry within their walls, to Alexander and the Persians alike', if he would raise the siege. In other words, Miletus was to be made an open city. Alexander turned this proposal down flat. Then he began his assault. While the League fleet blockaded the harbour mouth to prevent any assistance reaching the defenders from their Persian allies, the King's siege-engines battered away at the city walls. The defences were breached and the Macedonians surged through. Some of the garrison, including 300 mercenaries, escaped to a small island; the rest surrendered. Alexander, in accordance with his new policy, treated all Milesian citizens mercifully, though any foreigners who fell into his hands were sold as slaves. The Greek mercenaries he offered to spare ('moved to pity by their courage and loyalty', we are told) on condition that they entered his service.

For a while the Great King's fleet continued to ride off Mt Mycale, in the hope of provoking an engagement. But apart from some minor skirmishes, their attempts came to nothing; and since they were still cut off from all shore supplies, they found themselves in a virtual state of siege. Finally they gave up, weighed anchor, and sailed south to Halicarnassus (Bodrum), where the Persians were establishing a fresh line of defence. But the threat

right: Sardis: Alexander's first target after the Battle of the Granicus. It was the seat of a Persian satrap and stood at the head of the Royal Road to Susa. Excavations are currently in progress there.

overleaf: Through the valleys and uplands of Pisidia Alexander's Macedonians marched north to Celaenae and Gordium.

Miletus: little remains today of the once-great Ionian commercial port which was captured and sacked by the Persians in 494, and quickly fell to Alexander during his southward march from Sardis.

they represented had not been destroyed. It is in this context that we must view the momentous decision which Alexander now took: to disband his own fleet and stake everything on a land-based campaign. The Athenian detachment, plus one or two other vessels, were retained to serve as transports – and as hostages. Alexander also kept his squadrons in the Dardanelles. (Six months later they were back on naval operations in the Aegean.) But the bulk of the League's naval contingents were now paid off and sent home.

Alexander was taking an enormous calculated risk. Darius' squadrons were still at liberty to raid the Greek mainland, cut Alexander's lines of communication, and stir up trouble generally from one end of the Aegean to the other. (Most of these things in due course they did.) With 400 Phoenician warships at large, a Persian-backed Greek revolt was by no means impossible; and if it succeeded, Alexander's chances against Darius would not look at all rosy. The truth of the matter was that Alexander distrusted his Greek allies so profoundly – and with good reason – that he 'preferred to risk the collapse of his campaign in a spate of rebellion rather than entrust its safety to a Greek fleet'. He was also banking – again with good reason – on the chronic inability of the mainland city-states to take concerted action of any sort, even to secure their own freedom. But for a time, we shall see, it was touch and go.

After Miletus After the fall of Miletus, the surviving Persian forces withdrew south to Halicarnassus in Caria: a large, well-fortified stronghold, with a first-class harbour and every facility for withstanding a prolonged siege. The Great King appointed Memnon – who now had a score of his own to settle with Alexander – 'controller of lower Asia and commander of the fleet'. This was to be no sinecure: Halicarnassus, which he had made his base, stood squarely

right: A stone lion from the Mausoleum at Halicarnassus.

in the path of Alexander's advancing army. The Macedonians approached from the north-east, pitching camp about half a mile outside the Mylasa Gate. The more Alexander studied the city's defences, the less he liked what he saw. On the landward side rose huge crenellated walls, with guard-towers at regular intervals, protected by a moat forty-five feet wide and over twenty feet in depth. There were no fewer than three separate fortified citadels, which could – and did – hold out long after the city itself had fallen. One stood on the ancient acropolis, at the north-west bastion. The other two – the fortress of Salmacis and the tiny off-shore island of Arconnesus – commanded the harbour entrance.

This harbour was further protected by the Great King's fleet, which now rode at anchor there. Since Alexander had disbanded his own squadrons, he could not enforce a blockade from the seaward side. Thus Halicarnassus was not liable to run short of supplies, let alone be starved into surrender. The King's one hope was to take it by direct assault. But here he faced another difficulty: his siege equipment had not arrived. For some days, while his transport vessels sought to elude the Phoenician naval blockade, Alexander made fruitless efforts to carry Halicarnassus by direct assault. But at last the ships got through, presumably beaching in some deserted cove along the coast of the Ceramic Gulf. From that moment the siege was on in earnest.

Memnon's mercenaries were well trained, and had the further advantage of heavy covering fire from catapults set up on the walls. Several assaults were made by the Macedonians, and all, after a tremendous struggle, were driven back. During the night, while builders worked in relays to mask the gaps made by heavy battering rams Memnon sent out a commando force to burn Alexander's towers and engines. Another desperate battle ensued. Finally the Persians were forced to retreat – but not before some 300 Macedonians had been severely wounded.

Alexander now moved his siege-train against the nothern end of the city. Relentless pounding by rams and artillery at length brought down two towers and the intervening rampart. Alexander thereupon decided to attempt a night attack. This operation proved an expensive failure, largely because the Macedonians found their way blocked by an inner curtain-wall. They managed to extricate themselves, but next morning Alexander was forced to ask Memnon for a truce so that he could recover his dead. The commanders of the garrison – Memnon, Orontobates, and two Athenians, Ephialtes and Thrasybulus – now held a council of war. Ephialtes, a man of great personal strength and courage, insisted that if Halicarnassus was to be saved, they must take the offensive themselves. Memnon, reasonably enough, agreed. Between them they worked out a highly ingenious operation, which came very close indeed to success.

From the mercenaries in the garrison they selected 2000 men, and divided them into two commando forces. The first group, armed with torches and pitch-buckets, sallied out from behind the curtain-wall at dawn, and set fire to Alexander's siege equipment. The King, as Memnon had anticipated, brought up his infantry battalions to deal with this threat. Once Alexander's infantry was engaged, the second mercenary force charged out from the

This statue, from the Mausoleum at Halicarnassus, is probably that of Mausolus himself.

main city gate nearby, and took them in flank and rear. At the same time Memnon brought a new piece of siege equipment into play – a wooden tower 150 feet high, every platform bristling with artillery and javelin-men. While Ephialtes led the attack below, laying about him with murderous energy, a shower of missiles rained down on the phalanx from above.

Memnon now threw in his Persian infantry reserves. Hemmed in on all sides, Alexander could do nothing but fight a last-ditch action. He was saved, finally, by his reserve battalion of veterans. Shields locked, spear-line bristling, they now moved into the fray, a solid unbreakable line. Just as Ephialtes and his men thought victory was in their grasp, they found themselves faced with the prospect of fighting a second action. They wavered; the Macedonians pressed home their advantage; and by a great piece of luck Ephialtes himself was killed. In a matter of minutes the whole Persian assault-group crumbled, and began a stampede back to the city. There was savage hand-to-hand fighting by the curtain-wall, while so many men crowded on to the bridge across the moat that it collapsed.

The defenders had had enough. That night Memnon and Orontobates decided to pull out. Their best surviving troops they left behind to garrison the harbour fortresses. The remainder of the defence force, together with all easily moveable stores and equipment, they evacuated by sea to Cos. Before leaving they set fire to the armouries, to the great wooden tower that contained their siege artillery, and to houses abutting on the walls. A strong wind was blowing – the autumn *meltemi* that still scours Bodrum – and the blaze rapidly spread. Alexander saw it, but was helpless. Nor could he do a thing to stop the evacuation. He had no real fleet of his own, and the fortresses at the harbour mouth were still in Persian hands. He and his army were forced to stand and watch, by the lurid glare of the burning city, while Memnon shipped out all the men, stores and equipment he could cram aboard.

The army divides All newly married men were now sent home on winter leave, an act which won the King much popularity. Cleander and Coenus, who went with them as escorting officers, were instructed to collect fresh reinforcements from Macedonia and the Peloponnese.

The expeditionary force was divided into two separate commands. Parmenio, with the Thessalian cavalry, the Allied contingents, and the baggage-train – including Alexander's heavy siege equipment – was to march back north to Sardis, and from here conduct a campaign against the tribes of the central Anatolian plateau. The King himself, meanwhile, would advance eastward into Lycia and Pamphylia, 'to establish control of the coast and so immobilise the enemy's fleet'. Having done this, he would take his column up through the Pisidian hinterland (see map, p. 93), and rejoin Parmenio early the following spring, at Gordium. This was also to be the rendezvous for troops coming back off leave.

Alexander marched south-east to Telmessus, and then struck north, up one of the passes that circumvent the Xanthus gorges. (His object was to break through to the trunk road linking Phrygia with the coast, and thus regain contact with Parmenio.) Here, between mountain snows and hostile tribesmen, he bogged down, still short of his objective. Envoys from Phaselis

overleaf: The Anatolian plain east of Ankara: this was the route Alexander followed during his southward march towards the Cilician Gates.

and other towns in eastern Lycia now arrived, 'bringing him a gold crown and offer of friendship', together with useful information about local routes and hazards. Alexander weighed up the odds, and decided to let his communications go hang for the time being. He marched back to the coast, and here, at Xanthus, an incident took place which convinced him that the risk he was taking was justified. As the result of some subterranean upheaval, a spring near the city boiled up like a geyser, spewing forth a bronze tablet inscribed with ancient symbols – perhaps a long-lost *ex voto* offering. For any diviner with his wits about him this was a godsend. Aristander, the King's diviner, duly interpreted the mysterious inscription: it said (and who was to contradict him?) that 'the empire of the Persians would one day be destroyed by the Greeks and come to an end'. Much encouraged, Alexander set off again, in an easterly direction this time: by the coast road as far as Phoenice (Finike), and thence across the Chelidonian peninsula to Phaselis.

The land-route between Phaselis and Side went by way of the pass over Mt Climax, a narrow, precipitous track rising from the Kemer Chay through high-walled limestone defiles, and emerging on the Pamphylian plain south of Beldibi. Alexander, remembering the device he had employed to negotiate Mt Ossa (see above, p. 72), now set his Thracian pioneers to work, cutting steps and widening the gorge. The main body of the army then toiled in column up this rocky defile while Alexander himself, accompanied by a small escort, rode along the shore. This passage was only negotiable with a strong north wind blowing, and for some while now there had been heavy southerly gales, which made it impossible. However, Alexander decided to trust his luck. According to Callisthenes and others, the wind veered round to the north at the appropriate moment, so that the King and his party negotiated the passage without difficulty.

Once past Mt Climax, the army emerged into the rich and beautiful Pamphylian plain – the modern Turkish Riviera – a well-watered crescent some sixty miles long by eighteen deep, in splendid isolation between the sea and a high enclosing rampart of mountains. This marked the eastward limit of Alexander's foray along the coast. From Side as far as Cilicia stretched a wild, rugged, uninhabited region, without harbours or adequate land communications. No military intervention was needed here. After a brief brush with brigands, the expedition followed the coast as far as Perga, which surrendered without trouble. From here Alexander pushed on towards Aspendus. Outside the city he was met by a deputation, offering submission, but asking at the same time to be spared the indignity of a garrison. Alexander – who had been well briefed on Aspendus' resources, and was by now running short of cavalry mounts as well as cash – agreed not to garrison the city; but he exacted a steep price for the privilege. The Aspendians were to turn over to him all the horses they bred for Darius in their famous stud-farms, and, on top of this, to 'contribute fifty talents towards the men's pay'.

The citizens, on learning his extortionate terms, repudiated the treaty made in their name. When Alexander's commissariat party arrived to collect horses and 'contributions', they found the gates barred against them. Aspendus stood on a hill overlooking the Eurymedon, with a walled suburb down by the river itself. The citizens now evacuated this lower quarter, shut themselves in the citadel, and hoped against hope that the King would be too busy elsewhere to come back and deal with them. Unfortunately, he was not. He needed money and horses, and he had every intention of getting them. All too soon, the Aspendians saw Alexander and his troops bivouacking in the deserted lower town. At this their nerve failed them, and they sent down a herald, asking permission to surrender on the terms previously agreed. Alexander, however, had no intention of letting them off so lightly. The horses, he said, they were to supply as before. But their already exorbitant 'contribution' was doubled, and on top of this they now had to pay an annual sum as tribute – not, be it noted, to the League, but to Macedonia. Aspendus was placed under direct satrapal control, a step which surely included the imposition of a garrison. All leading citizens were to be surrendered as hostages.

The case of Aspendus exposes, with harsh clarity, Alexander's fundamental objectives in Asia Minor. So long as he received willing cooperation the pretence of a Panhellenic crusade could be kept up. But any resistance, the least opposition to his will, met with instant and savage reprisals. *Sois mon frère ou je te tue*: Alexander's conduct has since become a grim cliché, an anti-revolutionary joke. But it was no joke for those who, like the Aspendians, happened to become its victims.

North through Pisidia   From Aspendus the Macedonians marched north, through the uplands of Pisidia. The last real opposition Alexander encountered in this region was at Sagalassus. Here he had to fight that most tricky of all engagements   an uphill attack against an entrenched position and without cavalry support, since the ground was too steep and rough. But Macedonian training and discipline won out in the end. After a fierce struggle Sagalassus fell. Alexander, having mopped up a few more minor hill forts, now pressed on over the plateau. Skirting Lake Burdur, with its desolate salt-flats, he came in five days to Celaenae, at the headwaters of two rivers, the Maeander and the Marsyas.

Celaenae's position made it of great strategic importance, lying as it did at the junction of the main roads crossing the plateau – south to Pamphylia, by the route Alexander had followed; west to the Hermus and Maeander valleys; north to Gordium. The two latter itineraries formed a section of the Persian Royal Road; Xerxes had passed through Celaenae on his march to Sardis. Before Alexander moved on, Celaenae had to be made secure. Through this narrow 'corridor', with unsubdued tribes to the north and south, would run his only lines of communication between the Middle East and Ionia. The city soon fell, though the acropolis continued to hold out for some while.

Leaving a garrison under one of his best generals, Antigonus the One-eyed, Alexander set off once more, reaching Gordium early in March 333. Here he was joined by Parmenio's corps, together with the troops who had been sent home on winter furlough. They brought him welcome reinforcements – 3000 Macedonian infantrymen, 500 cavalry, 150 volunteers from Elis. But the general situation in Greece and the Aegean, as his returning officers now reported it, was sheerly disastrous, far worse than anything he could have feared; and once again the man responsible was Alexander's most dangerous opponent, that resourceful and elusive mercenary commander, Memnon of Rhodes.

After the fall of Halicarnassus, Memnon had been authorised by Darius (better late than never) to implement the strategy he had proposed before the Granicus: that of carrying the war over into Macedonia and Greece. The Persian fleet was already at his disposal. Now Darius furnished him, in addition, with funds substantial enough to raise a professional mercenary army. While Memnon systematically set about reducing the eastern islands of the Aegean, his agents were busy in Greece itself, handing out the Great King's gold to prospective supporters, and promising that Memnon would soon descend on Euboea, with a large army and a fleet of 300 warships.

Alexander was faced with a crucial decision. If he went on, he might well lose the Dardanelles, perhaps even Macedonia: Greece stood on the very brink of revolt. But if he turned back, the odds against his carrying the Persian crusade through to a successful conclusion would lengthen immeasurably. It was now, while the young King was still debating this problem, that the famous episode of the Gordian Knot took place. Like many men faced with a seemingly impossible choice, Alexander was ready to stake everything on a divine portent. Now, if ever, was the moment for the voice from heaven.

In Gordium, by the temple of Zeus Basileus, he found what he sought. There was an ancient waggon – supposedly dedicated by Gordius' son Midas when he became King of Phrygia – which still stood, a much-revered relic, on the acropolis. It had one very odd feature: its yoke was fastened to the pole with numerous thongs of cornel-bark, in a complex multiple knot of the kind known by sailors as a Turk's-head. An ancient oracle had foretold that anyone who contrived to loose this knot would become Lord of all Asia. Here was a challenge which Alexander found irresistible.

One characteristic of a Turk's-head knot is that it leaves no loose ends visible. For a long while Alexander struggled with this labyrinthine tangle to little effect. At last he gave up, 'at a loss how to proceed'. A failure would have been the worst possible omen: something drastic had to be done. Aristobulus says that Alexander drew out the dowel-peg which ran through pole and yoke, thus releasing the thongs. This sounds like *ex post facto* propaganda. According to our other sources, Alexander, exclaiming 'What difference does it make *how* I loose it?' drew his sword and slashed through the tangle at a single stroke – thus revealing the ends carefully tucked away inside.

That night there came thunder and lightning, which Alexander and the seers took to mean that Zeus approved the King's action (it could, of course, just as well have signified divine wrath). In any case, Alexander's mind was now made up. He would continue his campaign at all costs. Amphoterus was appointed admiral of the Dardanelles squadrons, while Hegelochus took command of the land forces based on Abydos. Alexander gave them 500 talents to raise a fresh fleet from the Greek allies – a thankless task – and sent a further 600 to Antipater for garrison pay and home defence. Then he moved on once more. From Gordium he marched north-east to Ancyra

Ancient Gordium, where Alexander cut the famous 'Gordian knot'.

(Ankara), on the borders of Cappadocia and Paphlagonia. While he was in Ancyra, the King received one more than welcome piece of news: shortly after the siege of Mytilene, Memnon had fallen sick and died. He was the only first-class general Darius possessed in Asia Minor, and his disappearance from the scene was an extraordinary piece of luck for Alexander. The threatened invasion of Greece had depended entirely on the Rhodian's skill and initiative; now the whole project might well collapse overnight.

Memnon's successors

After Memnon's death the command of his expeditionary force passed to two Persian nobles: Pharnabazus, his nephew by marriage, and Autophradates. While Autophradates went on with the campaign among the Aegean islands, Pharnabazus took a strong mercenary force by sea to Lycia, with the clear aim of winning back Alexander's conquest along the coast. But this very promising strategy was soon cut short by Darius, who knew as well as Alexander that Memnon's invasion plans had appreciably less chance of success without Memnon himself to direct operations. The Great King therefore summoned a meeting of his Privy Council and put the problem before them. Should he still attempt to carry the war into Europe? Or would it be better to force a direct trial of strength with the Macedonian army? The general feeling among his Persian councillors was that Darius should bring Alexander to battle, but this view was opposed with more force than tact by the Athenian commander Charidemus. He said, quite rightly, that it would be lunacy for Darius to stake his throne on such a gamble: he should remain at Susa, in charge of the war effort as a whole, while a professional general dealt with Alexander. He also hinted, in pretty broad terms, that he was more than ready to assume supreme command himself. Darius' councillors reacted sharply. Charidemus, they hinted, only wanted this job so that he could the more easily betray them to the Macedonians. At this point, fatally, Charidemus lost his temper: as a mercenary he was more vulnerable than most to such allegations. The meeting degenerated into a shouting match. Some of his remarks about Iranian cowardice and incompetence so incensed Darius (who could speak Greek fluently) that he 'seized him by the girdle according to the custom of the Persians' and ordered his instant execution. As he was dragged away, Charidemus cried out that Darius would pay for his unjust punishment with the loss of his throne and kingdom.

Once Darius' temper had cooled, he bitterly regretted having killed his best surviving general, and was forced to admit that no suitable replacement could be found. As a result the European invasion was now officially abandoned in favour of a direct confrontation with Alexander. Pharnabazus found himself officially confirmed as Memnon's successor; but the empty nature of this honour was made plain by the simultaneous recall of all his mercenaries, whom Darius badly needed to stiffen the Persian infantry line. Making the best of a bad job, he rejoined Autophradates and the two commanders pooled their forces. While ten triremes under Datames were detached to raid the Cyclades, the remainder sailed north and captured Tenedos. The Macedonians had still failed to raise an adequate fleet, and there was little opposition.

While Darius awaited his reinforcements in Babylon, Alexander was thrusting south across the rocky, volcanic uplands of Cappadocia, under a burning August sun. Between them and the coastal plain stretched the great barrier of the Taurus Mountains. The only pass was a deep, twisting canyon. Alexander, understandably, anticipated trouble at the Gates; but there was no other feasible route. He was saved a good deal of trouble – unintentionally – by Arsames, the Persian governor of Cilicia. The Gates provided Arsames with a defence-line of unparalleled strength. If he had brought up all his troops, and staked everything on holding the pass, Alexander would have had no option but to retreat. Instead, bent on imitating Memnon's strategy and avoiding a head-on collision, Arsames left only a small force at the Gates, and devoted much time and energy to devastating the Cilician plain behind them. The entire Macedonian army was able to advance through the defile, four abreast, and down into the plain. Alexander himself said afterwards that he never had a more amazing piece of luck in his entire career.

The rocky, volcanic uplands of Cappadocia, which Alexander traversed *en route* for Tarsus.

left: The Cilician Gates: Alexander's successful passage through this defile was one of the biggest strokes of luck in his entire career.

below: Approaching the Taurus Mountains.

He now heard reports that Arsames was evacuating Tarsus. In accordance with his chosen policy, the Persian intended to loot the city of its treasure, and then burn it down. Alexander at once sent Parmenio on ahead with the cavalry and the light-armed troops. Arsames, learning of his approach, took off in some haste, leaving both city and treasure intact. Darius was on the march from Babylon, and the satrap now made his way east to join him.

Alexander entered Tarsus on 3 September 333, sweating hot and exhausted after a rapid forced march from the foothills of the Taurus. Through the city itself ran the River Cydnus (Tersus-Tchai), clear, fast-flowing, and ice-cold with melted mountain snows. When he reached its banks, the young King at once stripped off and plunged in. Almost immediately he suffered an attack of cramp so severe that those watching took it for some sort of convulsion. His aides rushed into the water and pulled him out half-conscious. He was ashy-white, chilled to the bone. Before he took his bathe he seems to have been suffering from some kind of bronchial infection, which now quickly turned into acute pneumonia. For days he lay helpless, with a raging fever. His physicians were so pessimistic about his chances of recovery that they withheld their services, in case they should be accused of negligence – or, worse, of murder.

One doctor only, Philip of Acarnania, offered to treat him. This was Alexander's confidential physician, whom he had known since childhood. There were certain quick-acting drugs, Philip told him, but they involved an element of risk. The King, his mind running feverishly on Darius' advance, raised no objection. Philip's cure worked; but it was touch and go. The purge had an immediate and violent effect. The King's voice failed, and he began to have great difficulty in breathing; soon he lapsed into a semi-coma. Philip massaged him, and applied a series of hot fomentations. Alexander's tough constitution pulled him through the crisis, and the drug did the rest. Presently his fever dropped, and after three days he had sufficiently recovered to show himself to his anxious troops.

He now sent Parmenio, with the allied infantry, the Greek mercenaries, and the Thracian and Thessalian horse, to report on Darius' movements and to block the passes. Meanwhile he himself spent another week or two convalescing in Tarsus. Sick or well, he was never idle. For the first time, he took over a major mint, and used it to strike his own coins – a highly significant innovation. Until he crossed the Taurus, he could still claim to be 'liberating' the Greeks. But from Cilicia onwards he came as a conqueror. If he wanted Syrians or Phoenicians to acknowledge his overlordship, he had to build up an authority similar to that wielded by the Great King himself.

It was now that Harpalus, his Treasurer and Quartermaster General, supposedly defected – though the evidence is ambiguous, and Harpalus may in fact have been on a secret mission to watch the political situation in Greece, with defection as his cover-story. The whole affair remains shrouded in mystery and propaganda. Whatever Harpalus was up to in Greece did not prevent his subsequent reinstatement: he is by far the most enigmatic member of Alexander's *entourage*, and we have by no means heard the last of him.

Encouraging news from Parmenio meant that there was time to make at least a perfunctory show of 'subjugating' Cilicia. Alexander first visited Anchialus, a day's march west of Tarsus, then the nearby town of Soli, and then returned to Tarsus. Philotas and the cavalry were sent ahead as far as the Pyramus River, on the west side of the Gulf of Alexandretta. Alexander himself followed with the Royal Squadron and the infantry. He seems to have been much concerned to win support from the Cilician towns *en route*; but this did not noticeably delay his advance. Less than two days later he arrived in Castabala, where Parmenio met him with the latest news.

Darius had pitched camp at Sochi, somewhere east of the Syrian Gates (Beilan Pass) in the open plain. Parmenio urged Alexander to marshal his forces at Issus, and wait for Darius there. In so narrow a space, between the mountains and the sea, there was less danger of the Macedonians being out-flanked. Also (a vital point not mentioned by our sources) from Issus Alexander could anticipate Darius *whichever pass he chose to come through* (see map, p. 93). Yet Alexander seems to have convinced himself that if Darius moved at all, it would be through the Syrian Gates. At all events, the King did not wait at Issus. He took the rest of the army south through the Pillar of Jonah to Myriandrus, pitched camp opposite the pass, and waited for an enemy who never came.

This, clearly, was just the move that Darius had been hoping he would make. While Alexander was held up at Myriandrus by a violent thunder-storm (a very lame excuse, this: the Macedonian army afterwards marched mile after mile through Indian monsoon rains) Darius set out north on a lightning dash for the Amanic Gates (the modern Bogtche Pass). Having got through the pass unopposed, he swooped down from Castabala on Issus, where he captured most of Alexander's hospital cases. Their hands were cut off and seared with pitch; they were then taken on a tour of the Persian army, turned loose, and told to report what they had seen to Alexander. From Issus the Great King advanced as far as the Pinarus River (probably the Payas rather than the Deli) and took up a defensive position on its northern bank. He now lay in Alexander's rear, squarely across his lines of communication, and could thus force him to fight a reversed-front engagement. Alexander had been caught in an almost perfect trap. There was nothing for it but to fight, and in highly unfavourable circumstances. Nor did he have much choice of tactics: it was a frontal assault or nothing. His own Macedonians had marched nearly seventy miles in two days, and at the end of this marathon effort torrential rains had washed them out of their tents. They were sodden, exhausted and resentful. Yet somehow Alexander's outrageous optimism – well conveyed in the rousing pep-talk he now gave them – proved infectious: when he finished with a reference to Xenophon and the Ten Thousand, they cheered wildly.

At dawn the Macedonian army began its descent from the Jonah pass towards Issus. It took Alexander three miles to get clear of the pass, after which he had to march another nine before reaching the Pinarus River. He began his march in column of route. Then, as the ground opened out before him, he deployed battalion after battalion of the infantry into line, keeping his left flank close by the shore (Parmenio had strict instructions

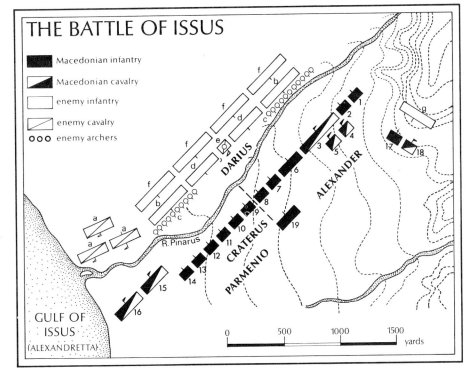

THE BATTLE OF ISSUS

Macedonian infantry

Macedonian cavalry

enemy infantry

enemy cavalry

enemy archers

DARIUS

ALEXANDER

CRATERUS

PARMENIO

R. Pinarus

GULF OF
ISSUS
(ALEXANDRETTA)

0   500   1000   1500
                          yards

never to lose contact with the sea) and pushing his right up into the foothills.
When all the line-regiments had been brought up, Alexander began to
feed in the cavalry squadrons. Most of them, Thessalians included, he massed
on the right wing, under his own command. Parmenio, for the moment, had
to make do with the Greek allies.

As usual, the Persians' great weakness lay in their infantry. Darius'
Asiatic levies were worse than useless against the Macedonian phalanx; he
sensibly lumped them together in the rear as reserves and camp-guards.
To make up his front line (see plan above) was something of a problem. In
the very centre he placed his Royal Bodyguard, a crack Iranian corps 2000
strong, whose spear-butts were decorated with golden quinces. He himself,
as tradition required, was stationed immediately behind them, in his great
ornamental chariot. Flanking the Bodyguard on either side were Darius'
indispensable Greek mercenaries: 30,000 of them, if we can trust our sources,
though this figure is generally regarded as an exaggeration. Finally, on the
wings, came two divisions of light-armed Persian infantry, the so-called
'Cardaces'. These appear to have been Iranian youths who were undergoing
or had just completed their military training.

By the time Darius had moved all his infantry units into battle-formation,
it was mid-afternoon, and the Macedonians were getting uncomfortably
close. Not that Alexander showed any impatience. He led his troops forward
at a very leisurely pace, with frequent halts to check their dressing and
observe the movements of the enemy. Darius' intentions were still far from
clear. Then, abruptly, the Persian cavalry squadrons that had been acting
as a screen were signalled back across the river, and dispatched to their
final battle-stations. At this point Darius' intentions became very clear

123

indeed, and Alexander had to carry out a last-minute reorganisation of his own line. Instead of massing the Iranian cavalry opposite Alexander's right, where it had been expected, the Great King was moving all his best squadrons down to the seashore, against Parmenio.

Alexander at once sent the Thessalians back across to his left, as reinforcements, ordering them to ride behind the phalanx so that their movements would remain unobserved. Reports now came in that the Persian forces up on the ridge had occupied a projecting spur of the mountain, and were now actually *behind* the Macedonian right wing. Alexander sent a mixed force of light-armed troops to deal with them. He himself (for whatever reason) was still far more concerned by the possibility of a frontal outflanking movement. He pushed forward his cavalry patrols, and brought across two squadrons from the centre to strengthen his right wing. The Persians in the hills, however, made no attempt to fight, and a quick commando assault soon routed them. Alexander left 300 cavalry to watch their movements, but recalled the archers and Agrianians as extra protection for his flank.

So the Macedonian army, now deployed on a three-mile front, continued its steady advance. When it was just beyond bow-shot Alexander halted in the hope that the Persians might charge. They did not. Darius had a first-class defensive position, and – very reasonably – was not in the least inclined to abandon it. Alexander saw now that any further delay would be useless. It was already late afternoon. After a final inspection he led on once more, slowly at first, in close formation, until they came within range of the Persian archers. These now loosed off a tremendous volley, 'such a shower of missiles that they collided with one another in the air'. Then a trumpet rang out, and Alexander, at the head of the Companions, charged across the river, scattering Darius' archers and driving them back among the light-armed Persian infantry. It was a magnificently successful assault: the battle on the right wing was won in the first few moments.

In the centre things did not go nearly so well. The phalanx had great difficulty in getting across the river at all. For a while neither side could advance more than a few feet. Then came the inevitable aftermath of Alexander's headlong charge: a dangerous gap opened up on the right flank of the phalanx. This was too good a chance for the mercenaries to miss. They drove a deep wedge into the Macedonian line: during the desperate fighting that followed Ptolemy son of Seleucus and some 120 Macedonian officers lost their lives.

Meanwhile Alexander, having rolled up the Persian left wing, now swung his wedge of cavalry inward against the rear files of the mercenaries and the Royal Bodyguard. From this moment he and his men strained every nerve to kill or capture Darius. The Great King offered the best – perhaps the only – focal point for any future resistance involving all the provinces of the empire. His loss would cripple the Persian cause. Besides, the vast majority of his subjects cared little who ruled them as long as their own local interests were left intact.

The moment he located the Great King's chariot, Alexander charged straight for it. Oxathres, Darius' brother, leading the Royal Household Cavalry, fought desperately to protect him. Dying men and horses lay piled in wild confusion. Alexander received a wound in the thigh – from Darius

right: A Persian soldier, a detail from the 'Issus Mosaic'.

overleaf: Traditionally this scene represents the turning-point at Issus when Darius fled the battle; but Philoxenus, the artist from whose painting the mosaic was copied, may have incorporated elements from other battles. Alexander's personal moment of peril seems borrowed from the Granicus, and the confrontation also has echoes of Gaugamela. Note the sharp and unflattering realism of both main portraits.

himself, it was claimed. For a moment there was a real danger that the horses of Darius' chariot might carry the Great King headlong through Alexander's lines. Darius, abandoning royal protocol in this emergency, grabbed the reins with his own hands. A second, lighter chariot was somehow found and brought up. Darius, seeing himself in imminent danger of capture, scrambled into it and fled the field.

By now Alexander's centre and left were both seriously threatened, and he had no option but to postpone his pursuit of the Great King. He must have been in a fury of frustration; nevertheless he acted promptly and with crushing effectiveness. He swung his whole right wing round in a wedge against the mercenaries' flank, and drove them out of the river with heavy casualties. When Nabarzanes' heavy cavalry saw their own centre being cut to pieces, and heard of the Great King's flight, they wheeled their horses about and followed him. The retreat soon became a rout. The Persians were encumbered by their heavy scale-armour, and the Thessalians harried them relentlessly.

As soon as Alexander saw that the phalanx and the Thessalians were out of danger, he and his Companions set off on a headlong chase after Darius. But everything was against them. The Great King had over half a mile's start on them. Worse, the route he had taken – probably the mountain track to Dörtyol and Hassa – was now jammed with the disorganised remnants of the Persian Imperial Army. Nevertheless, the pursuers kept going for some twenty-five miles. Only when it was completely dark did Alexander give up and turn back. Despite everything, he did not reach camp empty-handed. Darius had very soon abandoned his chariot, and fled over the mountains on horseback, stripping off his royal mantle and all other insignia by which he might be recognised. These, together with his shield and bow, Alexander found and kept as trophies.

He got back to camp about midnight, dusty and exhausted after his breakneck ride. Just as he was settling down to dinner – he must have had a ravenous appetite after his exertions – there came the sound of wailing and lamentation from a nearby tent. He dispatched an attendant to find out what all the uproar was about. It appeared that one of the Persian court eunuchs, having seen the Great King's chariot and royal insignia, jumped to the conclusion that he was dead; and now Darius' mother, wife and children were mourning for their lord. Alexander hastened to reassure them. They were given to understand that they had nothing to fear. Darius was not dead; Alexander, moreover, had not fought against him out of personal enmity, but 'had made legitimate war for the sovereignty of Asia'. They were to retain all the titles, ceremonial, and insignia befitting their royal status, and would receive whatever allowances they had been granted by Darius himself.

Issus was a great victory, but very far from a decisive one. It had enabled Alexander to extricate himself from a very dangerous position. It brought in welcome spoils, and had excellent value for purposes of propaganda. But more than 10,000 Greek mercenaries had got away, in good order, to form the nucleus of another Persian army; the Eastern provinces, such as Bactria, were still intact; and – most important of all – so long as Darius himself remained at large, there was no question of the war being over.

A highly individualistic study of Darius: one would like to believe that it portrays the man as he was, perhaps from contemporary portraits or medallions. It is even possible that Philoxenus accompanied Alexander's expedition and was able to paint the Great King from life.

7 Intimations of immortality

Hour after hour Darius kept up his headlong flight, over bad mountain roads, in pitch darkness, accompanied only by a few staff officers and attendants, determined to put as many miles between himself and Alexander as he could before daybreak. Next morning he was joined by other disorganised groups of fugitives, including some 4000 Greek mercenaries. With this scratch force he rode on eastward, never slackening rein until he had crossed the Euphrates and reached Babylon.

The Great King was, for the moment, a very frightened man. He clearly expected Alexander to be hammering at the gates of Babylon within a matter of days, and his own shattered forces were in no condition to fight another battle. Since he could not fight, he decided, he must try diplomacy. So, with many misgivings, the fugitive Lord of Asia drafted a memorandum to Alexander, proposing terms for a settlement. The offer he made was, as we shall see, extremely generous: it can never have occurred to him that his adversary might reject it out of hand. He had yet to learn the scope and intensity of Alexander's ambitions.

Meanwhile the Macedonians were revelling in their first real taste of Oriental luxury. Darius' camp had yielded plunder beyond their wildest dreams. Alexander himself might despise such fripperies, but his officers and men did not. From now on their passion for good living steadily increased. Once the battle was over, Alexander had told them, nothing would remain but to crown their many labours with the sovereignty of Asia. This, in the event, proved an infinitely expandable programme. If they were expecting a quick chase after Darius, another share-out of Persian loot, and a triumphant homecoming, they were doomed to disappointment. At this critical stage in the campaign Alexander had to consider his future strategy very carefully indeed.

The one way in which he could finally crush Darius was by provoking him into another set battle – a battle, moreover, in which the full strength of the Persian empire was deployed. He therefore decided, very shrewdly, to attend to other matters for the time being. The Great King's pride was such that there would be no difficulty in forcing a show-down when the time came. Meanwhile he had to be given ample leisure to reassemble and strengthen his shattered forces. This suited Alexander's own plans very well. While

A gold coin of Alexander, showing the head (obverse) of Athena.

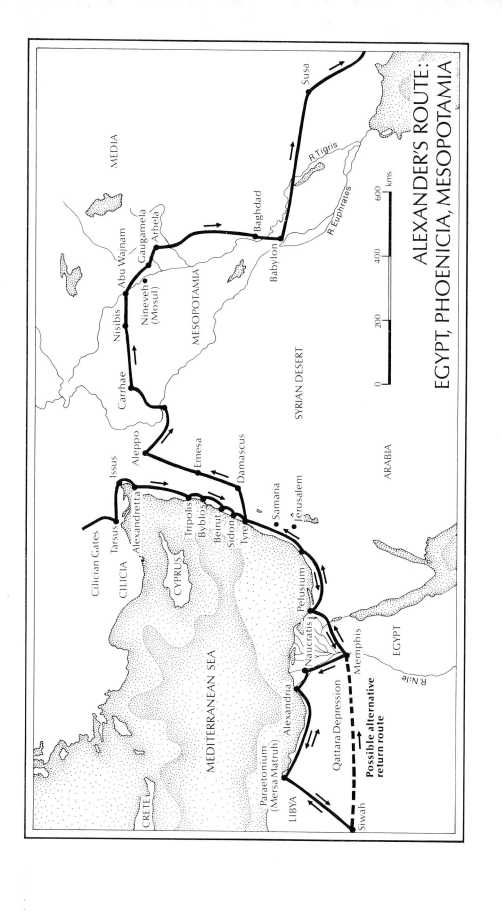

ALEXANDER'S ROUTE:
EGYPT, PHOENICIA, MESOPOTAMIA

Darius was thus occupied, he himself – undisturbed by any major opposition – would complete his interrupted project of reducing the Phoenician seaboard. As usual, he wasted no time. Only a few days after Issus, the Macedonian army struck camp and set out down the road into Syria. Marathus surrendered without a struggle; and it was here that two Persian envoys reached Alexander, bearing Darius' armistice proposals. If Alexander would restore his wife, mother, and children, he was ready to pay an appropriate ransom. Furthermore, if Alexander agreed to sign a treaty of friendship and alliance with Persia, the Great King would cede him 'the territories and cities of Asia west of the Halys River'.

This document placed Alexander in a somewhat delicate predicament. What Darius now offered him was all that Philip had aimed to conquer – 'Asia from Cilicia to Sinope', as Isocrates phrased it. Alexander's own ambitions, however, looked far beyond so modest a goal. Nothing would satisfy him, ultimately, but the utter overthrow of Darius and his own establishment as Lord of Asia, heir by right of conquest to the Achaemenid throne and empire. With this end in view, it was essential that the Persian offer should be turned down. Alexander therefore suppressed the original document and forged a substitute, which was not only offensively arrogant in tone, but – more important – omitted any reference to territorial concessions. This the King's military council rejected on sight; and Alexander then drafted a reply which began, very much *de haut en bas*, 'King Alexander to Darius'. But it is the concluding words which are most remarkable: 'In future', he wrote, 'let any communication you wish to make with me be addressed to the King of all Asia. Do not write to me as an equal. Everything you possess is now mine; so, if you should want anything, let me know in the proper terms, or I shall take steps to deal with you as a criminal. If, on the other hand, you wish to dispute your throne, stand and fight for it and do not run away. Wherever you may hide yourself, be sure I shall seek you out.' The envoy chosen to deliver this scathing broadside had strict instructions 'to discuss no question whatever which might arise from it' – a very necessary precaution.

Alexander's final threat was, at the time of writing, no more than a monumental piece of bluff. Yet it might well sting Darius into further military action – the one way of ensuring his downfall. Meanwhile, the mere fact that he had offered to surrender Asia Minor showed how badly Issus had shaken him. It was an encouraging sign for any future negotiations.

When Darius received Alexander's reply, he at once began planning a fresh campaign. The eastern provinces contained vast untapped reserves of manpower. All he needed was time in which to organise them. Meanwhile, Memnon's scheme for carrying the war into Europe – temporarily shelved at the instance of the Persian High Command – was now given a fresh airing. If Darius could cut Alexander's land communications in Asia Minor, win complete control of the Dardanelles, and persuade the Greek states to launch a general revolt against Antipater, the Macedonian army's position would become virtually untenable. In this way, the Great King calculated, he might force Alexander to withdraw without fighting another major engagement. At the very least he would win valuable time. He therefore

issued operational orders aimed at undermining the Macedonian position in Greece, the Aegean and Asia Minor.

Alexander's lines of communication, as we have seen (cf. above, p. 115), ran through a narrow bottleneck by way of Celaenae. With the aid of the mountain tribes, Darius calculated, it should not take long to close this bottleneck altogether. If Alexander found himself cut off from Europe, he might prove more amenable to argument. But this (though Darius could not have known it) was a false assumption. Alexander had already made his crucial decision, at Gordium: Greece and Macedonia were, in the last resort, expendable. The victory of Issus can only have reinforced such an attitude.

Parmenio rounded up the Great King's treasure and baggage train from Damascus without opposition; and early in January 332 Alexander continued his march. Byblos surrendered without any trouble. The Macedonians tramped on south beside the sea, to the great commercial port of Sidon. Here the inhabitants welcomed Alexander – out of hatred for Darius and the Persians, says Arrian; but Sidon's long-standing rivalry with Tyre, a few miles further on down the coast, must surely have been the true deciding factor.

From Sidon Alexander continued towards Tyre, the most powerful naval and commercial port between Cilicia and Egypt. It stood on a rocky island half a mile off-shore, protected by great walls which on the landward side

Sidon, Tyre's neighbour and rival on the Phoenician coast, which welcomed the advancing Macedonian army.

The march to Tyre

High-relief statues of weeping women on a sarcophagus found together with the 'Alexander sarcophagus' in the Royal Cemetery at Sidon. Fourth century BC.

rose to a height of about 150 feet. As his army approached, a group of ambassadors, including the King's son, came out to greet him, with the usual gold crown and many protestations of allegiance. But their hospitable manner was deceptive. They had not the slightest intention of handing over Tyre to the Macedonians: on the contrary, they meant to hold this island fortress for Darius and the Phoenician fleet. If they could avoid trouble by a little diplomatic bribery, well and good. But they were not prepared to compromise. If Alexander proved obstinate, he could go ahead and besiege them. They had worn out besiegers before, and the Macedonians did not even have the advantage of a fleet. Besides, the longer they delayed Alexander, the more time Darius would have to mobilise a new army and carry out his military operations in Asia Minor. Before very long Alexander saw that the Tyrians were 'more inclined to accept an alliance with him than to submit to his rule'. He thanked the envoys for their gifts. Then, very blandly, he said what great pleasure it would give him, as a royal descendant of Heracles, to visit the island and sacrifice to their god Melkart, in his great temple there.

The Tyrians were well aware that Heracles was generally identified with the Phoenician god Melkart, and probably also knew just how Alexander hoped to exploit this equation for his own benefit. Now was the time of Melkart's great annual festival, which attracted many visitors, especially from Carthage. To let Alexander have his way would be tantamount to acknowledging him as their rightful king. So the envoys, with charming aplomb, told him that another temple, just as good, existed on the mainland, at Old Tyre. Perhaps he would like to sacrifice there? At this Alexander flew into a rage and dismissed them out of hand, with all manner of dire threats. On returning home they advised their government to think twice before taking on so formidable an opponent. But the Tyrians had complete confidence in their natural and man-made defences. The channel between Tyre and the mainland was over twenty feet deep and frequently lashed by violent south-west winds. Their fortifications, they believed, would resist the strongest battering-ram yet devised. The city walls stood sheer above the sea: how could any army without ships scale them? Shore-based artillery was useless at such a range. The Tyrians decided to stand firm, encouraged by their visitors from Carthage, who promised them massive reinforcements. Alexander was now faced with what was to prove the longest and most gruelling military operation of his entire career.

He began by demolishing Old Tyre to provide foundation stones and rubble for a mole across the strait. A pioneering party was sent inland through the lower Beqaa Valley to fetch timber, cedars in particular, from the slopes of Antilebanon. Not only Alexander's troops, but all able-bodied men from the surrounding towns and villages found themselves drafted into a vast emergency labour force, estimated at 'many tens of thousands'.

At first the Tyrians treated his project as a joke. But the rapid, efficient progress of the work soon made them change their tune. They evacuated some of their women and children, and began to construct extra artillery for the landward defences. Far from laughing at Alexander's mole, they now made a vigorous attempt to destroy it before it could become a real menace. Eighty vessels crammed with archers, slingers, and light catapults sailed down either side of the construction, and poured a concentrated cross-fire into the thousands of labourers swarming over it. At such short range they could hardly miss, and Alexander's men – who wore no armour – suffered heavy casualties.

As a counter-measure the King rigged up protective screens of hide and canvas, and placed two tall wooden towers near the end of the mole. From these his archers and artillerymen could shoot straight down into the enemy's boats. Such precautions were now doubly necessary. The work was so far advanced that very soon it would come within range of the catapults on the walls. But at the same time, since it had reached the deepest part of the channel, its rate of progress had slowed almost to a standstill. Endless tons of rock went into the sea without appreciably raising the foundation level. Supplies of timber were not coming through as fast as they should, since the forestry section had constantly to fight off attacks by Arab marauders. On top of everything else the Tyrians, whose resourcefulness was only matched by their sense of timing, chose this moment to carry out a highly successful commando raid.

They took a broadbeamed old horse-transport and crammed it to the gunwales with dry firewood, over which they poured large quantities of liquid pitch. From the projecting yard-arm of each mast they hung a cauldron full of some highly inflammable substance, probably naphtha. When a good

Tyre, scene of Alexander's seven-month siege in 332 BC. Centuries of silting have progressively widened his original causeway from the shore.

on-shore wind began blowing, they put a skeleton crew aboard, and towed this improvised fireship towards the mole with a pair of fast triremes, the crews rowing flat out so as to work up maximum speed. At the last moment the triremes sheered off, to port and starboard respectively, while those aboard the transport let go the tow-ropes. Then they hurled flaming torches into the midst of the combustible material, and quickly dived overboard. The barge, now a mass of flames, bore straight down on the mole, close to Alexander's wooden towers. These caught fire at once. Meanwhile the two triremes had put about and now lay alongside the mole, sniping at any Macedonian who put his head outside the towers, or attempted to extinguish the fire.

Then the ropes holding the cauldrons burnt through, and a torrent of naphtha came pouring down. The result must have been like a small-scale explosion in an oil-refinery. Both towers were engulfed by a raging inferno. At the same time a flotilla of small craft which had been following the fireship ran in on the mole from all sides. One commando party slaughtered the men carrying rocks from the shore. Others tore down Alexander's protective palisades and set fire to any siege equipment that had escaped the original conflagration. The whole attack was carried out in a matter of minutes. Then the raiders withdrew, leaving behind them a smoke-blackened trail of carnage and destruction. For its entire length the mole was littered with charred corpses and blazing, shapeless piles of timber.

This expensive set-back made one thing abundantly clear to Alexander: without a strong fleet he might as well give up altogether. Only an amphibious assault stood any real chance of success. To obtain ships was not so hopeless a task as might be supposed. The kings of Byblos and Aradus (Arwad), learning that their cities were in Macedonian hands, both withdrew their contingents from the Persian fleet and sailed back to Sidon. Ten triremes arrived from Rhodes (hitherto a Persian stronghold), ten more from Lycia, and three from Soli. Together with Sidon's own squadrons, this at once gave Alexander 103 vessels. A day or two later the kings of Cyprus sailed in, leading a combined flotilla of no less than 120 warships. Desertions on this scale meant that the Persian fleet would very soon cease to be an effective force.

Alexander had every reason to be pleased. In a week or two he had mustered a far more powerful fleet than that of the Tyrians; and the situation in Greece and Ionia seemed to be, at long last, taking a turn for the better.

A rhyton in the form of a trireme's prow. Hellenistic, found at Vulci.

He at once collected fresh engineers from Cyprus and Phoenicia: these were set to work mounting siege artillery (including rams) on barges or old transport vessels. While the fleet was being fitted out, Alexander himself took a flying column up into the snow-clad wastes of the Lebanon ranges, and spent ten days harrying the tribesmen who had threatened his timber supplies.

By the end of this period the fleet was ready for active service. Alexander at once put to sea in battle formation. At the sight of the gigantic Macedonian armada the Tyrian squadrons put about and made for home. Immediately Alexander crammed on all speed in a bid to reach the North Harbour before them. A desperate race now ensued. Most of Tyre's best troops had been packed aboard the galleys to fight as marines, and if Alexander could force his way into the harbour, he had an excellent chance of capturing the city there and then. The Tyrians, in line-ahead formation, just managed to squeeze through the harbour entrance in front of Alexander's leading vessels. Three Tyrian triremes put about to hold off the attack, and were sunk one after the other. But meanwhile, behind them, a solid array of ships had been jammed bows on across the harbour mouth. Similar defensive tactics were adopted at the Egyptian Harbour, on the south-east side of the island.

Alexander, seeing there was nothing he could do to force an entry, brought his fleet to anchor on the lee side of the mole. Early next morning he sent the Cyprian and Phoenician squadrons to blockade both harbour mouths. This effectively bottled up Tyre's entire naval force, and gave Alexander mastery of the sea. He was now free to press on at full speed with the mole, his workers protected from attack by a thick defensive screen of ships. But Poseidon, it seemed, was fighting on the Tyrian side. A strong north-west gale blew up, which not only made further progress impossible, but caused serious damage to the existing structure. Alexander, however, refused to admit defeat. A number of giant untrimmed Lebanon cedars were floated into position on the windward side, and absorbed the most violent impact of the waves. After the storm subsided, these huge trees were built into the mole as bulwarks. The damage was soon made good, and Alexander, surmounting every obstacle, at last found himself within missile range of the walls.

He now proceeded to launch the ancient equivalent of a saturation barrage. Stone-throwers and light catapults were brought up in force to the end of the mole. While the stone-throwers pounded away at Tyre's fortifications, the catapults, reinforced by archers and slingers, concentrated on those defenders who were manning the battlements. At the same time, no less vigorous an assault was being pressed home from the seaward side. Alexander's engineers had constructed a number of naval battering-rams. Each of these was mounted on a large platform lashed across two barges. Other similar floating platforms carried heavy catapults and manganels. All were well protected against attack from above. These craft, escorted by more orthodox vessels, now formed a tight circle right round the island fortress, and subjected it to the most violent, unremitting assault. The great rams smashed their way through loose blocks of masonry, while a deadly hail of bolts and arrows picked off the defenders on the walls.

The Tyrians fought back as best they could. They hung up hides and other yielding materials to break the force of the stone balls. They built wooden towers on their battlements, and filled them with archers who shot fire-arrows into the assault-craft below. They worked at feverish speed to repair the breaches made by Alexander's rams, or (where this proved impracticable) to build curtain-walls behind them. The defences opposite the mole still stood firm. Alexander now decided to attempt a night assault by sea. Under cover of darkness his whole task force moved into position. Then, for the second time, Tyre was saved by bad weather. A gale got up, and violent waves began to pound Alexander's floating platforms. Some of these actually broke up: they were unwieldy at the best of times, and quite unmanageable in a storm. Alexander had no choice but to cancel the operation. Most of his fleet got back safely, though many vessels had suffered serious damage.

This set-back gave the Tyrians a brief but valuable breathing-space. With considerable ingenuity, they now dumped heavy blocks of stone and masonry in the shallow water below the walls. This should suffice to keep Alexander's floating rams out of range. Nevertheless, they had to face the fact that very soon (unless something quite unforeseen happened) Alexander's mole would reach the island. This is why many of their devices were designed for hand-to-hand combat. They included drop-beams (which swung down on the ships from a derrick), grappling-irons or barbed tridents attached to cords with which assailants could be hooked off their towers, fire-throwers that discharged large quantities of molten metal, scythes on poles to cut the ropes which worked the rams, and – simple but effective – lead-shot fishing-nets to entangle any who might rush the fortifications by means of bridge-ladders.

One reason for all this urgent work was an embassy which had just arrived from Carthage, bearing highly unwelcome news. Those Carthaginians still in the city had doubtless sent home increasingly gloomy reports on Tyre's chances of survival. Their government, sensing an imminent débâcle, did not want to involve Carthage in what might prove a long and expensive war. They remembered, suddenly and conveniently, that Carthage had troubles of her own at home, and would not, therefore, much though they regretted it, be able to send Tyre any reinforcements. This news caused considerable alarm throughout the beleaguered city.

Alexander, meanwhile, was making vast efforts to winch up the heaps of stone and masonry which had been dropped in the sea beneath the walls. This work could only be done from securely anchored transport vessels with strong derricks. Tyrian divers held up the salvage work by cutting these ships' anchor-cables. Only when Alexander replaced the cables with chains could the crews go ahead. They finally cleared all the stones, catapulting them into deep water where no one could retrieve them. Now, once again, the assault-craft could come in close under the walls. About the same time, after a sustained effort of which Heracles himself might well have been proud, the mole finally reached Tyre. Alexander's promise that he would join Tyre's fortress to the mainland had been fulfilled. At this point he would have been less than human had he not attempted a direct assault. The great siege-towers, over 150 feet high, were wheeled into position, the boarding-gangways were made ready, and a tremendous attack launched against the walls.

Besieging a fourth-century city, a detail from the Xanthus Nereid monument: while fighting goes on before the walls, guards man the battlements, and an anxious woman can be glimpsed behind them.

The Tyrians, who had long been awaiting this moment, fought back with ferocious courage. The most ingenious and horrific device at their disposal was also the simplest. Sand and fine gravel were heated in huge metal bowls and then emptied over any assailant who came within range. The red-hot sand sifted down inside breastplates and shirts, burning deep into the flesh, an appallingly effective forerunner of napalm. Finally, Alexander was forced to retreat. For nearly six months he had laboured before the walls of Tyre, and all in vain. The cost in men and materials had been prodigious; and day by day Darius was steadily building and training a new Grand Army. If Alexander held on now, it was because he had long ago passed the point of no return. To give up the siege would be more costly than to go through with it.

The King now (28 July) moved his whole task-force round to the southeast side of Tyre, just below the Egyptian Harbour. Concentrated bombardment broke down one section of the wall, and badly shook what remained. Alexander, desperate to follow up this opening, at once threw assault-bridges across from his ships, and ordered a spearhead of crack troops into the breach. They were driven back by a violent and well-aimed hail of missiles. Yet despite this he knew, beyond any doubt, that he had at last found the vulnerable point in Tyre's defences.

Alexander rested his men for a couple of days before the final assault. The sea had become choppy again; but on the third night the wind dropped, and at dawn Alexander began a tremendous bombardment of the wall, choosing the same point that he had breached earlier. When a wide section had been battered into rubble, he withdrew his unwieldy artillery barges, and brought up two special assault-craft crammed with shock-troops. While this was going on, the Cyprian and Phoenician squadrons launched a powerful attack against both harbours, and numerous other vessels loaded with archers and ammunition kept circling the island, lending a hand wherever it was needed.

As soon as the assault-craft were in position and the gangways run out, a wave of Macedonians charged across on to the battlements, where fierce hand-to-hand fighting continued for some time. Then there came a sound of cheering from the harbours below them: the Cyprian and Phoenician squadrons had successfully smashed their way through. The Tyrians on the wall, afraid of being caught front and rear, now retreated to the centre of the city, barricading the narrow streets as they went. When the last organised resistance was broken, Alexander's veterans ranged through the city on a ferocious manhunt, all restraint abandoned, hysterical and half-crazy after the long rigours of that dreadful siege, mere butchers now, striking and trampling and tearing limb from limb until Tyre became a bloody, reeking abattoir.

Some citizens locked themselves in their houses and committed suicide. Alexander had ordered that all save those who sought sanctuary were to be slain, and his commands were executed with savage relish. The air grew thick with smoke from burning buildings. Seven thousand Tyrians died in this frightful orgy of destruction; the number would have been far higher had it not been for the men of Sidon, who entered the city alongside Alexander's troops. Even though Tyre had been Sidon's rival for centuries, these neighbours of the victims, horrified by what they now witnessed, managed to smuggle some 15,000 of them to safety.

The great city over which Hiram had once held sway was now utterly destroyed. Her king, Azimilik, and various other notables – including envoys from Carthage – had taken refuge in the temple of Melkart, and Alexander spared their lives. The remaining survivors, some 30,000 in number, he sold into slavery. Two thousand men of military age were crucified. Then Alexander went up into the temple, and made his long-delayed sacrifice: the most costly blood-offering even Melkart had ever received.

Against Alexander's mole, quiet now under the summer sky, sand began to drift from the coastal dunes, softening the sharp outline of blocks and joists, linking Tyre ever more closely to the mainland. With each passing century the peninsula grew wider. Today, deep under asphalt streets and apartment blocks, the stone core of that fantastic causeway still stands: one of Alexander's most tangible and permanent legacies to posterity.

Meanwhile Darius had done very little about raising a new Imperial army, preferring to stake everything on the success of his campaign in Asia Minor and the Aegean. All the front-line troops he had available were committed to one of these two theatres. By the summer of 332, however, shortly before Alexander stormed Tyre, Darius was forced to recognise that this campaign had proved an expensive failure. He therefore decided to approach Alexander again. The terms of his second offer were somewhat more generous. Territorial concessions remained unaltered: he would cede all the provinces west of the Halys. But the ransom proposed for his family was now doubled, from ten to twenty thousand talents; and on top of this he offered Alexander the hand in marriage of his daughter Stateira, with all the emoluments proper to the Great King's son-in-law. His letter ended on an admonitory note. The Persian empire was vast; sooner or later Alexander's small army would have to emerge into the steppes, where it would be far more vulnerable.

Alexander, securely in control at Tyre, had no qualms about rejecting these new proposals. Darius, he told the Persian envoys, was offering him a wife he could marry whenever he chose, and a dowry which he had already won for himself. He had not crossed the sea to pick up such minor fringe benefits as Lydia or Cilicia. His goal now was Persepolis, and the eastern provinces. If Darius wanted to keep his empire, Alexander repeated, he must fight for it: because the Macedonians would hunt him down wherever he took refuge. On receipt of this message, the Great King abandoned his attempt to secure a settlement by diplomatic means, and 'set to work on vast preparations for war.'

Gaza   Alexander was now ready to continue his march south. When the fall of Tyre became known, every coastal city along the direct route to Egypt had made its submission – with one important exception. This was Gaza, a powerful walled stronghold at the edge of the desert, built on a tell a couple of miles inland, with deep sand-dunes all round it. The last commander to take Gaza by direct assault had been Cambyses, some two centuries before. Alexander succeeded in emulating Cambyses; though not without a very hard fight, and not before he himself had been severely wounded.

The portal of a temple at Syene, showing Alexander with the crown of Egypt.

At this point he sent Amyntas son of Andromenes home to Pella, with ten triremes, on a fresh recruiting drive. Local volunteers and mercenaries were well enough in their way; but the backbone of Alexander's army remained the phalanx, and only Macedonians could adequately fill the many gaps in its ranks.

From Gaza Alexander marched for the Nile Delta, covering the 130 miles to Pelusium in just under a week. As before, he sent the fleet on ahead, and when he arrived it was already there to welcome him – together with a rapturous throng of Egyptians, for whom Alexander truly came as a liberator. The Persians had maintained an uneasy and intermittent rule over Egypt ever since 525, when the mad Cambyses had first acquired it for his empire. They had treated this province all the more harshly because they – like the Romans after them – regarded it as little more than a gigantic free granary.

Alexander, therefore, had everything in his favour when he arrived. If he took care not to offend local religious susceptibilities – better still, if he participated in some kind of public ritual to symbolise the transfer of power – he could count on enthusiastic support from the entire population. In the event, he got rather more than he bargained for. What had been conceived as a piece of political diplomacy turned into a profoundly felt emotional and spiritual experience. It is no exaggeration to say that the months Alexander spent in Egypt – from late October 332 to April 331 – marked a psychological turning-point in his life.

From Pelusium the Macedonian fleet and army advanced up the Nile in stately procession towards Memphis. The Persian garrison offered no resistance. Mazaces, Darius' governor, came out to meet Alexander, presenting him with '800 talents and all the royal furniture'. This obliging service won Mazaces an administrative post in the new regime. But when Alexander reached Memphis, he found a still greater tribute awaiting him. The Persian kings had been, *ex officio* as it were, Pharaohs of Egypt, by right of conquest over the native dynasty. Alexander had put down Darius: in the priests' eyes he now became their legitimate ruler. So, on 14 November 332, the young Macedonian was solemnly instated as Pharaoh. The impact of this revelation on Alexander can well be imagined. Here, at last, Olympias' belief in his divine birth found a wholly acceptable context.

Too much success can be dangerous: power breeds its own special isolation. There are signs that after Issus Alexander began to lose touch with his Macedonians, and such an infusion of superhuman charisma must surely have accelerated the process. Already his achievements had outrivalled those of Heracles. Now, amid the ancient splendours of Egypt – a civilisation which invariably bred semi-mystical awe in the Greek mind – he learnt that he was in truth a god, and the son of a god. Greek tradition distinguished sharply between the two. Egypt did not. For Alexander this was to have interesting consequences.

As Pharaoh, he lost no time in emphasising the contrast between his own régime and that of his Persian predecessors. Before leaving Memphis, in January 331, he ordered the restoration of at least two temples, at Karnak and Luxor. (Both, in all likelihood, had been destroyed by Cambyses.) Then he sailed back down the Nile, this time along the western, or Canopic,

right: Memphis, the age-old capital of Egypt: cruelly ravaged by the Persians, and the scene of Alexander's enthronement as Pharaoh.

overleaf: Byblos in the Egyptian Delta: the principal source of papyrus in antiquity.

tributary. His object was to visit Naucratis, the international Greek trading port, and assess its value as a commercial centre. Having eliminated Tyre he now meant to divert the Eastern Mediterranean's highly profitable flow of maritime traffic from Phoenicia to Egypt. Naucratis, perhaps because of its isolated inland position, did not impress him. When he reached the coast, and sailed round Lake Mareotis, he found a far better site, on a narrow limestone ridge between lake and sea, opposite the island of Pharos.

The harbour here was deep, and provided excellent shelter. Both land approaches could be easily blocked against invasion. Cool prevailing winds would ensure a pleasant, healthy climate, even at the height of summer. After examining the site Alexander had a prophetic dream, in which some hoary sage declaimed Homer's lines alluding to Pharos. As his first royal act,

Columns of the Temple of Karnak, which forms the northern half of the ruins of ancient Thebes on the east bank of the Nile. Alexander restored a chamber in the festival hall of Thothmes II.

Egypt's Macedonian Pharaoh decided to build a city there: Alexandria, the most famous of those many foundations which afterwards bore his name.

It was at this point that Alexander expressed a particular desire (*pothos*: see above, p. 77) to consult the oracle of Zeus-Ammon in the Siwah Oasis. Since Siwah lay some 300 miles distant across the burning wastes of the Libyan desert, his motives must have been very compelling. He did not make a habit of wasting six weeks or more on some mere casual whim. On the other hand, he did tend to consult an oracle before each major advance in his career of conquest. He had made a special detour to Delphi; the incident at Gordium had left a profound impression on him. Now once again he hoped to lift the veil that covered his future.

Alexander reached Siwah in late February, some three weeks after setting out. When he emerged from the oracular consultation all he would say, in answer to a chorus of eager questions, was that 'he had been told what his heart desired'. In a subsequent letter to his mother, he wrote that he had learnt certain secret matters which he would impart to her, and her alone, on his return. But since he died without ever again setting foot on Macedonian soil, these secrets went to the grave with him. Nevertheless, it seems very likely that the traditional answers are not too wide of the mark. Alexander's status as son of a god now became more generally known and accepted: other oracles hastened to endorse the claim. If Ammon did not actually promise him the Achaemenid empire, at least he was told to which gods

above left: The Temple of Luxor, the southern part of the ruins of ancient Thebes. Built by Amenhotep III and dedicated to the three Theban deities Amen, Mut and Khansu. Alexander rebuilt the sanctuary.

above right: The sole remains of the oracular shrine at Siwah where Alexander made a pilgrimage to hear prophecies about his future. Though many guesses have been made as to the questions he asked and the responses he got, he never divulged either.

right: Modern Alexandria: the island (as it was in Alexander's day) of Pharos is in the foreground, with the Great Harbour beyond it.

he should sacrifice if, or when, he became Lord of Asia (see below, p. 162). The future site of Alexandria must have been approved. But whatever Alexander heard at Siwah, one thing is certain: it struck him with the force of a revelation, and left a permanent mark on his entire future career.

By the time he got back the King clearly had the whole plan of Alexandria worked out. It was to be built along the isthmus, in the symbolically appropriate shape of a Macedonian military cloak. Deinochares, the city-planner who had redesigned Ephesus, persuaded Alexander to adopt the axial-grid system, with a great central boulevard running from east to west, intersected by numerous streets at right-angles. But the King had his own ideas about such matters as the exact line of the outer fortifications, the position of the central market, and the sites to be reserved for various temples – including shrines to the Egyptian deities Isis and Sarapis. The city's official foundation date was 7 April. After the first bricks had been laid Alexander left the builders to get on with it and sailed back up-river to Memphis.

Among many embassies awaiting him on his return was one from Miletus, with remarkable news concerning Apollo's oracle at nearby Didyma. No prophecies had issued from this shrine since its destruction during the Persian Wars. Even the sacred spring dried up. But with the coming of Alexander – or so the envoys said – miracle of miracles, the spring began to flow again, and the god to prophesy. Since the Milesians were anxious to excuse themselves for having supported the Persian Pharnabazus during his Aegean campaign, the King probably took all this with a fairly large grain of salt. Nevertheless, it made very useful political propaganda. The oracular responses which the envoys brought with them were certainly designed to please. Apollo

Carved stone lion from the great Temple of Apollo at Didyma. This temple was rebuilt in or soon after Alexander's day, and probably at his expense: flattering predictions by Apollo's oracle reaped their due reward. The original structure had been destroyed during the Persian Wars. Obviously it made good propaganda for Alexander to repair the effects of Persian vandalism.

ratified Alexander's descent from Zeus, predicted great future victories for him (not to mention the death of Darius), and saw no future in King Agis' threatened Spartan revolt.

From now on Alexander began to take a noticeably softer line with embassies from mainland Greece. Success – combined with what he had learnt at Siwah – may have put him in a more generous mood. But it is hard to believe that he was not also influenced by the explosive situation in the Peloponnese. Anything that might prevent a general revolt of the Greek states was worth trying.

The holiday in Egypt was over by mid-April. Callisthenes, who had been travelling round Ethiopia and speculating (with remarkable prescience) on the sources of the Nile, prepared to resume his more serious official labours. Alexander, having made arrangements for the administration of Egypt (leaving much in Egyptian hands), set out back for Tyre. There he found the fleet awaiting him, together with envoys from Athens, Rhodes and Chios. The Athenians had come to make a second application (the first having been refused) for the release of their fellow-countrymen captured at the Granicus. This time the request was granted at once, without argument. The Chians and Rhodians had complaints about their Macedonian garrisons: these complaints, after investigation, the King upheld.

A new policy

Alexander's new policy of conciliation shows diplomatic foresight; but it was also dictated, to a very great extent, by the alarming news from mainland Greece. During the winter Agis and his brother Agesilaus had managed to win over most of Crete. Before leaving Egypt, Alexander dispatched a naval task-force under Amphoterus (who had reported back from the Dardanelles) with orders to 'liberate' the island and clear the sea of pirates – the latter term doubtless including any pro-Spartan squadrons they might encounter. But at Tyre Alexander learnt that Agis was now in open revolt. He had gathered a large mercenary force, and was appealing for all the Greek states to join him. A number of them, however, were either undecided or actively hostile.

This gave Alexander his opening. A hundred Cypriot and Phoenician triremes now sailed for Crete to rendezvous with Amphoterus. The combined fleet would then move into Peloponnesian waters, and do everything possible to unite the still uncommitted city-states against Sparta. Rumours were coming in about a revolt in Thrace. But Alexander could waste no further time or reserves on Greece: from now on it was up to Antipater.

In early summer 331 Alexander led his whole army north-east through Syria, reaching Thapsacus on the Euphrates not earlier than 10 July. Darius knew very well that Babylon itself must be Alexander's next objective. This great city on the Lower Euphrates was the economic centre of the empire, the strategic bastion protecting Susa, Persepolis and the eastern provinces. Nor was there much doubt in the Great King's mind as to the route his adversary would take. Alexander, he knew, struck hard, fast, and with maximum economy. It was therefore odds-on that he would come straight down the east bank of the Euphrates – just as Cyrus had done in 401, to meet disastrous defeat at Cunaxa.

There is every sign that Darius had studied the battle of Cunaxa with some care, and hoped to repeat it in detail. Mazaeus' advance force was similarly ordered to retreat before the invader, burning all crops and fodder as it went. The plain at Cunaxa, some sixty miles north-west of Babylon, was ideal for cavalry manoeuvres – and the Great King now had some 34,000 armed horsemen at his disposal. Alexander's troops, he calculated, would reach Cunaxa hot, exhausted, and underfed. Between Mazaeus' scorched-

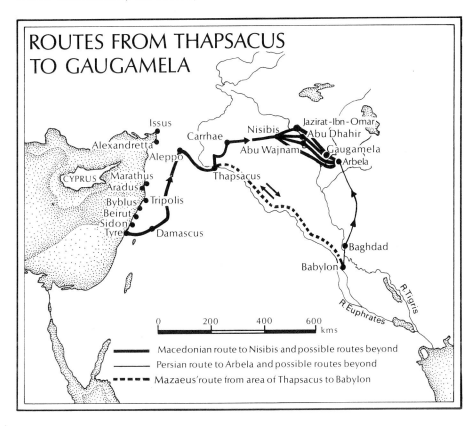

ROUTES FROM THAPSACUS TO GAUGAMELA

Macedonian route to Nisibis and possible routes beyond
Persian route to Arbela and possible routes beyond
Mazaeus' route from area of Thapsacus to Babylon

earth policy and the blazing Mesopotamian sun, they would fall easy victims to his own fresh, well-armed and numerically superior divisions, just as Cyrus' expedition had done. But this whole elaborate fantasy depended on Alexander doing what he was expected to do: always a dangerous premiss, and especially foolish in the present case.

Alexander, who knew his *Anabasis* almost by heart, was the last man to walk into such a trap when he had Cyrus' example to warn him off. Besides, the narrow green strip of the Euphrates Valley would barely support his army, even if Mazaeus failed to lay it waste. So when two pontoon bridges had been built across the Euphrates, the Macedonian army, instead of marching downstream as predicted, struck out in a north-easterly direction across the Mesopotamian plain. Mazaeus watched them go, horror-struck. Then he rode the 440 miles back to Babylon with the news. Darius could forget his dreams of a second Cunaxa.

A quick change of strategy was now made. Darius decided to hold Alexander at the Tigris (see map, p. 132): a bold but risky plan, since no one could be sure where he intended to cross. Four main fords were possible. The nearest of these to Babylon was at Mosul, 356 miles away. From Thapsacus the march to Mosul was slightly longer, 371 miles. But as one went further north, the ratio of distances changed in Alexander's favour. The most remote crossing-point from Babylon was also the nearest to Thapsacus, 308 miles as opposed to 422. It looks as though Darius was concentrating almost entirely on the Mosul ford. With his unwieldy army this was the only crossing-point where he could hope to be in position before Alexander arrived. Even so he was going to have remarkable luck if he made it with any margin to spare. The overall plan depended on perfect coordination between Mazaeus, the scouts, and Command H.Q. The Imperial army had, at all costs, to reach Arbela on schedule. Most important of all, Alexander must get no inkling of this revised strategy: a security leak would be fatal.

The Great King got his forces to Arbela, and prepared to march on Mosul. Meanwhile Alexander, following the northern route across Mesopotamia, had been lucky enough to capture some of Darius' scouts. Under interrogation they not only revealed the entire Persian plan of campaign, but also provided valuable details concerning the size and composition of the Great King's army. (How far Alexander believed what he was told is another matter, as we shall see.) If the Macedonians had, in fact, been making for the Mosul ford, which seems likely, there was now a quick change of route. They turned off in the direction of Abu Wajnam, some forty miles to the north.

The Macedonians encountered no opposition at Abu Wajnam, which they reached on 18 September. A few frightened scouts fled south with the news, and the Great King – already across the Greater Zab and approaching Mosul – had to change his plans yet again. He no longer had the Tigris between Alexander's army and his own. The Macedonians were little more than fifty miles away. His best chance was to locate another open plain, suitable for cavalry and chariots, and bring Alexander to battle there. Persian scouts found what he needed at Gaugamela (Tell Gomel), a village between the Khazir River and the ruins of Nineveh. Darius brought up his troops, inspected the plain, and at once set sappers to work clearing it of

Macedonians
Right flank guard
1 Greek Mercenary Cavalry—Menidas
2 Lancers—Aretes
3 Paeonian Cavalry—Ariston
4 ½ Agrianians—Attalus
5 ½ Macedonian Archers—Briso
6 Veteran Mercenaries—Cleander
Right wing
7 Companion Cavalry—Philotas
8 Javelin-men—Balacrus
9 ½ Macedonian Archers—Briso
10 ½ Agrianians—Attalus
11 Hypaspists—Nicanor
12 Phalanx—Coenus
13 Phalanx—Perdiccas
14 Phalanx—Meleager
15 Phalanx—Polyperchon
Left wing
16 Phalanx—Simmias
17 Phalanx—Craterus
18 Allied Greek Cavalry—Erigyius
19 Thessalian Cavalry—Philip
20 Cretan Archers—Clearchus
21 Achaian Mercenary Infantry
Left flank guard
22 Greek Mercenary Cavalry—Andromachus
23 Thracian Horse—Sitalces
24 Allied Greek Horse—Coeranus
25 Odrysian Horse—Agathon

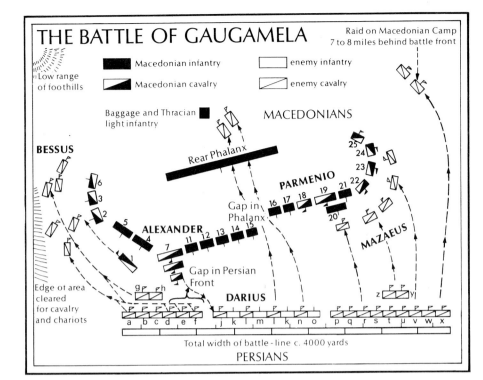

THE BATTLE OF GAUGAMELA

Raid on Macedonian Camp
7 to 8 miles behind battle front

Low range of foothills

■ Macedonian infantry   □ enemy infantry

◨ Macedonian cavalry   ◨ enemy cavalry

Baggage and Thracian light infantry ■

MACEDONIANS

BESSUS

Rear Phalanx

PARMENIO

ALEXANDER

Gap in Phalanx

MAZAEUS

Gap in Persian Front

DARIUS

Edge of area cleared for cavalry and chariots

Total width of battle-line c. 4000 yards

PERSIANS

Persians

Left wing
a Bactrian Cavalry
b Dahae Cavalry
c Arachosian Cavalry
d Persian Cavalry
e Susian Cavalry
f Cadusian Cavalry
g Bactrian Cavalry
h Scythian Cavalry
i Chariots

Centre
j Carian Cavalry
k Greek Mercenaries
l Persian Horse Guards
m Persian Foot Guards
n Indian Cavalry
o Mardian Archers

Right wing
p Coelo-Syrian Cavalry
q Mesopotamian Cavalry
r Median Cavalry
s Parthian Cavalry
t Sacian Cavalry
u Tapurian Cavalry
v Hyrcanian Cavalry
w Albanian Cavalry
x Sacesinian Cavalry
y Cappadocian Cavalry
z Armenian Cavalry

any trees, rocks, or awkward hummocks. What he did *not* do – an omission which afterwards cost him dear – was to occupy the low hills some three miles to the north-west. From this convenient vantage-point Alexander's reconnaissance troops subsequently observed, and reported on, all his military dispositions.

Shortly after crossing the Tigris, Alexander made contact with a regiment of Mazaeus' cavalry. The Paeonian mounted scouts, under their leader Ariston, were sent to deal with this nuisance. The Persians fled; Ariston speared their colonel, cut off his head, and 'amid great applause laid it at the King's feet'. The Macedonians were then given forty-eight hours' rest. Four days later (24 September) Mazaeus' cavalry was sighted again. Could this indicate the presence of the whole Persian army? A quick cavalry raid, led by the King himself, succeeded in taking one or two prisoners. These soon told him what he wanted to know. Darius now lay at Gaugamela, no more than eight miles away beyond the hills. His ground-levelling operations proved that he did not intend moving far from his present camp.

Alexander therefore, very sensibly, gave his own troops another four days' rest, from 25–8 September. The heat down in the plain was gruelling, and he wanted them as fit and fresh as possible for the final battle. During this period Darius' agents tried to smuggle in leaflets, offering the Macedonians rich rewards if they would kill or betray Alexander. These were intercepted and (on Parmenio's advice) suppressed. The camp was also strengthened with a ditch and a palisade.

It was now that Darius made his third and final attempt to reach a settlement with Alexander by peaceful negotiation. This time he offered more, far more, than previously – all territories west of the Euphrates; 30,000 talents as ransom for his mother and daughters; the hand of one daughter in marriage, and the retention of his son Ochus as a permanent hostage. Alexander placed these proposals before his War Council – though this time the decision was never seriously in doubt. 'If I were Alexander,' Parmenio declared, 'I should accept this offer, and make a treaty.' 'So should I,' said Alexander, 'if I were Parmenio.'

Alexander had not yet actually set eyes on Darius' new army for himself, and was clearly sceptical of what he had heard concerning it. He seems to have assumed that it would be neither very much larger nor noticeably more efficient than the force which he had smashed at Issus. His own army had been built up since then to a total of about 47,000 men. Before dawn on 29 September he breasted the low ridge of hills above Gaugamela, and got the first glimpse of what he was up against. It stopped him dead in his tracks. Darius' army consisted, to all intents and purposes, entirely of cavalry, and armoured cavalry at that. A snap count suggested that in this vital arm the Macedonians were outnumbered by at least five to one. The Great King, unable to raise a competent infantry force, had decided to give up the idea of front-line foot-soldiers altogether. Not only was this highly unconventional force stronger and better-armed than Alexander had anticipated: its order of battle also took him somewhat aback. Darius, this time, was determined that the Macedonians should not repeat those tactics which had brought them victory at Issus and the Granicus. On his left wing he had stationed a considerable force of Bactrian and Scythian cavalry, together with half his scythed chariots.

The more he studied these Persian dispositions, the less Alexander liked them. He spent much of the 29th riding round the prospective battlefield with a strong cavalry escort, examining the ground – and Darius' lines – with a very sharp eye. The Persians made no attempt to stop him. Then (like his hero Achilles, but for very different reasons) he retired to his tent. While his men ate and slept, Alexander sat up hour after hour, 'casting over in his mind the number of the Persian forces', considering and discarding one tactical scheme after another. After much thought, he worked out the last details of his master-strategy – and having done so, at once fell into a deep untroubled sleep. The sun rose, but the King did not. Company officers, on their own initiative, sounded reveille and issued orders for the men to take breakfast. Still Alexander slumbered on. Finally Parmenio shook him awake. It was high time to form up in battle order – and only Alexander himself knew what that order was.

The King yawned and stretched. When Parmenio expressed surprise at his having slept so soundly, Alexander retorted: 'It is not remarkable at all. When Darius was scorching the earth, razing villages, destroying foodstuffs, I was beside myself; but now what am I to fear, when he is preparing to fight a pitched battle? By Heracles, he has done exactly what I wanted.' This was the most superb bravado. Darius had 34,000 front-line cavalry to Alexander's 7,250: no amount of strategy – or so it might have been thought – could get round that one basic fact. Alexander was going to be outflanked, and knew it. There were no mountains to protect him as at Issus, and no sea either. Darius'

A certain amount of idealisation is detectable in this late second-century statue of Alexander (probably by the sculptor Menas) found in Magnesia.

above: Soldiers marching in formation, a detail from the Nereid monument of Xanthus in Lycia. Fourth century BC.

line overlapped his by nearly a mile. So while his basic order of battle remained unchanged (see plan, p. 155), he took special pains to protect his flanks and rear – and also to make his line look weaker here than in fact it was. He stationed a powerful force of mercenaries on his right wing, carefully masking them with cavalry squadrons. He echeloned both wings back at an angle of 45° from his main battle-line. Finally, he placed the League infantry and the rest of the Greek mercenaries to cover his rear.

He was, in fact, making a virtue of necessity. Alone in his lamp-lit tent, by sheer intuitive genius, he had invented a tactical plan that was to be imitated, centuries afterwards, by Marlborough at Blenheim and Napoleon at Austerlitz, but which no other general had hitherto conceived. To reduce the vast numerical odds against him, and to create an opening for his decisive charge, he planned to draw as many Persian cavalry units as possible away from the centre, into engagement with his flank-guards. When the flanks were fully committed, he would strike at Darius' weakened centre.

So, on the morning of 30 September 331 BC, the Macedonian and Persian armies moved forward, crabwise and with apparent reluctance, into an engagement which, as it turned out, 'gave Alexander the chance to secure the whole Persian empire from the Euphrates to the Hindu Kush': his military masterpiece, both in design and execution. The Macedonians advanced, as usual, with their left wing progressively echeloned back, trying to lure the Persian right, under Mazaeus, into a premature flank engagement. At the same time the Persian left – commanded by Bessus, satrap of Bactria and would-be Great King – outflanked Alexander so far that he and the Companion Cavalry were almost opposite Darius' central command-post.

Neither side wanted to engage first. But someone had to act; and in the end it was Darius. Anxious to halt this dangerous drift towards rough ground, he ordered Bessus to launch a flank attack against Alexander's advancing

Alexander portrayed as Heracles, with a lion's mane headdress, on a tetradrachm from the mint of Amphipolis. *c.* 333 BC.

159

right wing. This was the move for which Alexander had been waiting. Once Bessus' cavalry was committed, the King, with superb timing, kept feeding in further units from his deep flank-guard. To counter this increasing pressure, Bessus brought up squadron after squadron, determined now to penetrate or roll up Alexander's flank, and probably still unaware of the 6,700 mercenaries waiting in reserve behind the Macedonian cavalry. A point came when this force – Alexander's cavalry numbered no more than 1100 – was holding (for just long enough) ten times its own strength of front-line Persian horsemen. Meanwhile Darius, as a diversionary measure, launched his scythed chariots. They proved, on the whole, remarkably ineffective. The screen of light-armed troops which Alexander had posted in front of his main line caused havoc among them by pelting the horses with javelins, and stabbing the drivers as they whirled past. The well-drilled ranks of the phalanx opened wide, and the survivors were rounded up by Alexander's grooms.

By now almost all the Persian cavalry on both flanks was engaged. Parmenio was fighting a desperate defensive action against Mazaeus, while Alexander had just flung in his last mounted reserves, the Rangers, to hold Bessus. At this crucial moment the King's keen eye detected a thinning of the ranks, perhaps even a gap, momentarily opening in Darius' left centre. It was now or never. Gathering all his remaining forces into one gigantic wedge, Alexander charged. In two or three minutes the whole course of the battle was transformed. Bessus, still fully engaged against Alexander's right, found his own flank dangerously exposed by the force of the Companions' charge; he had lost touch with Darius, and feared that at any moment Alexander's wedge might swing round to take him in the rear. He therefore, with good justification, sounded a retreat, and began to withdraw his forces.

At the same time Darius, hard-pressed by Alexander's cavalry and infantry, and seeing himself in danger of being cut off, fled the field as he had done at Issus. This time he only just managed to escape before the ring closed on him, and vanished across the plain towards Arbela, dust-clouds swirling behind his chariot. Mazaeus, seeing him go, at once broke off the long and desperate struggle against Parmenio. Bessus was already withdrawing, in comparatively good order, on the further flank. The whole Persian line now rapidly broke up.

Once again, however, Alexander's efforts to kill or capture Darius were frustrated. While Parmenio rounded up the Persian baggage-train, with its elephants and camels, the King rode on into the gathering dusk, still hoping to overtake Darius' party. When darkness fell he rested his weary men and horses for an hour or two, resuming the chase about midnight. The Macedonian party rode into Arbela as dawn broke, having covered some seventy-five miles during the night, only to find Darius gone. As at Issus, he had left his chariot and bow behind him, together with no less than 4000 talents in coined money. This was a substantial consolation prize; and in any case the Great King's prestige had suffered such a catastrophic blow that his personal escape was of comparatively little moment. The Achaemenid empire had been split in two, and its ruler's authority ripped to

Graeco-Roman bust of Alexander, showing the hair characteristically raised above the forehead (*anastole*) and falling down both sides of the face in the 'lion's mane' pattern. It has been suggested that this is a formalised representation of Alexander as Helios, the Sun-god.

shreds. If Alexander now proclaimed himself Great King in Darius' stead, who would deny his right to the title?

Macedonian intelligence officers soon pieced together the story of the Great King's escape. He and his retinue had retreated headlong to Arbela, not even bothering to break down the river-bridges as they fled. Here they were joined by Bessus and the Bactrian cavalry, 2000 loyal Greek mercenaries, and a few survivors from The Royal Guard. Soon after midnight these battered remnants of the Persian Grand Army set out from Arbela, taking the road east through the Armenian mountains, and eventually descending on Ecbatana from the north. Here Darius halted for a while, to let stragglers rejoin him. He made sporadic efforts to reorganise and rearm them; he also sent palpably nervous notes to his governors and generals in Bactria and the upper satrapies, urging them to remain loyal. But Gaugamela had broken his nerve, and he never recovered it.

8 The Lord of Asia

Gaugamela marked a turning-point for Alexander in more ways than one. To the Greeks he had always been a type-cast example of the ambitious tyrant, and now he was proceeding to vindicate their judgment. But the effect on his Macedonian troops was profound. From this time on, relations between Alexander and his army steadily deteriorated, culminating – as we shall see – in ugly episodes of mutiny and murder. The Macedonian Old Guard, in particular, were shocked by their King's visible drift towards Oriental despotism. For them Alexander's task in Asia was done, and the sooner he took them all home again, the better. But the King's own horizon of conquest was continually expanding; Macedonia had begun to seem very small and far away.

Hitherto Alexander had been able to present himself as a liberator. But once he set out on the road to Susa and Persepolis, he would have to think up a different line. He could hardly claim to be liberating the Persians from themselves. Thus he soon became (as the Marxists say) involved in a contradiction. His dispatches home now placed more emphasis on revenge than liberation as a motive for the crusade. This, no doubt, was also the line he took with the Macedonian army. However, if he was to prevent trouble in his rear – let alone pose as Darius' successor – he would have to conciliate the Persian nobility in no uncertain fashion; which, again, would not endear him to his own men. He could scarcely lay claim to the throne of Persia without observing Persian court etiquette. The Great King was hedged about with endless taboos and religious ritual – in sharp contrast to the easy-going, rough and ready relationship that prevailed between a Macedonian monarch and his peers. To combine these roles was, ultimately, impossible. Sooner or later he would have to chose between them.

The front of one of the few extant 'Alexander tablets'; the inscription, in Babylonian, concerns payment in silver in lieu of labour on the removal of sand from Esagila (Temple of Marduk, Babylon).

After Gaugamela

Alexander stayed no more than a day or two in Arbela. He buried his own dead, but left the Persians where they lay. A force under Philoxenus was sent ahead to Susa, by the direct route, with orders to accept the city's surrender and safeguard its treasure. Meanwhile Alexander himself crossed the Tigris and marched for Babylon, some 300 miles away to the south. As the Macedonians approached, some hard private bargaining went on between Alexander and Mazaeus, who after Gaugamela had returned to his

right: An archer of the Imperial Bodyguard, on the Tripylon staircase at Persepolis.

Mythical animals moulded onto the brick walls of Babylon.

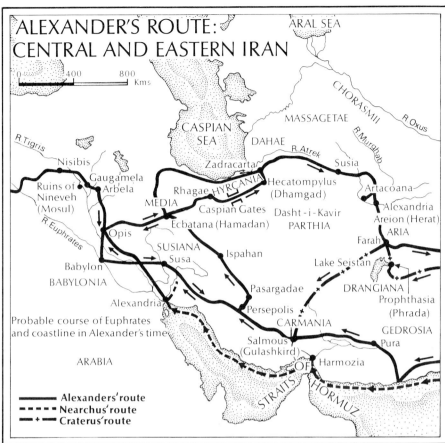

ALEXANDER'S ROUTE: CENTRAL AND EASTERN IRAN

Probable course of Euphrates and coastline in Alexander's time

—————— Alexanders' route
- - - - - - Nearchus' route
—·—·—· Craterus' route

duties as satrap of Babylon. Alexander wanted a bloodless surrender of the city; Mazaeus hoped to continue in office under the new regime. A provisional deal was made. Nevertheless, Alexander did not trust his late opponent one inch; he approached Babylon in battle-formation, ready for any kind of treachery or surprise attack.

To those dusty soldiers trudging along beside the Euphrates, Babylon must have appeared like some shimmering mirage across the plain; a vista of high white terraces, luxuriant greenery, great crenellated walls and towers. Its outer fortifications were of mud-brick formed with bitumen, and so broad on top that two four-horse chariots could pass abreast on them. Hardly less impressive was the colourful procession which now came trailing along the royal road – with much trumpet-blowing and clashing of cymbals – to greet Alexander and his men. At its head rode the renegade satrap Mazaeus, who formally made over city, citadel, and treasure into the King's hands. Alexander now mounted a chariot, formed his men into hollow columns (he still seems to have suspected some sort of trap) and made a superb triumphal entry. The whole route was strewn with flowers and garlands. Silver altars, heaped high with rich spices, burnt sweetly in honour of the conqueror. As Alexander rode under the high gold and lapis splendours of the Ishtar Gate, with its heraldic bulls and dragons, crowds on the parapet cheered and showered roses down on him.

165

PLAN OF BABYLON

A - ISHTAR GATE
B - NEO-BABYLONIAN PALACES
C - ZIGGURAT

R. Euphrates

0   500   1000
                M
0 1000 2000 3000
                F

Alexander's welcome was due, in part, to his promise – which no doubt Mazaeus had passed on – that he would honour the gods of Babylon, and, in particular, that he would restore the ziggurat and shrine of Esagila, which had been destroyed by Xerxes' general Megabyxus in 482. Once more – for the last time – he could present himself as the deliverer from Persian injustice and oppression, and the Babylonians, in gratitude, proved more than generous hosts. Officers and men alike were billeted in luxurious private houses, and never lacked for food, wine, or women. Babylon's professional courtesans were reinforced by countless enthusiastic amateurs, including the daughters and wives of many leading citizens. Their guests were shown the usual tourist sights, including the fabulous Hanging Gardens – a stone-terraced forest of trees and shrubs, built by an Assyrian king whose wife pined for the forests and uplands of her native Iran.

A Persian bodyguard, in glazed brick, from the palace at Susa.

166

A winged-bull relief, in glazed brick, from the palace at Susa.

While his troops enjoyed themselves, and Callisthenes laboriously transcribed the Babylonian priests' astronomical records (if they really went back for 31,000 years he must have had his time cut out), the King plunged into problems of administration. His first and undoubtedly his most important step was to confirm Mazaeus as satrap of Babylon, with the traditional right of coining silver. The choice of Mazaeus was particularly astute. He had a Babylonian wife, and strong local connections. Not that Alexander was foolish enough to give him a completely free hand. The garrison commander in Babylon was a Macedonian; so was the officer left in charge of the satrapal levies. Mazaeus might have had the right to issue coins, but not to collect taxes. This job went to a Macedonian finance officer, working under Harpalus, Alexander's Treasurer, who had mysteriously reappeared and been reinstated – when the army returned to Tyre.

To judge from the massive donations we find Alexander paying out at this point he must have had some difficulty in persuading his troops to abandon the flesh-pots of Babylon. Each Macedonian cavalryman received 600 drachmas – not far short of a year's pay – and other ranks proportionate amounts. The total expenditure was well over 2000 talents; but Babylon's treasury footed the bill.

The advance on Susa Susa, the second of the Great King's palatial capitals, lay some 375 miles south-east from Babylon, close to the Persian Gulf. The plain in which it stood was immensely fertile but ringed about with mountains, so that for nine months of the year it formed a natural oven. By mid-November, when Alexander finally set out, the winds had veered round to south or south-east, and the first rains had fallen. The army was overtaken *en route* by massive reinforcements from Greece, under Amyntas: 1500 cavalry and no less than 13,500 infantry, of whom nearly a third had been recruited in Macedonia itself. The arrival of this force prompted Alexander to halt his march for a day or two and carry out certain innovations in the command

right: A miniature gold chariot from the Treasure of the Oxus. While the two occupants are clearly Iranian, the vehicle itself suggests the influence of the Great Eurasian steppes, in Bactriana and beyond. Sixth to fourth century BC.

structure. Infantry reinforcements were still distributed territorially among the battalions of the phalanx; a new seventh battalion was now formed in addition. But with the cavalry Alexander went out of his way to break down all territorial groupings. The squadrons were now subdivided into two troops [*lochoi*], each under its own troop commander, and brought up to strength with reinforcements chosen on a random, non-regional basis. Promotion in future was to be by merit rather than seniority – which again gave the King far closer control over all military appointments. This kind of shake-up, taken in conjunction with the donations at Babylon, suggests that Alexander was already faced by considerable lack of enthusiasm – to put it no more strongly – among his officers and men. The reorganisation had two objects: increased efficiency and increased loyalty.

While he was still on the road to Susa, a messenger reached him from Philoxenus with the news that the city had capitulated. Once again the Macedonian army received a royal welcome. When they reached the city Alexander was conducted into the royal palace, through the great hypostyle hall with its vivid glazed-brick reliefs – horned lions, winged griffins, long rows of gorgeously apparelled Persian archers – to the treasury. Here the satrap, Abuleites, formally made over to him between forty and fifty thousand talents of minted gold Darics. But this was only the beginning. The treasury also held more than a hundred tons of purple-dyed cloth from Hermione, nearly two centuries old, its colour still unfaded. There was all the loot that Xerxes had amassed from Greece; jars of Nile and Danube water sent in by vassal monarchs as tokens of fealty; and the furnishings, gold plate and jewellery in the palace itself. If Darius was, in fact, hoping to distract Alexander with dazzling riches while he himself once more prepared for battle, he could hardly have baited the trap more effectively.

The tomb of Cyrus the Great at Pasargadae. The plinth is 48 by 44 feet at the base, and the tomb itself is made of white limestone blocks held together by iron clamps. It is shaped like a northern-type house, with a gable. Onesicritus, who inspected it with Alexander, reported that its inscription, in Greek and Persian, read simply: 'Here lie, I, Cyrus, King of Kings.'

Alexander's personal ambitions, however, reached further than mere loot, which never held any great attraction for him. After he had inspected the treasury, his first act – no doubt a calculated gesture – was to seat himself on Darius' throne, under its famous golden canopy. This, as Alexander must have known, meant death for any other than the legitimate occupant. Old Demaratus of Corinth shed tears of joy at the sight, and died shortly afterwards: *nunc dimittis*. But despite its symbolic impact, this incident also had a streak of unintentional comedy about it. Darius was a very tall man, and Alexander somewhat under average height; so when the latter sat down, his feet dangled in space above the royal footstool. One of the Royal Pages, with considerable presence of mind, removed the footstool and substituted a table. At this a Persian eunuch standing by began to weep noisily. Alexander asked him what the trouble was, and he explained that this was the royal table from which his master Darius had formerly eaten. Alexander, anxious not to offend any Achaemenid religious taboos, was on the point of having the table removed again. But Philotas, shrewdly, pointed out that his act, being committed unknowingly, counted as an omen. Alexander had (in true Biblical style) made his enemy's board his footstool. The table stayed where it was.

A winter campaign   By now it was January, and bitterly cold up in the passes. The Macedonians, Darius assumed, would go into winter quarters at Susa. With the coming of spring they would set out again: either north-east to Ecbatana, where Darius now lay, or south-east to Persepolis and Pasargadae. But Alexander made a speciality of winter campaigns, and he intended to exploit his victory at Gaugamela to the full. This did not include offering Darius a gentlemanly three months in which to get his wind back.

About mid-January the Macedonian army took the road, marching south-east from Susa. The only Persian who seems to have guessed Alexander's intentions was the satrap Ariobarzanes. Since Gaugamela he had raised an infantry force 25,000 strong, with 700 cavalry. The moment he learnt that Alexander was on the move, he occupied a deep mountain gorge known as the Susian Gates, and built a defensive wall across it. There were two possible routes to Persepolis of which this was the more direct. If Alexander made a frontal assault up the gorge, Ariobarzanes calculated, he was bound to be repelled with heavy losses. On the other hand, if he chose the easier southern route (almost identical with the modern motor-road through Kazerun and Shiraz) there would be ample time for the Persians to fall back on Persepolis. City and gold reserves could be evacuated long before the Macedonians got there. Ariobarzanes' plan was admirable: it only contained two fallacies. He believed his position at the Susian Gates to be impregnable; and he did not allow for the possibility that Alexander might divide his forces.

Parmenio, with the baggage train, the Thessalians, and all the heavy-armed troops, was dispatched by the main southern road, while Alexander himself took a light mobile column of shock-troops over the mountains to deal with Ariobarzanes. After five days' hard marching this force reached the Susian Gates. An attempt to carry the wall by direct assault failed disastrously. Ariobarzanes had artillery mounted above the wall; his men rolled

great boulders down on the Macedonians and poured a hail of arrows and javelins into their ranks from the steep spurs of the gorge. Alexander was forced to retreat, with numerous casualties. He had taken some prisoners, however; and one of them, a local herdsman, volunteered to guide him by an extremely difficult pass over the mountains, which would bring him out behind Ariobarzanes' position.

This mountain detour was only twelve miles round, but it took Alexander's commando force a gruelling day and two nights to negotiate it. They got there just before dawn on the third day. Two guard-pickets were silently massacred. Then the trumpets blared out, and Craterus' waiting troops launched a fierce frontal attack on the wall. At the same moment Alexander and his men came swarming down the crags behind Ariobarzanes' camp. After a hard and vicious struggle, the Gates were forced.

The north door of the Hall of the Hundred Columns, Persepolis. The scene represents a royal audience, with the monarch, larger than lifesize, in the top row.

Even now the victorious army made slow progress. Its route was seamed with lateral ravines and water-courses, and often obliterated by heavy snow-drifts. About this time, however, a messenger got through to the King from Tiridates, the garrison commander of Persepolis. Tiridates promised to surrender the city, but warned Alexander that he and his Macedonians must get there without delay: otherwise the inhabitants might well plunder the royal treasury before they left. Ordering the infantry to follow as best they could, Alexander set off on an all-night, breakneck cavalry dash which reached the Araxes River at dawn. There was no bridge; the King and his men built one in record time by the simple expedient of knocking down a nearby village, and using the timbers and dressed stone blocks from the houses they demolished. Then they rode on.

Alexander entered Persepolis on 31 January 330 BC. This was a Holy City, akin to Mecca or Jerusalem, and equally rich in solemn religious associations. If Alexander still cherished hopes of inheriting the Achaemenid crown according to legitimate precedent, backed by the Great King's nobles and the priestly caste of the Magi, he would treat this, of all places, with extreme propriety and respect. Anything less would permanently antagonise those whom he most needed to conciliate. There are signs, however, that by the time Alexander reached Persepolis, he had given up all hope of persuading the Iranian *élite* to endorse his claims. What he had not reckoned on was a purely religious or ideological opposition – something to which his own pragmatic nature tended to blind him. Many Iranian aristocrats were ready enough to collaborate. But to recognise Alexander as the Chosen One of Ahura Mazda was quite another matter.

This may explain why, despite Tiridates' formal surrender, he now gave his troops *carte blanche* to sack Persepolis – all but the palaces and the citadel, where Darius' treasures were stored. The King made an inflammatory speech to his officers beforehand, ranting on about Persian crimes against Greece, and describing Persepolis as 'the most hateful of the cities of Asia'. The Macedonians needed no further encouragement. Their last real taste of wholesale rape and plunder had been at Gaza. Ever since then, in particular at Babylon and Susa, Alexander's policy of conciliation had placed them under heavy disciplinary restraint. Now, unleashed at last, they went completely berserk.

Meanwhile, Alexander himself was inspecting the royal treasure-vaults, which contained an accumulated surplus of no less than 120,000 talents, dating back to the time of Cyrus the Great. From the Great King's bed-chamber came 8000 talents in gold, besides the jewelled golden vine – which, as Alexander surely knew, was also a symbolic Tree of Life, representing 'the rightful, proper continuity of Achaemenid government under Ahura Mazda'. This fantastic fortune was now to finance Alexander's further adventures in the East. Taking the pound sterling at its 1913 value, the accumulated bullion of Persepolis was worth something like £44,000,000 – which represents the national income of the Athenian empire, in its fifth-century heyday, for very nearly three hundred years.

Alexander's supremacy was now assured. With brilliant panache he had struck, through freezing winter snows, at the very heart and nerve-centre of

Darius' crumbling empire. The Zagros mountains had been neatly by-passed: the fall of Persepolis opened the road to Ecbatana. Any reasonable person, working on precedent, could have deduced what Alexander would do next – head straight north, capture Darius whatever the cost, and wind up this already overlong Persian campaign. But – once again – Alexander's behaviour proved totally unpredictable: he did not leave Persepolis until late May or early June. There was only one motive that could possibly have held him there so long; and that was the Persian New Year Festival. He had shown his Iranian subjects that he was not a man to be trifled with; the sacking of Persepolis proved that. But the vandalism of the Macedonian army had been most carefully controlled. The palaces and temples, the great apadana or audience hall, the whole complex of buildings which formed the city's spiritual centre, on that vast, stage-like terrace backed by the Kuh-i-Rahmet mountains – none of these had been touched. In other words, *the New Year Festival could still be held.* Perhaps even now, Alexander argued, common sense would prevail, and he would be acclaimed, with all due ceremonial, as Ahura Mazda's representative on earth.

But Alexander found himself up against a people who took their religion (including the divinity that hedged the Great King) very seriously indeed. March passed into April, and soon it became plain that Persepolis would see no procession that year, no ritual renewal of kingship.

By late May, his mind was finally made up. The city must be destroyed. It symbolised centuries of Achaemenid rule: once Alexander moved on eastward it would form the obvious rallying-point, both religious and

above left: This, among the most famous representations of Alexander, is a Roman copy of an original statue by Lysippus (see p. 80), the 'Alexander with the spear', perhaps commissioned for the foundation of Alexandria. On the base of this bronze original someone chiselled the following comment, in verse:

The image, gazing Zeuswards, might almost be saying:
'Earth is *my* footstool: Zeus, you can keep Olympus."'

above: A giant capital with *protomae* in the form of griffins' heads, at Persepolis.

political, for any nationalist resistance movement. Its great friezes and palaces and fire-altars embodied something to which the Macedonian conqueror had no effective answer: a purely spiritual and ideological opposition. 'My own view', says Arrian, stung into voicing a personal opinion for once, 'is that this was bad policy.' But the destruction of Persepolis finally removed any chance Alexander might have had of legitimising himself as an Achaemenid by peaceful means. It also provoked a desperate last-ditch stand in the eastern provinces. Because of this, many have been tempted to see the burning of the palaces as an accident, suggested during a drunken orgy, and regretted immediately afterwards.

Such is the version of events which has passed into history (or legend), and no arguments now are likely to dislodge it. The *mise-en-scène* is justly famous. Alexander held a great feast, at which he got very drunk. Thaïs, Ptolemy's mistress, speaking as an Athenian, said how marvellous it would be to burn down Xerxes' palace – thus, of course, shifting the initial onus of responsibility away from Alexander himself. Torches were called for, and a wavering, garlanded procession set off, to the skirling of flutes and pipes. As the revellers approached the palace doors, there was a moment's hesitation. This, cried some sedulous ape, was a deed worthy of Alexander alone. The King, with drunken enthusiasm – and perhaps glad to feel himself once more the champion of Hellas, a role he had been progressively abandoning – cast the first torch. Flames licked out, consuming rich tapestry-work, eating into the dry cedar cross-beams. Guards who came hurrying up with water-buckets stayed instead to watch the fun. Very soon the entire terrace was one roaring inferno.

right: Persepolis: in the foreground, Xerxes' gateway, guarded by winged bulls.

Overleaf
left: A relief at Persepolis portraying a human-headed bull.
right: A horsehead capital at Persepolis.

Median nobles bringing offerings to the Great King at the time of the New Year Festival, in a relief on the Tripylon staircase at Persepolis.

The palaces had already been systematically looted before their destruction. Macedonian soldiers found and removed almost all the coins, gold-work, and jewellery. They raided the armoury for swords and daggers and deliberately smashed up innumerable exquisite stone vases. They decapitated statues and defaced reliefs. The Hellenic crusade against Asiatic barbarism was now approaching its final triumph. What remains today, solid and indisputable, is the evidence of the fire itself – and all that it preserved. 'Burned beams of the roof still lay their print across stairways and against sculptures. Heaps of ashes are all that remain of the cedar panelling.' But that vast conflagration also hard-baked hundreds of clay tablets (which would otherwise have long since fallen to dust), besides firing the marvellous glaze on Xerxes' processional reliefs. When Alexander left these smoking ruins behind him, he could hardly know that his act of incendiarism had immortalised Persepolis for all time.

Alexander struck north from Persepolis at the beginning of June, leaving 3000 Macedonians behind to garrison the city and province – an unusually strong force. Three days' march from Ecbatana, after Alexander had already covered more than 400 miles, a renegade Persian nobleman appeared with the news that Darius was in retreat. His expected reinforcements had failed to arrive: he had taken off eastward, five days before, with the Bactrian cavalry, 6000 picked infantrymen, and 7000 talents from the Ecbatana palace treasury; his immediate destination seemed to be the Caspian Gates [Kotal-e-Dochtar].

Alexander had to move fast. Darius' intention (his informant said) was to retreat by the shores of the Caspian as far as Bactria, ravaging the land as he went. This would leave the Macedonians with a serious supply problem, since their route lay round the northern edge of the great salt desert. If they could be lured into the desolate wilderness of mountain and steppe beyond Hyrcania, a fresh satrapal army, familiar with local conditions, might very easily wear them down.

When he reached Ecbatana, Alexander took rapid stock of the situation. He was now embarking on a new phase of his campaign. The burning of Persepolis had written *finis* to the Hellenic crusade as such, and he used this excuse to pay off all his League troops – including Parmenio's Thessalians. What he now envisaged was a streamlined professional army, loyal to him alone, and prepared to follow him wherever he might lead. Accordingly, a tempting bait was dangled before these demobilised troops. Any man who wished might re-enlist with Alexander as a soldier of fortune, and those who did so received a bounty of no less than *three talents* (18,000 drachmas) on enrolment. It would take a very high-minded man indeed to resist such princely terms. The whole deal cost Alexander some 12,000–13,000 talents. Almost as much again was embezzled by his light-fingered financial officers – an ominous symptom of things to come.

By applying his money so skilfully, Alexander had purchased himself a mercenary army overnight. He had also fatally loosened Parmenio's hold on the military command structure. In future, he calculated, his troops' first allegiance would be to their royal paymaster. In fact Alexander lost no time in cutting Parmenio down to size. The old general remained behind at Ecbatana as area military commander: his career as Chief of Staff was over. Alexander dealt with him very tactfully. Parmenio was, after all, seventy years old, and – as the King doubtless assured him – had earned a rest from front-line campaigning. This did not mean that he was off the active list. His first task would be to convey the Great King's treasure to Ecbatana. After this he was to take an expeditionary force – Alexander had left him something like 6000 mercenaries – and pacify the tribes round the south and south-west Caspian.

It all sounded very sensible: on the face of it, Parmenio's position had lost nothing in dignity or prestige. But his effective power – as he himself well knew – had been drastically curtailed. He had lost his Thessalian cavalry as a unit, and it was to Harpalus, as Imperial Quartermaster General, that the mercenaries who had replaced them now looked for their pay. When the treasure convoy reached Ecbatana, it was Harpalus who would have charge of it, and issue Alexander's coinage from the royal mint. Parmenio's own new second-in-command, Cleander, was the King's nominee.

It has been said that Ecbatana marks the point at which Alexander's tragedy begins, 'the tragedy of an increasing loneliness, of a growing impatience with those who could not understand'. In fact his Macedonian officers, Parmenio included, understood only too well. All absolute autocrats end in spiritual isolation, creating their own world, their own version of the truth: Alexander was no exception. From now on, those few friends who dared criticise him to his face most often paid a heavy price for their honesty. Such a state of affairs encouraged gross adulation among the King's more sycophantic courtiers; and this, in turn, reinforced Alexander's own latent delusions of grandeur. In 330 the process had barely begun. But during the years that followed, it developed with alarming speed and intensity.

Alexander wasted not a moment more than was necessary in Ecbatana. His arrangements made, he at once went on after Darius. With luck he might yet overtake the Persians before they were through the Caspian Gates. But at Rhagae, about fifty miles from the Gates, Alexander learnt that Darius had already passed through them, and was now making for Hecatompylus (Damghan). To continue his forced march, under a burning July sun, without rest or adequate preparation, would be suicidal as well as pointless. Alexander bivouacked at Rhagae for five days, and then advanced as far as the Gates. Beyond them, south of the Elburz Mountains, lay that desolate tract of salt desert known today as the Dasht-e-Kavir.

While the cavalry, under Coenus, was sent out on a foraging expedition, two Babylonian noblemen – one of them Mazaeus' son – rode in with the dramatic news that Darius had been deposed, and was now a prisoner. The *coup* had been planned jointly by Bessus, satrap of Bactria, and the Grand Vizier, Nabarzanes. Without even waiting for Coenus to get back, the King set off after the Persian column, taking his best cavalry and the Guards Brigade. They force-marched for two nights and a day. When they reached the camp where Darius had been put under arrest, they found his aged Greek interpreter, who gave Alexander further details.

Nabarzanes had suggested, to begin with, that the Great King might – temporarily, of course – resign his title in favour of Bessus. But the Great

The Caspian Gates
(Kotal-e-Dochtar), which
formed a crucial stage in
Alexander's headlong
final pursuit of Darius.
Beyond this pass lay the
great salt desert, backed
by the Elburz Mountains.

King, weakly resentful, flew into a rage, drew his sword, and tried to kill
Nabarzanes. The council broke up in some disorder. This left the retreating
army split into two hostile camps. The Bactrians and other Eastern contingents looked to Bessus as their natural leader, while the Persians, under
Artabazus, and the Greek mercenaries stuck loyally by Darius. An open trial
of strength at this juncture was out of the question. The conspirators therefore
swore formal oaths of fealty to Darius, and were officially reconciled. A night
or two later, however, they abducted Darius to the Bactrian camp and
placed him under close arrest. The loyalists were now left with only two
alternatives, to pull out or capitulate. At first they chose the former, but two
days later most of the Persians drifted back to Bessus, seduced by his lavish
promises, and 'because there was no one else to follow'.

Bessus now declared himself Great King, taking the title of Artaxerxes IV,
and was enthusiastically acclaimed by his troops. His predecessor found
himself chained up in an old covered waggon: as good a way as any of
camouflaging his whereabouts on the march. Darius was also, of course,
the rebels' insurance ticket: as Arrian says, they 'had determined to hand
him over if they heard that Alexander was after them, and thus get favourable
terms for themselves'.

On the receipt of this information, Alexander saw that there was not a
moment to lose. About noon the next day the Macedonian party reached a
village where Darius and his captives had rested the previous day. At this
rate the pursuers were going to collapse from fatigue and heat-exhaustion
before they overtook their quarry. At all costs Alexander had to head the
Persians off. Was there, he enquired, any kind of short cut? Yes, the villagers

told him, a trail did exist, but it ran through uninhabited desert, and there were no water-points. Alexander swept these objections aside, commandeered local guides, dismounted 500 of his cavalry, and gave their horses to his toughest, fittest infantrymen. Then he set off on a fantastic all-night cross-country chase, covering fifty miles by dawn.

He overtook the Persians just as first light broke. His sudden appearance completely shattered them. Their one thought was to get away, and as fast as possible. Darius' heavy waggon slowed them down considerably. Bessus and Nabarzanes urged their prisoner to mount a horse and escape with them. The Great King refused. If he could not hold his empire, at least he would die with dignity. He would not accompany traitors, he said. Divine vengeance was at hand: he cast himself on Alexander's mercy. There was no time for prolonged argument. At any moment the retreating column might be surrounded. Bessus and Nabarzanes could do nothing now but ensure that Darius did not fall into Alexander's hands alive. So they and their fellow-conspirators ran him through with their javelins, and then fled, each by a different route – Nabarzanes to Hyrcania, Bessus to his own province of Bactria, while others made off southward, to Areia and Drangiana [Seistan].

Their behaviour set Alexander a nice problem. If the Great King was still a prisoner, which of the various retreating columns had charge of him? It was impossible to tell. At this point a thirsty Macedonian soldier called Polystratus, directed by peasants to the spring in a nearby valley, saw a driverless waggon standing there, and thought it odd that the oxen should have been stabbed rather than rounded up as booty. Then he heard the groans of a dying man. Naturally curious, he went over and drew back the hide curtains. There on the floor lay King Darius, still in chains, his royal mantle sodden with blood, the murderers' javelins protruding from his breast, alone except for one faithful dog crouching beside him. He asked, weakly, for water. Polystratus fetched some in his helmet. Clasping the Macedonian's hand, Darius gave thanks to heaven that he had not died utterly alone and abandoned. Soon after this his laboured breathing dwindled into silence, and all was over.

When Alexander stood, at last, before the broken corpse of his adversary, and saw the sordid, agonising circumstances in which he had died, his distress was obvious and genuine. Taking off his own royal cloak, he placed it over the body. At his express command, Darius was borne back in state to Persepolis, and given a King's burial, beside his Achaemenid forebears. But Alexander's chivalrous gesture – perhaps prompted in part by a twinge of personal remorse – had other, more practical motives as well. With Darius dead – and therefore unable to abdicate in his favour – Alexander's claim on the Achaemenid throne remained that of a foreign usurper. Worse still, he was now up against a genuine, and far more formidable, Achaemenid competitor in the person of Bessus, or King Artaxerxes, as he now styled himself. If Bessus managed to rally the West behind him, Alexander could still be in serious trouble. As it was, he would have to fight for the Eastern provinces instead of receiving their surrender under a general settlement.

Alexander's only possible line was to behave, from the moment of Darius' death, as though he were in fact the Great King's chosen and legitimate

Zeus with an eagle in his right hand and a staff in his left, on the reverse of a coin of Alexander.

184

successor. He must hunt down Bessus, not as a rival for the throne, but as a rebel and a regicide. Bessus, unfortunately, had too long a start, and the chase was soon abandoned. Alexander thereupon took his troops back to the nearby city of Hecatompylus [Damghan], and gave them a few days' rest. A rumour – very understandable in the circumstances – got around the camp that this was the end of the crusade. Wishful thinking crystallised into firm belief. Alexander woke one morning to hear the sound of waggons being loaded up for the homeward march.

Since he was already planning ahead in terms of a long Eastern campaign, this attitude caused him considerable alarm. He summoned his staff-commanders, 'and, with tears in his eyes, complained that he was being recalled from the mid-course of his glory'. They agreed to do what they could, but advised the King to be tactful and conciliatory when he made his general address to the troops. Alexander did something even more effective: he scared them silly. His whole speech emphasised the insecurity of the conquests they had made, the unwillingness of the Persians to accept their overlordship. 'It is by your arms that they are restrained, not by their dispositions, and those who fear us when we are present, in our absence will be enemies. We stand on the very threshold of victory.' Once Bessus was destroyed, Persian submission would be a foregone conclusion. Besides, the satrap's capital lay no more than four days' march away (a plain lie: the distance was 462 miles). What was that after all they had been through together? His troops cheered him to the echo: yet another crisis had been surmounted.

Two days later the army struck camp and marched north into Hyrcania, a wild, mountainous, but fertile district bordering on the Caspian. During his march on Zadracarta [Gorgan], the capital, Alexander received a letter from Nabarzanes. The Grand Vizier, after much specious self-exculpation for the part he had played in Darius' murder, offered to give himself up if he was granted a safe-conduct and reasonable terms. Alexander at once sent him the assurances he required. The more defections of this sort he could encourage, the more isolated Bessus' position would become. On his arrival in Zadracarta he found a number of high-ranking Persians, Artabazus among them, waiting to offer him their submission. This was a most encouraging sign. Some time later, after the King's return from a punitive expedition against a local tribe, Nabarzanes duly arrived on the scene. The Grand Vizier had brought numerous costly offerings to sweeten his reception, including 'a eunuch of remarkable beauty and in the very flower of boyhood, who had been loved by Darius and was afterwards to be loved by Alexander'. The name of this sinister youth was Bagoas: his entreaties are said to have tipped the scales in the Grand Vizier's favour.

One highly suspect development, in Macedonian eyes, was Alexander's ever-increasing Orientalisation: his adoption of Persian dress and protocol, the way he was beginning to confer on Iranian noblemen honours previously reserved for Macedonians, the progressive infiltration of ex-enemy troops into his own field army. Alexander even took over the traditional retinue of 365 concubines (one for each night of the year) who had served Darius, and were hand-picked from the most beautiful women in all Asia. We may doubt

185

whether Alexander made any of these innovations from active choice or preferences. But if the Persians were ever to accept his dynastic pretensions, he must play the part of Great King in an acceptable manner. By so doing, of course, he ran a grave risk of alienating his own Macedonians. His dilemma is well symbolised by the two seal-rings he used from now on. For European correspondence he employed his old Macedonian ring, while letters inside the Persian empire he stamped with the royal signet of Darius. He made his Companions – much against their will in some cases – wear purple-bordered white Persian cloaks, and (when all else failed) tried to silence his more vociferous critics by increasingly lavish hand-outs and bonanzas.

However, any ruler who made so blatant an effort to run with the hare and hunt with the hounds could hardly avoid trouble in the long run. A few of Alexander's close friends, such as Hephaestion, together with the usual clique of court toadies, actively supported his new integrationist line. The professional career officers – Craterus is a good example – were indifferent so long as their own status and prospects did not suffer. But Philip's hard-bitten veterans fiercely resented the whole experiment. So far as they were concerned, the war ended with Darius' death, and Alexander's grandiose dreams of further Eastern conquest left them cold. The sooner they got home the better. Any leader offering a reversal of Alexander's policy, coupled with speedy repatriation, could almost certainly count on their backing. The air was electric, ready to spark an explosion at any moment.

Alexander took several steps to lessen the tension. Like most personally austere leaders, he had an ill-disguised contempt for humanity in the mass, and seems to have felt he could manipulate his troops as he pleased simply by indulging their grosser appetites. It was now that vast luxurious feasts and drinking-parties first became a regular feature of camp life: the idea of bread-and-circuses was by no means a Roman invention. Immediate action, however, was the best antidote to any threat of mutiny. The army marched on eastward, from Zadracarta to Susia, in Areia. Here the satrap, Satibarzanes, who had been one of Darius' murderers, came forward and made his submission. The news he brought was that Bessus had been widely acclaimed as Lord of Asia. Recruits were joining him, not only in Bactria itself, but from the wild nomadic tribes beyond the Oxus. This was a threat that had to be dealt with as soon as possible, before it got completely out of hand. Alexander therefore confirmed Satibarzanes as satrap – a decision he soon had cause to regret – and pressed on at top speed towards Bactria.

At the Margus [Murghab] river, Alexander heard that Satibarzanes had massacred his Macedonian garrison, and was raising Areia in revolt. The King at once halted his advance into Bactria. Leaving Craterus in command of the main army, he took a flying column southward towards Artacoana, the satrapal seat, where Satibarzanes was gathering his forces. In two days Alexander covered nearly 100 miles. Satibarzanes, caught off-guard, fled to Bactria with 2000 cavalry. His remaining troops dug themselves in on a nearby wooded mountain. It was now August: Alexander set the forest alight and roasted the lot of them. Another Persian, Arsaces, was appointed satrap of Areia in Satibarzanes' place. To help prevent further trouble,

Alexander founded a settlement near Artacoana, which he called Alexandria-of-the-Areians [Herat] – the first of many such military garrisons planted at strategic points throughout the Eastern provinces. The Macedonians were now advancing into regions where towns, as a Westerner would conceive them, were largely non-existent, and of which their geographical knowledge was hazy in the extreme. Here they endured three years of mountain guerilla fighting (330–27) from Afghanistan to Bokhara, from Lake Seistan to the Hindu Kush, against the fiercest, most indomitable opposition Alexander had yet been called upon to face. Bessus, and his successor Spitamenes, were fighting a nationalist war, with strong religious overtones; between them they gave Alexander more continuous trouble than all the embattled hosts of Darius.

Having dealt with troublesome opposition in the remote area extending eastward from Seistan to the Indus (see map, p. 193), the Macedonian army was rested for a while at the capital of Drangiana, on the eastern shore of Lake Seistan – a city afterwards occupied by the Parthians, who called it Phrada. Here, during the autumn of 330 (in circumstances hardly less mysterious than those surrounding the Dreyfus Affair) Alexander finally destroyed both Parmenio and his one surviving son, the arrogant, ambitious Philotas.

For a long while now, as we have seen, the King had been steadily undermining Parmenio's power and authority. Nevertheless Parmenio still enjoyed great popularity with the troops, and any direct attack on him might well provoke a riot, or worse. Alexander's obvious line was to get at the old marshal through his son, Philotas, a far less likeable character. Tactless, overbearing, and ostentatious, Philotas caused deep resentment among officers and men alike by his caustic tongue and high-handed manners. For some while now Alexander had been steadily advancing Craterus and Perdiccas at his expense.

Philotas' worst fault seems to have been his outspoken bluntness. If we can believe Curtius, he wrote to Alexander after the Siwah episode, congratulating the King on his divine parentage, and commiserating (perhaps only half in jest) with all those who would in future be under such more-than-human authority. This kind of shrewd deflation was hardly calculated to increase Alexander's liking for him. But – at least until after Gaugamela – one quality Philotas possessed guaranteed his position. He was a brilliant cavalry commander, who led the Companions with superb panache and assurance. Now, however, as Alexander's destiny called him away from the plains into the mountains, and guerilla fighting became the order of the day, Philotas had become expendable. It did not take long to have him liquidated on trumped-up evidence which, incidentally, also implicated Parmenio.

The King had no intention of carrying out a wholesale pogrom of dissident Macedonian officers. He had attained his immediate objective, and knew when to stop. Only one thing – perhaps the most important – still remained to be done. Polydamas, one of the Companions, was dispatched across the deserts of central Iran, in Arab costume and with two Arabs as guides, bearing Parmenio's death-warrant. To ensure that they reached Ecbatana before the old general could hear any rumour of his son's death, the party travelled on racing-camels, covering the distance in eleven days rather than the usual thirty. Polydamas carried two letters for Parmenio himself, so that this sudden visit should not arouse any untimely suspicions. One was from Alexander, while the other bore Philotas' seal, and may indeed have been written by him after torture, at the same time as his 'confession'. As the old general opened it, in self-evident delight, Cleander stabbed him twice, first through the ribs and then in the throat. His fellow-officers followed suit. Blows continued to rain down on him even after he was dead.

For Alexander, it had been touch and go. He had got the army to act against Philotas, and had destroyed Parmenio in the backwash of that carefully staged condemnation. The incubus that had lain on him for so long was now at long last removed. But the whole episode left an unpleasant aftermath of suspicion and hatred behind it. From now on Alexander never completely trusted his troops: all those who expressed criticism of him and his policies, or were (in his opinion) unduly distressed by Parmenio's death, or groused about their prolonged military service, he 'assembled into one unit which he called the Disciplinary Company, so that the rest of the Macedonians might not be corrupted by their improper remarks and criticism'. The ultimate purpose of this group (or so Justin alleges) was to supply men for particularly dangerous missions, or remote military settlements on the Eastern frontiers.

At the same time Alexander determined (though he changed his mind later), never again to leave his all-important Companion Cavalry under one man's control. He therefore split Philotas' command between Black Cleitus – an appointment clearly designed to placate Old Guard conservatives – and his own closest personal friend, Hephaestion. This was Hephaestion's first major post. Henceforward his rise to power was steady, progressive, and by no means based entirely on nepotism: he seems to have been a competent, if uninspired, cavalry commander.

The 'Alexander sarcophagus' from Sidon, showing a warrior most often identified, from his age and prominence, as Parmenio.

9 The quest for Ocean

It was winter by the time Alexander resumed his march. If he had simply wanted to pursue Bessus he could have back-tracked north to the point where he left the Murghab River [see map, p. 165], and then have continued his advance on Zariaspa [Balkh]. Instead, he swung north-east through Arachosia, which meant that he would now be forced to cross the Hindu Kush. His main reason for picking this long, difficult route seems to have been the still-unpacified state of the southern satrapies – including Arachosia itself.

Alexander reached Kandahar in February 329, and began his crossing of the Hindu Kush about the beginning of April. During their winter march through the highlands of eastern Afghanistan his troops had suffered severely from frostbite, snow blindness, and chronic fatigue – the latter probably due to oxygen shortage at high altitudes. Somewhere near Kabul the King gave them a short and well-earned rest. Then, after establishing a third garrison town (which received the name Alexandria-in-the-Caucasus) he took his army over the Khawak Pass (11,600 ft), and struck north along the Surkhab River towards Drapsaca [Kunduz]. The crossing is said to have been accomplished in seventeen days.

Bessus, together with 7000 Bactrians and some strong Soghdian levies – the latter under two great feudal barons, Spitamenes and Oxyartes – was confidently awaiting Alexander at Aornus [Tashkurgan]. There are seven passes from Kabul to the Oxus valley; Bessus assumed, very reasonably, that the Macedonians would choose the lowest. But Alexander, unpredictable as always, did nothing of the sort. The Khawak Pass is not only the easternmost of the seven (which was why Alexander chose it) but also the highest and the most heavily snowbound. His army negotiated it with fantastic speed, and Bessus, eighty miles away to the west, found himself outflanked. He therefore decided to abandon Bactria altogether, retreat across the Oxus, and base his defence on Soghdiana (see map, p. 193).

After a short rest at Drapsaca, Alexander went on to occupy both Aornus and Zariaspa, the capital of Bactria – and Zoroaster's birthplace – without encountering any real opposition. Then, leaving old Artabazus as satrap of the newly conquered province, he passed on towards the Oxus. It was now June, the dry season, and his route lay across a burning waterless desert.

The frostbitten suddenly found themselves suffering from heatstroke.

As a result of this experience the Thessalian volunteers (already restive as a result of Parmenio's murder) mutinied *en masse*, and many of Philip's older veterans followed their example. They were four thousand miles from home: they had had enough. The King had no option but to release them all, with severance pay and bonuses. This unexpected demobilisation left him dangerously short of first-class troops. To make matters worse, a great number – more than he had lost in any battle – now died as a result of dehydration followed by frenetic over-drinking. He therefore took a gamble, and, for the first time, recruited local 'barbarian' auxiliaries on a large scale. The gamble paid off handsomely – though what Alexander's remaining Macedonians made of it is quite another matter.

The Oxus [Amu Darya] presented a formidable obstacle. At Kelif, where Alexander made his crossing, it was three-quarters of a mile wide, and deep in proportion, with a sandy bottom and a swift-flowing current. The King's engineers tried to sink piles for a bridge, but these were quickly carried away. Finally Alexander fell back on the expedient he had adopted at the Danube – except that this time he had no fleet to help him. All the leather tent-covers were stuffed with dry chaff and then stitched up carefully to make floats. By this makeshift method the King got his forces across the river, though it took him five days.

Alexandria-of-the-Arachosians, garrisoned by Alexander during his march to the Hindu Kush. This was one of many such military settlements in the East which were named after him; its remains are close to the modern city of Kandahar.

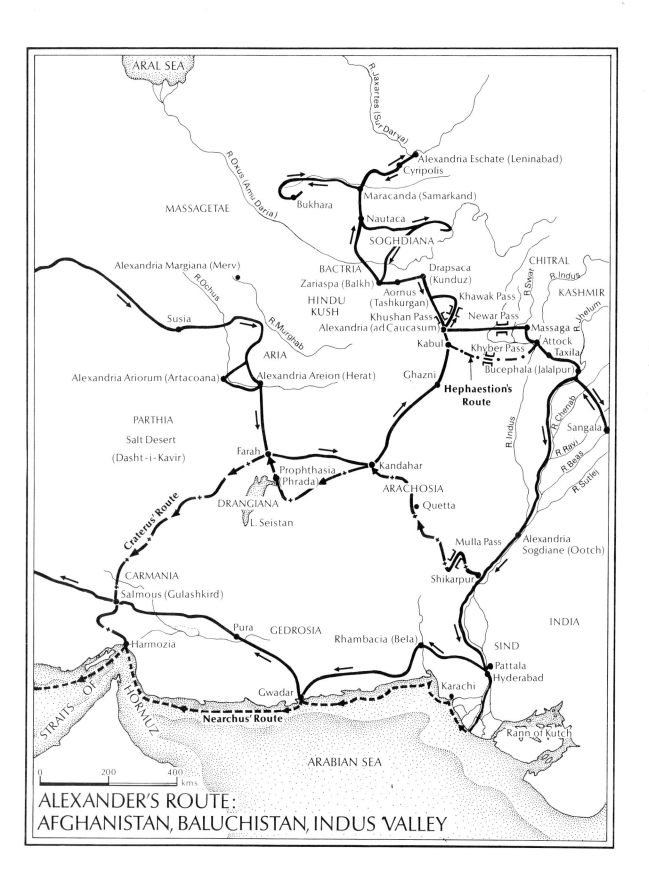

ALEXANDER'S ROUTE:
AFGHANISTAN, BALUCHISTAN, INDUS VALLEY

Ruins of the Nabhcar
Gate at Zariaspa (Balkh,
in Afghanistan). It was
built by the Graeco-
Bactrian dynasty that
ruled here in the third
century BC.

Bessus assumed that Alexander would be held up at the Oxus until he could collect a transport fleet – just as he had earlier deduced, with erroneous confidence, which pass the Macedonians would follow from Kabul. His reputation, already shaky after the evacuation of Bactria, sank to zero when Alexander's latest exploit became known. Spitamenes and the Soghdian barons decided, at this point, that a change of leadership was advisable. They therefore placed Bessus under arrest, and sent messengers to tell Alexander that if a Macedonian officer and escort came to a certain rendez-vous, the regicide would be handed over to them. This was an extremely clever move. It not only rid the new junta of Bessus himself, but convinced Alexander of their willingness to collaborate. Nevertheless he was cautious: the message might be some sort of trap.

Ptolemy, son of Lagus, was entrusted with this delicate mission. He was directed to a remote village, where he found Bessus under armed guard. Anxious not to commit any *faux pas*, he sent a dispatch back to Alexander, asking how Bessus should be brought into his presence. The King's instructions were very specific. Bessus was to be placed by the roadside where Alexander and his troops would pass, naked, bound to a post, and with a slave's wooden collar round his neck. The King meant to make an example of him, primarily for the benefit of the Iranian nobility.

When Alexander came abreast of Bessus, he stepped down from his royal chariot, and asked the prisoner why he had first enchained and then slain Darius 'his King, kinsman and benefactor'. Bessus replied that it had been a joint decision 'to win Alexander's favour and so save their lives'. But such favours (as everyone knew) would only be welcomed as such by a foreign usurper – the one title Alexander was determined to avoid. As proof of the abhorrence with which he regarded Bessus' betrayal, Alexander first had him scourged, and then sent back to Zariaspa, where his nose and ears were cut off; finally he was publicly executed in Ecbatana, before a full assembly of the Medes and Persians.

The ancient fortifications
of Zariaspa – perhaps
those erected as a special
defence measure (initially
against Eastern nomads)
by Bactria's powerful
usurping monarch, Euthy-
demus of Magnesia (died
c. 190 BC), who stood
siege for two years against
Antiochus the Great
(209–7) and made an
alliance with him at the
end of it. Zariaspa was
also known in antiquity
as Bactra, of which its
modern name is a
corruption.

Under the happy but mistaken impression that Spitamenes was now his subject-ally, and all south-west Soghdiana peacefully subdued, Alexander struck north for Maracanda [Samarkand] and the Jaxartes [Syr-Darya]. This river marked the furthermost north-eastern boundary of the Persian empire. Beyond it lay limitless 'Scythian' steppe and mountain, inhabited by wild nomadic tribesman – Dahae, Sacae, Massagetae. Here Alexander found an outpost and a chain of seven forts, supposedly built by Cyrus. These he garrisoned with mercenaries. He also planned to construct a new military settlement of his own, 'both as an excellent base for a possible future invasion of Scythia and as a defensive position against raiding tribes from across the river'. Its name was Alexandria-the-Furthest [Leninabad].

It was now that the real trouble began. Alexander summoned Spitamenes and his colleagues to a meeting in Zariaspa. Spitamenes refused, and the whole province rose in revolt under him. Local commandos recaptured Cyrus' outpost and its string of forts, massacring the Macedonian garrisons. Spitamenes himself laid siege to Maracanda. The King acted fast enough, but he does not seem, as yet, to have fully appreciated what he was up against. The relief force he sent to Maracanda was hopelessly inadequate for its task. Indeed, its titular commander, Pharnuches, a Lydian interpreter, had with him only sixty Companion Cavalry, 800 mercenary horsemen, and 1500 mercenary foot-soldiers, under three Macedonian officers.

Alexander dealt with the river-forts himself. He had been shot through the leg-bone by a stray arrow on the march to Maracanda: this probably did not improve his temper. Five of the seven forts he retook in three days, butchering the defenders. The main outpost, Cyropolis, fell after a raiding-party squeezed in through a dry river-course that ran under the wall. Shortly afterwards, irritated by the taunts and threats of the tribesmen across the river, he carried out a tactically brilliant raid into their territory. During the pursuit that followed, he was unwise enough to drink some infected water. When he recrossed the Jaxartes he had gastro-enteritis to contend with on top of his other troubles.

But the worst news was yet to come. When Pharnuches and his relief column approached, Spitamenes had withdrawn from Maracanda, skilfully luring his pursuers on towards Bokhara, across the Zarafshen River, into the wild territory of the Massagetae. Here they were ambushed, surrounded, and shot down almost to a man (accounts differ as to the exact circumstances). Only 300 foot-soldiers and about forty cavalry escaped. Spitamenes at once took his troops back to Maracanda, and resumed the siege. When Alexander heard this grim story from the survivors, he threatened them with the death penalty if they breathed a word about what had happened. One thing stood out clearly: Spitamenes was the most dangerous opponent Alexander had been called upon to face since Memnon of Rhodes.

The Macedonians now marched along the Jaxartes, across the Golod'naya Steppe, and into the valley of the Zarafshen, reaching Maracanda at dawn on the fourth day – a distance of about 160 miles. Spitamenes and his horsemen promptly raised their siege and faded away into the desert. Alexander pursued them for a while, but in the end gave up the chase as hopeless. He recrossed the Oxus and went into winter quarters at Zariaspa (329–8). It was now that final sentence was pronounced on Bessus. During that same winter welcome reinforcements, mostly mercenaries, arrived from the coast. With them came such men as Parmenio's brother Asander, and Nearchus, Alexander's boyhood friend, till recently satrap of Lycia. Nearchus now became a battalion commander in the Guards Brigade. Asander is never heard of again.

Meanwhile, before he could move on, there was the elusive Spitamenes to be dealt with. Early in spring 328 Alexander, leaving Craterus and four battalions of the phalanx to police Bactria, set about this frustrating task. At the crossing of the Oxus two springs, one of water and the other of oil, were revealed when a trench was being dug for the King's tent. Aristander the seer (with that singular gift for an apt platitude which characterises all his pronouncements) interpreted this as 'a sign of difficulties to come and of eventual victory'. The King now split up his forces into five mobile columns, under Hephaestion, Ptolemy, Perdiccas, Coenus and himself. These columns ranged through the countryside, mopping up pockets of local resistance and establishing a linked network of military outposts. Either now or shortly afterwards a similar system was set up in Margiane [western Bactria].

The River Jaxartes, now the Syr-Darya, or Yellow River, rises in the Tien-shan Mountains and has its outfall in the Aral Sea, after traversing some 1500 miles of the wildest country – both steppe and mountain – in the world. It marked the northern-most limits of Alexander's conquests.

Existing hill-forts were taken over and fresh ones built, all within easy reach of each other.

Spitamenes, meanwhile, had kept well beyond Alexander's reach, among the Massagetae nomads, where he was reputed to be raising a large cavalry force. When the five Macedonian columns made their prearranged rendez-vous in Maracanda, about mid-summer, the King sent off Coenus and old Artabazus to keep an eye on his activities. Spitamenes dodged their scouts with insolent ease, swept south into Bactria, captured a border fortress, ravaged the land round Zariaspa, and carved up a scratch force of Mace-donian veterans who ventured out against him. When this news reached Craterus (who had been up-country with his four phalanx-battalions) he hurried after Spitamenes, overtaking him just on the edge of the desert. There was a fierce engagement, during which about 150 Massagetae horse-men lost their lives. But the remainder – Spitamenes included – did their usual vanishing trick into the steppe, where Craterus found it impracticable to pursue them.

The atmosphere in headquarters that summer was strained and irritable. What should have been a quick minor campaign continued to drag on in-conclusively. Two unprecedented defeats did not improve matters. The hatred and jealousy between Philip's Old Guard and the King's Graeco-Oriental courtiers reached a fresh peak of intensity. The heavy carousing which fol-lowed one particular Macedonian banquet soon set resentful tongues wagging freely. *In vino veritas* – and the truth came out with more violence for being so long suppressed, as it had done during Philip's last and fatal marriage-feast.

The evening began, like so many others, with an uproarious drinking-party. Alexander, more than half-tipsy, and egged on by the sycophants who crowded round him, began to boast immoderately of his own achievements. Flatterers compared the King's exploits – favourably – with those of Heracles. This vainglorious attitude might have been consciously calculated to provoke the Old Guard. If so, it achieved its object. Black Cleitus (who found Alexander's Orientalism and the gross adulation of his courtiers equally repellent) now remarked, sourly, that such talk was blasphemous. In any case, they were exaggerating. Most of Alexander's successes were due to the Macedonian army as a whole. When he heard this the King 'was deeply hurt'. One can imagine the scene all too clearly.

Alexander's clique now launched into a wholesale denunciation of Philip. The King himself needed little encouragement to develop such a theme. Cleitus, by now angry-drunk himself, vigorously upheld Philip's achievements in Greece, 'rating them all higher than the present victories'. 'From this,' says Curtius, 'there arose a dispute between the younger and the older soldiers.' But the division was not merely one of youth and age; it was fundamental, irreconcilable – nationalism against Orientalism, simplicity against sophistication, blunt free speech against sedulous conformism.

Alexander now poured fuel on the flames by giving the floor to a Greek singer, who proceeded to entertain the company with a malicious skit aimed at certain (unnamed) Macedonian commanders who had recently been defeated in battle. Cleitus, stung beyond endurance, cried out that it was a shameful thing, in the hearing of enemies and barbarians (by which he meant the King's Persian guests), 'to insult Macedonians who were far better men than those who laughed at them, even though they had met with misfortune'. Cleitus, clearly, had been one of the commanders involved – and now he was rising to the bait. Silkily, the King murmured that to call cowardice 'misfortune' sounded uncommonly like special pleading. 'It was my cowardice, as you call it, that saved your life at the Granicus,' Cleitus shouted. 'It is by the blood of the Macedonians, and by these wounds of ours, that you have risen so high – disowning Philip, claiming Ammon as your father.'

Alexander's reply is highly revealing: '*That's how you talk about me the whole time, isn't it?* That's what causes all this bad blood between the Macedonians. You needn't think you're going to get away with it'.

'Look, Alexander,' Cleitus said – carefully addressing the King by his bare name, according to Philip's practice – 'we *don't* get away with it, even now. What rewards have we for our labours? Those who died are the luckiest – they never lived to see Macedonians thrashed with Median rods, or kow-towing to Persians before they could have an audience of their own King.'

This speech caused a tremendous uproar, during which Alexander – perhaps not quite so drunk as he made out – turned to two Greek courtiers and observed, scathingly : 'Don't you feel that Greeks go about among Macedonians like demi-gods among wild beasts?' There was so much noise that Cleitus missed the King's exact words – which may in fact have been a deliberate aside, designed to provoke him further. The old warrior bellowed at Alexander that he either ought to say what he meant openly, or else not invite to supper 'men who were free and spoke their minds', but rather consort with slaves and barbarians, creatures who would prostrate themselves before his white robe and Persian sash.

Alexander, half out of his mind with rage, picked up the first thing that came to hand, an apple, hurled it at Cleitus, and began looking round for his sword. One of the Gentlemen of the Bodyguard had prudently removed it. The King's close friends – Perdiccas, Lysimachus, Leonnatus – scenting trouble, crowded round and forcibly held him down. A violent struggle developed, with Alexander screaming that this was a plot, that he had been betrayed like Darius. Cleitus, who had broken loose once more, now lurched back in by another door, shouting a line from Euripides' *Andromache*: 'Alas, what evil government in Hellas!' Alexander would have had no trouble in continuing Cleitus' all too apt quotation:

> When the public sets a war memorial up
> Do those who really sweated get the credit?
> Oh no! Some general wangles the prestige! –
> Who, brandishing his one spear among thousands,
> Did one man's work, but gets a world of praise.
> These self-important fathers of their country
> Think they're above the people. Why, they're nothing!

An East Scythian vase (electrum) found at Kabul Oba, showing a warrior bandaging his wounded companion.

Alexander leapt up, seized a spear from one of his guards, and ran Cleitus through, killing him instantly.

Struck by sudden overwhelming remorse, the King plucked the spear from his old comrade's dead body and tried to impale himself on it. Once more, however, his friends forcibly restrained him. Alexander now shut himself up in his private quarters, without food or drink, and lay there for three days. The point at which genuine grief began to merge into calculated play-acting is very hard to determine. We can only judge by results: and the results were of great interest and significance. Once it sank into the minds of Alexander's followers that he might *really* starve himself to death, leaving them leaderless in this remote and barbarous country, they did everything they could to make him change his mind. What the King sought was a combined absolution and vote of confidence: he got both. The Macedonians, taking their cue from the King's reaction, 'decreed that Cleitus had been justly put to death', presumably for treason. His crime thus retrospectively legitimised – and conscious that henceforth he could, at a pinch, get the army's endorsement for almost anything – Alexander consented to sit up and take nourishment. But all those who were present at that fatal banquet knew the truth. Cleitus had been killed for daring to express open criticism of the King, and for no other reason.

Alexander had now spent two campaigning seasons in Bactria and Soghdiana, with very little to show for them. Spitamenes remained as elusive as ever. The King was grimly determined to finish him off before spring came: he had no intention of holding up his projected invasion of India a moment longer. There had been far too much delay as it was.

Administrative changes reveal a generally tougher line. Alexander himself took over Cleitus' vacant command in the Companion Cavalry. While

the bulk of the army moved into winter quarters at Nautaca (see map, p. 193) Coenus, with two battalions of the phalanx and a strong mixed cavalry force, was sent to cover the north-west frontier. Alexander's network of hill-forts now began to prove its worth. Spitamenes was finding even greater difficulties in obtaining provisions and horses, let alone a secure base. Finally, in desperation, he enlisted the support of 3000 Massagetae horsemen, and attempted a mass break-through – just as Alexander had foreseen when making his dispositions.

Coenus cut this large but ill-disciplined horde to pieces with professional zest, killing 800 enemy horsemen at almost no loss to himself. Spitamenes fled into the desert with the nomads, his prestige much lowered by this ignominious defeat. Indeed, when the Massagetae learnt that Alexander himself was coming after them, they lost no time in executing the fugitive, whose head they then dispatched to the King by way of a peace-offering. Their desert neighbours, the Dahae, hearing what had happened, promptly turned in Spitamenes' second-in-command, thus winning themselves a free pardon. With Spitamenes' death all organised resistance on the northen frontier collapsed.

Alexander had still to deal with the wild mountainous district of the south-east – Paraetecene, between modern Tadzhik and Badakhshan – where at least four great barons continued to defy him from their remote rock-fortresses. There was no time to be lost. After only two months at Nautaca the Macedonian army set off once more. It was early January, and weather conditions were appalling. During this march 2000 men froze to death or died of pneumonia. The first mountain stronghold to face Alexander's assault was that known as the 'Soghdian Rock'. Oxyartes, the local baron, had garrisoned it with up to 30,000 troops, and had sent his own wife and children there to ensure their safety. Provisions were stored up against a

above: A Graeco-Bactrian silver rhyton.

far left: A silver phalaron in Graeco-Bactrian style, portraying a winged griffin.

two-years' siege. Deep snow not only hampered the Macedonians' advance, but also ensured abundant drinking-water for the defenders. The rock itself was sheerfaced and (as its occupants believed) utterly inaccessible.

Their optimism became apparent when Alexander, at a preliminary parley, offered them safe-conduct to their homes if they agreed to surrender the fortress. They laughed rudely and asked whether his men could fly, adding that they would only surrender to winged soldiers, 'as no other sort of person could cause them the least anxiety'. The King's reputation should have made them think twice before issuing such a challenge: it simply put him on his mettle. He at once combed the entire army for experienced crags-men and mountaineers, of whom he found some three hundred. From these he called for volunteers to scale the sheer rock-face on the far side, offering vast rewards to the first twelve men up. When they reached the summit, above the fortress itself, they were to wave white flags as a signal.

The raiders roped themselves together and scaled the most difficult over-hangs with the aid of iron wedges and *pitons* driven into cracks in the rock-face. They made the ascent at night, an extra hazard. But at dawn a flutter of white flags broke out on the very summit of the rock; and Alexander sent a herald to tell the defenders that if they looked up, they would see he had found his winged men. Oxyartes' troops were so taken aback by this *coup de théâtre* that they capitulated on the spot – though they outnumbered the mountaineers (at a conservative estimate) by a hundred to one, and Alex-ander's main forces still had no clear road to the summit. Once again psychological insight had paid off handsomely. Alexander benefited further by marrying Oxyartes' daughter Roxane. His new father-in-law gave him considerable help in reducing the rest of Soghdiana.

Alexander was under no illusions as to the precarious nature of his hard-won victory. What else could he do to strengthen his position? One answer was suggested by the network of military garrisons he had built up. Some of these could be turned into permanent cities. At least six major foundations – all named Alexandria – are known from this area, including those of Margiane (Merv), Tarmita (Termez) on the Oxus, and Alexandria-the-Furthest (Leninabad). Their primary function was that of frontier defence. In addition, ample drafts of reinforcements (16,000 infantry alone during 328) made it possible to allow for an extra-strong garrison. Amyntas, the new satrap of Bactria, was eventually given 10,000 foot and 35,000 horse, a vast figure by previous standards. But perhaps the most significant step which Alexander took at this time (and the one which most clearly reveals Philip's influence) was the recruitment of 30,000 native youths, to be taught the Greek language and given a thorough military training, Macedonian style.

Eventually, these trainees would furnish replacements for the phalanx and Alexander's officer corps. The King later referred to them as his 'suc-cessors' by which, *bien entendu*, he meant successors of the Macedonian Old Guard. For the moment, however, while he marched on to India and the shores of Ocean, they would serve as admirable hostages. It was clearly impossible to keep this innovation a secret. Though Alexander doubtless emphasised the role of the 'successors' as hostages when discussing the matter with his staff officers, the Macedonian command structure clearly saw itself

threatened by direct competition from these barbarian upstarts. Indeed, it looks very much as though Alexander intended, for obvious reasons, to purge his royal *apparat* of all Macedonian influence whatsoever. The leaders of the Old Guard had, one by one, been eliminated. Persian nobles now formed the cornerstone of Alexander's administration.

Nevertheless, one major snag still remained. Where, except among the ranks of the Companions, the Guards Brigade, and the phalanx, were first-class battalion or divisional commanders to be found? Like it or not, Alexander had to put up with his officer corps; and it was these same officers whose blunt Macedonian irreverence kept pricking the bubble of his Oriental self-aggrandisement.

Nothing better exemplified the fundamental division in court circles than the matter of *proskynesis*, or obeisance. To Persians this was normal prescriptive etiquette. To the Greeks, however, *proskynesis*, if practised at all, was a gesture reserved exclusively for the adoration of a god. They therefore came to the erroneous conclusion that Persians, by prostrating themselves before the Great King, were *acknowledging his divinity*. Would it not be logical (the court sycophants argued) to grant Alexander such deified status too?

From the Persian viewpoint, Alexander could not abolish *proskynesis* without having his own *bona fides* as Great King called in question. On the other hand, there were far too many incidents of Macedonian officers roaring with laughter or otherwise showing unmannerly contempt when the act of

A cut-glass vase said to represent the Pharos (lighthouse) of Alexandria, from Begram, Afghanistan.

obeisance was performed; and these were the men on whom Alexander, in the last resort, depended. After much discussion, the divinisation project was, for the moment, abandoned, and Alexander, together with Hephaestion and one or two other close friends, devised an alternative plan for introducing *proskynesis* on a more or less secular basis. But the opposition of Aristotle's nephew Callisthenes, which reflected the feelings of the Macedonians and had been largely responsible for the failure of Alexander's first scheme, also sealed the fate of the second. Once again, Callisthenes had the Old Guard on his side, but this time his stand against Alexander cost him his life.

The land across the Indus

Alexander's ideas concerning India were, at this point, still sketchy in the extreme. To the Greeks of his day the land across the Indus was a shallow peninsula, bounded on the north by the Hindu Kush, and on the east by the great world-stream of Ocean, which ran (so they believed) at no great distance beyond the Sind Desert. Of the main Indian sub-continent, let alone the vast Far Eastern land-mass from China to Malaysia, they knew nothing. In general Alexander's ignorance of Indian geography remained profound, and his whole Eastern strategy rested on a false assumption. When enlightenment came, it was too late. The great Ganges plain, by its mere existence, shattered his dream more effectively than any army could have done.

Scylax (commissioned by Darius I to explore the Indian trade routes), Herodotus and Ctesias (a Greek doctor at the Persian court) had all written in some detail about India, but even if Alexander had familiarised himself with all this material (which is quite possible) he would not have been very much the wiser. By the fourth century Persia had abandoned her Indian satrapies: and even when it was officially part of the empire, the land beyond the Indus remained largely *terra incognita*, a region of myth and fable, like mediaeval Cathay. Alexander's main impulse in invading this mysterious wonderland was sheer curiosity, coupled with a determination to achieve world-dominion in the fullest sense. When he stood by the shore of Ocean, that ambition would be fulfilled. India once conquered, 'he would have Asia entirely in his hands'.

The final size of the army which recrossed the Hindu Kush in spring 327 is almost impossible to estimate. Alexander had with him not more than 15,000 Macedonians, of whom 2000 were cavalrymen. Total cavalry estimates, however, range between 6500 and 15,000. The infantry figures are equally uncertain, varying from 20,000 to 120,000. This vast horde streamed over the Kushan Pass [14,000 ft] to Alexandria-of-the-Caucasus in a mere ten days. While he was still in Bactria, Alexander had been joined by an Indian rajah, Sasigupta, a deserter from Bessus, who presumably had briefed him on the political situation beyond the Khyber. At all events, the King now sent envoys ahead to Ambhi, the rajah of Taxila [Takshaçila] and 'the Indians west of the Indus', asking them to meet him, at their convenience, in the Kabul Valley. Ambhi and several other minor princes duly arrived, with gifts, flattering speeches of welcome, and twenty-five elephants. It was the elephants that caught Alexander's eye, and eventually – under a certain amount of pressure, one suspects – the Indians agreed to make him a present of them. However, Ambhi had good reasons for keeping in with Alexander: he wanted the Macedonian army's support against his great rival Porus, a powerful monarch whose domains lay beyond the Hydaspes [Jhelum] River.

Alexander now divided his army. Hephaestion and Perdiccas, with rather

left: The mountains of the Hindu Kush.

centre: The Kabul River gorge, above Basauli, Afghanistan.

more than half the cavalry, three battalions of the phalanx, and the baggage-train, were to proceed down the Khyber Pass to the Indus. 'The instructions', says Arrian, 'were to take over either by force or agreement all places on their march, and on reaching the Indus to make suitable preparations for crossing'. Meanwhile Alexander himself, with Craterus as his second-in-command, planned to take a mobile column up the Choaspes [Kunar] River and to march through the hill country of Bajaur and Swat (see map, p. 193), reducing any enemy strongholds *en route*, and giving cover to the main army's left flank. The two forces would finally rendezvous at the Indus.

Alexander had a very rough passage during this campaign. Most of the walled towns he attacked, far from opening their gates at the first onset, put up a violent resistance. By way of retaliation, when they finally fell he took to butchering the inhabitants wholesale. At Massaga he treacherously massacred 7000 Indian mercenaries together with their wives and children. After dealing with the Aspasians [Açvakas] along the Kunar and Bajaur valleys, the Macedonians moved on north, into the rich forest-clad mountain region below Chitral. The first town they encountered surrendered after a short siege. It was called Nysa, a name intimately associated with Dionysus, and the god who founded it had (to judge from what the local inhabitants told Alexander) decidedly Dionysiac characteristics. Dionysus' presence was further confirmed, for the Macedonians, by a great mountain outside the town, where there grew not only vines but also ivy – a plant they had found nowhere else in the Far East. Alexander and his men climbed this mountain, crowned themselves with ivy-wreaths, and went on a ten-day Bacchic spree, feasting and drinking and revelling in splendid style. 'Hence', says Curtius, 'the mountain heights and valleys rang with the shouts of so many thousands, as they invoked the god who resided over that grove.'

There now followed Alexander's remarkable capture of the fortress which Arrian calls Aornus – perhaps a Greek attempt at Sanskrit *avarana*, 'a place

right: The Khyber Pass – the route followed by Hephaestion and Perdiccas to the Indus.

left: Chitral: the Bum-
boret Valley, home of the
modern Kalash Kaffirs,
whose dress, physical
features, wine-making
and religious practices all
suggest descent from an
isolated Greek community.
In this area was Nysa,
scene of Alexander's
famous Dionysiac revel.

of refuge'. This fortress stood on the great massif known as Pir-Sar, in a bend on the Indus about seventy-five miles north of Attock, and over 5000 feet above the river. Arrian gives its circumference as about twenty-five miles: it was well provided with water, and had only one ascent, which was steep and difficult. Local legend told of how a god (whom the Macedonians identified with Heracles) had tried, unsuccessfully, to capture this inaccessible strong-hold. Alexander, of course, at once conceived a violent desire (*pothos*) to capture Aornus himself – 'and the story about Heracles was not the least of his incentives'.

After making contact with Hephaestion (the rendezvous was at Ohind, sixteen miles above Attock) he at once set off up-river to tackle this ultra-Herculean labour. In the end, of course, he *did* capture the fortress (no story otherwise) with what Sir Aurel Stein adjudged 'such combined energy, skill and boldness as would be sought rather in a divine hero of legend than in a mortal leader of men'. In order to bring his catapult and artillery within range he was forced to run a great wooden crib-work causeway across the ravine between Una-Sar and a small hill dominating Pir-Sar. When the causeway was built, and Alexander's artillery in place, the defenders fled. With some difficulty a group of Macedonians reached the summit, and thus Alexander was left in possession of the Rock which had baffled Heracles.

Leaving Sasigupta as garrison commander of Aornus, Alexander carried out a quick reconnaissance of the surrounding countryside. His patrols were ordered to interrogate the natives and, 'in particular, to get what information they could about elephants, as this interested him more than anything'.

The Indus at Attock.

Most of the Indians had fled across the river: Alexander – whose retinue already included a group of hunters and mahouts – rounded up thirteen abandoned elephants and attached them to his own column. He then built rafts and shipped the entire force, elephants included, downstream to Ohind. His engineers had completed the bridge some time before, while Hephaestion had also collected a number of boats, including two thirty-oar galleys. Various rich presents, which ranged from bar silver to sacrificial sheep, had arrived from Ambhi, escorted by a crack native cavalry regiment, 7000 strong. The rajah also promised to surrender his capital, Taxila, the greatest city between the Indus and the Jhelum, and a former Persian satrapal seat.

It was now March (326). Alexander gave his troops a month's rest, ending with athletic contests and a cavalry tattoo. Then, after lavish sacrifices (and correspondingly favourable omens) the entire army crossed the Indus, and set out towards Taxila. Ambhi came out to welcome them, at the head of his own forces, in full battle-array and parading an impressive number of gaily caparisoned war-elephants. As they advanced across the plain they must have been a highly impressive spectacle. Alexander, however, still extremely jumpy after his Swat campaign, at once assumed that here was a dangerous trap. That the King could have entertained this nonsensical idea for one moment tells us a lot about his state of mind at the time. The rajah's army was five miles distant, and coming on in full view; it is hard to see how he could have hoped to surprise anyone. In fact, the moment he saw 'the excited activity of the Macedonians', and guessed its cause, he galloped ahead, alone except for a small cavalry escort, and formally submitted himself and his army to Alexander. The King, much relieved, now reinstated him with full sovereign rights, as rajah of Taxila.

The army spent between two and three months there, which in one respect was a near-fatal mistake on Alexander's part. It meant that by the time he embarked on the next stage of his expedition, about the beginning of June, the monsoon rains had begun. However, if he could reach some diplomatic accommodation with Porus and Abisares, the rajah of Kashmir, thus avoiding another major campaign, it would have been time well spent. By now he had a very clear idea of what he was up against; and he did not like it.

Immediately after the arrival of ambassadors from Abisares, in April, Alexander sent his own envoys to Porus: the timing would not be lost on him. The Paurava monarch was requested to meet Alexander at the Jhelum – which formed his frontiers – and to pay tribute in token of vassalage. The reply to this proposal was exactly what Alexander had feared and expected. Porus would indeed, he said, meet Alexander at the Jhelum – but in full military strength, and ready to do battle for his kingdom. Intelligence reports put his forces at 3000–4000 cavalry and up to 50,000 infantry, together with some 200 elephants and 300 war-chariots. He was expecting reinforcements from Abisares, and his troops had already begun to move up along the eastern bank of the river.

Alexander had no time to lose. His first urgent need was for a transport flotilla. Taxila lay miles from the nearest navigable river, and in any case building ships from scratch would take too long. Coenus was therefore sent back to the Indus, with orders to dismantle Alexander's pontoon-bridge, cut up the boats into sections, and load them on to ox-carts. They would then be carried overland for reassembly by the Jhelum. About the beginning of June the monsoon broke; and a few days later Alexander led his army southward to meet Porus, through steaming, torrential rains that continued, without a break, for over two months. His route lay across the Salt Range, by way of Chakawal and Ava. When he was through the Nandana Pass (see map, p. 215), he turned south-west and reached the Jhelum near Haranpur, having marched about 110 miles since leaving Taxila. He knew, from intelligence reports on the terrain ahead, that Haranpur was one of the few points at which he could hope to ford the Jhelum under monsoon conditions.

Porus, clearly, had been thinking along very similar lines. When Alexander reached the Haranpur ford, he found the opposite bank held in strength by a large force that included archers and chariots. Most alarming of all – especially to the horses – were Porus' elephants. A squadron of these great beasts, eighty-five strong, kept guard over the approaches, stamping and trumpeting as they moved ponderously to and fro. The river itself, swollen by monsoon rains, came roaring past in muddy spate, a good half-mile wide. There was no sign of the promised crossing-point.

Even if it were physically possible, to negotiate the river against such mass opposition would be suicidal. Alexander's cavalry horses would go mad with fright if brought anywhere near the elephants. It looked very much like stalemate; and Alexander deliberately encouraged this impression by having endless waggon-loads of corn and other supplies brought to his

right: The mountains of Afghanistan, twice crossed by Alexander and his men during their campaigns in the East.

overleaf: Ambhi's capital of Taxila, absorbed after Alexander's death into the Maurya Empire of Chandragupta. Four separate cities have been excavated in the area: that which Alexander saw was Taxila I, the so-called 'Bhir Mound' north-west of Sirkap.

208

camp, in full sight of the enemy. This would convince Porus, with luck, that his opponent – as he openly declared – meant to sweat it out on the Jhelum until the rains were over and the river became fordable once more. At the same time Macedonian troop activities continued to suggest the possibility of an immediate attack.

But as time passed, and no attack materialised, Porus began to pay less attention to Alexander's attempts at distracting him – which was, of course, just what Alexander had intended. Meanwhile Macedonian cavalry patrols were discreetly exploring the higher reaches of the Jhelum, as far east as Jalalpur (see map, p. 215). It was here, over seventeen miles upstream from their base-camp, that they found what Alexander wanted: a large, wooded island [Admana], with only a narrow channel flowing past either side of it, and a deep nullah on the near bank where troops and assault craft could be hidden. Since the King had decided to force the Jhelum under cover of darkness, he spent much time and ingenuity confusing Porus as to his real intentions. Every night fires would be lit over a wide area, with plenty of noise and bustle. At first Porus took these demonstrations very seriously. But after a while, when he found that nothing came of all the noise and clatter, he relaxed his vigilance.

Alexander now learnt that Abisares was no more than fifty miles off, with 'an army little smaller than that of Porus'. To let them join forces was out of the question. Porus, then, must be dealt with in the next forty-eight hours. Alexander's flotilla had already been transported piecemeal to Jalalpur and reassembled in the Kandar Kas nullah. The King now held an emergency staff conference and outlined his plan for the assault. The larger part of the army was to remain at base camp by the Haranpur ford, under Craterus' command. Preparations for crossing the river were to be carried out quite openly. The King's pavilion was to be pitched in a conspicuous position near the bank. A certain Macedonian officer, a near-double of Alexander, was to appear wearing his royal cloak, 'in order to give the impression that the King himself was encamped on that part of the bank'.

In fact the King, together with the main assault-group, would already be on his way to Jalalpur. This force, numbering 5000 horse and at least 10,000 foot, would cross the river before dawn, and advance down the southern bank on Porus' position. A second group – three battalions of the phalanx, plus the mercenary cavalry and infantry – was to take up a position between Haranpur and Admana Island, opposite the main fords, and only cross when battle had been joined. Craterus' holding force was not to attempt a crossing 'until Porus had moved from his position to attack Alexander' – and only then provided no elephants were left behind to defend the ford – 'or until he was sure that Porus was in retreat and the Greeks victorious'. Whichever way Porus moved, he left himself open to attack from the rear, either by Alexander or Craterus. His one possible defence was to detach a strong but limited force that could destroy Alexander's assault-group before it established a bridgehead – thus still leaving Porus himself in full control at Haranpur.

Alexander built up his 'turning force' from the following units: the Royal Squadron of the Companions; three cavalry divisions (hipparchies) under

The Swat Valley, scene of some of Alexander's toughest and most bloodily fought campaigns: known in antiquity as Assacenia.

Hephaestion, Perdiccas and Demetrius; the Guards Brigade; two phalanx battalions, commanded by Coenus and Cleitus the White; the archers and Agrianians; cavalry units from Bactria and Turkestan; and a special force of Scythian horse-archers. This whole body, some 15,000–16,000 strong, he brought to the crossing-point, and embarked on boats and rafts, by about 3 a.m. on the morning of the assault. He had to get this large force out of camp in broad daylight, without their departure being noticed by Porus' scouts; march them over seventeen miles (which, in monsoon conditions, he can hardly have done in less than six hours); reassemble and launch enough vessels to take them across the river; and embark the entire assault-group, horses included, well before dawn. To complicate matters further, the crucial part of this operation was carried out in darkness, during a particularly violent electric storm.

When dawn broke, and the wind and rain had become less violent, the flotilla was already sailing down the northern channel, still hidden from Porus' scouts by the wooded mass of Admana Island (see map opposite). But when they passed beyond its western tip, the alarm was given, and messengers rode off at full speed to warn Porus. It was now that Alexander made a miscalculation that could have cost him the battle. When he was clear of Admana Island he put in to shore and disembarked all his forces, cavalry leading. But, as he presently found, what he had taken for the river-bank was in fact another long, narrow island. Finally he managed to find a ford, but to get such a force ashore must have taken several hours, at the very least, by which time Porus would have known all about it.

Was Alexander's move a feint, or the prelude to a major attack? At this point no one could tell. Without hesitation Porus detached a force of 2000 cavalry and 120 chariots, under his own son, to ride east with all speed, and, if possible, destroy Alexander's assault-group before it was clear of the river. In the circumstances this was his only feasible move. But he had made it too late. His son was no match for the best cavalry units in the whole Macedonian army; besides, he was heavily outnumbered. After a brief skirmish – during which Bucephalas received the wound from which he subsequently died – the Indians fled, leaving four hundred dead behind, including young Porus himself. The chariots bogged down in thick mud and had to be abandoned.

When the news of his son's defeat reached Porus, the rajah had a brief moment of indecision. Either as a feint, or because they took the minor engagement across the river for a full-scale victory, Craterus' men were making vigorous preparations to force the Haranpur crossing. Finally, how-ever, Porus decided, rightly, that his show-down must be with Alexander. He left a holding force (with elephants) to keep Craterus in play, and marched the rest of his army upstream, ready for battle. At this point – allowing for detachments and losses – he probably had at his disposal 20,000 infantry, 2000 horse, 130 elephants and 180 war-chariots.

He picked his ground carefully: a level sandy plain, free from mud, where elephants and cavalry would have ample room to manoeuvre. Porus drew up his infantry battalions in a wide central front, stationing an elephant every hundred feet or so to strengthen them. On either wing he placed, first,

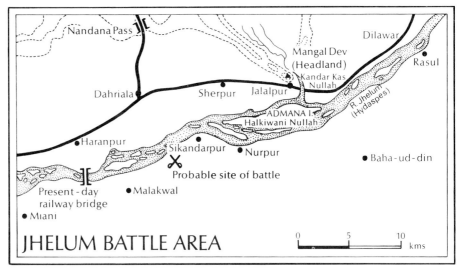

Map labels: Nandana Pass, Dilawar, Mangal Dev (Headland), Rasul, Dahriala, Sherpur, Jalalpur, Kandar Kas Nullah, R. Jhelum (Hydaspes), ADMANA I., Halkiwani Nullah, Haranpur, Sikandarpur, Nurpur, Baha-ud-din, Probable site of battle, Present-day railway bridge, Malakwal, Miani

0   5   10 kms

a flanking body of infantry, and then his cavalry, with a squadron of chariots masking them. The overall Indian battle-line must have been nearer four miles than three in length, of which the infantry accounted for at least two-thirds.

To defeat Porus' cavalry, Alexander adopted highly ingenious stratagem. If he launched a cavalry attack of his own against the Indian left wing, *with numbers just sufficiently less than Porus' own total mounted forces to convince the rajah that an all-out retaliation would annihilate them*, then Porus might well, as they say, take a swinger – which in this case would mean shifting his right-wing cavalry across to the left in the hope of achieving total victory (see plan, p. 216). The success of such a scheme depended on Alexander keeping two full cavalry divisions hidden from the enemy until Porus had committed his own forces irrevocably to a left-flank engagement. The commander of these divisions, Coenus, received very specific instructions. He was to circle Porus' right wing, still out of sight, and wait until battle was joined on the opposite flank. If Porus transferred his right-wing cavalry to feed this engagement, Coenus was to charge across behind the enemy lines, and take them in the rear – otherwise he would engage them normally.

The phalanx battalions and the Guards Brigade, in similar fashion, had orders 'not to engage until it was evident that the Indians, both horse and foot, had been thrown into confusion by the Macedonian cavalry'. His dispositions thus made, Alexander attacked at once. The mounted archers, a thousand strong, were launched against the Indian left, and knocked out almost all of Porus' chariots – a very useful softening-up process. Then the King charged, at the head of his massed cavalry divisions.

Porus did exactly what Alexander had hoped he would. From the howdah on top of his great war-elephant (an excellent command-post) the rajah made a lightning assessment of Macedonian cavalry strength, and brought across his own right-wing squadrons to deliver the *coup de grâce*. Coenus, with two fresh divisions, at once broke cover and rode in pursuit. The Indians engaged against Alexander suddenly found themselves forced to fight a rearguard action against Coenus as well.

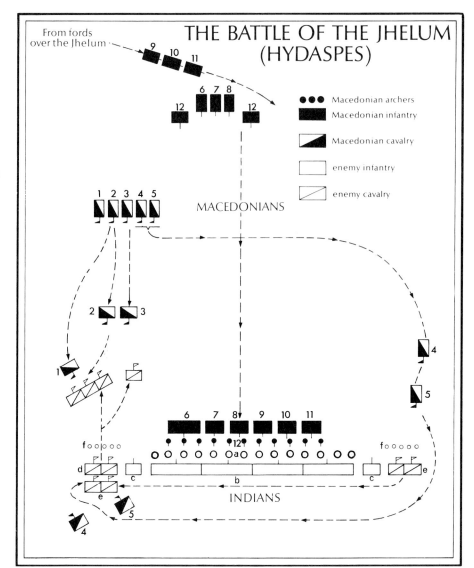

THE BATTLE OF THE JHELUM (HYDASPES)

From fords over the Jhelum

MACEDONIANS

INDIANS

●●● Macedonian archers

■ Macedonian infantry

◢ Macedonian cavalry

▭ enemy infantry

▱ enemy cavalry

The real nightmare facing the phalanx – one that haunted them for the rest of their days – was that row of maddened, trumpeting, furious elephants. Alexander had worked out a technique for dealing with these beasts: encircle them, let the archers pick off their mahouts, and then discharge volleys of javelins and spears into the most vulnerable parts of their anatomy. The infantrymen, meanwhile, slashed through their trunks with Persian scimitars, or chopped at their feet with axes. The elephants had several very effective tricks of their own. Some Macedonian soldiers they stamped underfoot, crushing them to a bloody pulp, armour and all. Others they caught up with their trunks and dashed to the ground. Others, again, found themselves impaled on the great beasts' tusks. As Porus' squadrons were pressed back, the elephants, hemmed in a narrowing space, began to trample their own side: the cavalry suffered particularly heavy losses because of them.

Indian miniature of Alexander and Roxane.

above: The obverse of a silver decadrachm, struck at Babylon to commemorate the victory of the Jhelum. It shows Alexander on Bucephalas, attacking Porus' war elephant with his lance.

far right: Silver tetradrachm, struck by Ptolemy I as satrap of Egypt (323–305 BC). The obverse, shown here, presents Alexander wearing the ram's horn of Zeus Ammon and the elephant-scalp headdress.

Alexander with the Brahmins, in an Indian miniature. Ancient romancers never wearied of dramatising the intellectual confrontation between East and West, and were particularly attracted by the Indian ascetics, whom they referred to as Gymnosophists, or 'naked philosophers'.

Porus led one last elephant-charge in person. It was not a success. By now the Macedonians were learning how to deal with these lumbering creatures at least risk to themselves, dodging them like so many huge bulls, and relentlessly slashing and shooting at them and their riders. Presently the elephants decided they had had enough; they 'began to back away, slowly, like ships going astern and with nothing worse than trumpetings'. At this Alexander drew his cavalry ring tighter round Porus' battered divisions, and signalled the Guards Brigade and the phalanx 'to lock shields and move up in a solid mass'. This final stage of the battle was pure butchery, but the Macedonians, after so traumatic an experience, were in no mood to give quarter. Indian casualties are variously estimated at 12,000 + and 23,000 (of which 3000 were mounted troops).

Porus fought to the bitter end. Then, when he saw further resistance was hopeless, he slowly rode off the field on his great elephant, weak from loss of blood (a javelin had pierced him though the right shoulder). Alexander, 'anxious to save the life of this great and gallant soldier', sent Ambhi after him with an immediate offer of terms – an appalling diplomatic blunder. Porus regarded Ambhi as a traitor and a quisling: when he approached, the wounded rajah made a valiant attempt to pig-stick him with his lance. Eventually a more suitable messenger was found. Porus now dismounted from his elephant, weak and thirsty, and was brought to Alexander. When Alexander asked him how he wished to be treated, the dignified Paurava warrior said: 'Like a King'. Alexander pressed him further. Was there nothing else he wanted for himself? He had only to ask. 'Everything,' Porus told his captor, 'is contained in that one request.'

Gaugamela was fought against heavier odds, and far more hung on its outcome. But at the Jhelum Alexander displayed a flexible resourcefulness of strategy which he never equalled on any other occasion, from his brilliant initial dispositions to the final ruse by which he outmanoeuvred Porus' cavalry. In addition, he had to cope with appalling weather – and, worst of all, with the Indian war-elephants. This frightful struggle left its mark on Alexander's men. Their nerve, if not broken, was severely shaken; and nothing Alexander said or did would ever reconcile them to facing elephants in battle again.

Perhaps only those with personal experience of the rainy season in India can fully appreciate its effects on equipment, terrain, and morale. When every piece of metal (be it sword or gun) rusts in five or six hours after polishing; when canvas, leather and fabric are patched with damp green mould, and rot in a matter of weeks; when every soldier in uniform suffers agonies from foot-rot and prickly heat; when the ground is a steaming morass, and the air whines like a band-saw with mosquitoes – then (in Alexander's day or Wingate's) there is mutinous talk in camp, and a damp collective *cafard* descends on old sweats yearning for the long voyage home.

Alexander's chivalrous treatment of Porus led the Indians to regard him as a *dharmavijayi*, or 'conqueror through righteousness' – an idea which still casts its spell over some modern historians. While the King undoubtedly felt strong personal admiration for his defeated opponent, he also saw him as a most useful ally, a source of first-class recruits, and the ideal counterweight to Ambhi of Taxila. Though Alexander staged a public reconciliation between the two rajahs, he meant each of them to keep a watchful eye on the other.

Bucephalas had died at last, of old age and wounds: Alexander gave his faithful charger a state funeral, leading the procession himself. One of the two new cities he now founded, on the site of the battle, was named Bucephala, as a memorial tribute.

While he spared Porus the indignity of a resident Macedonian satrap, he would at least, through these military garrison-towns, keep some kind of check on the rajah's activities. He need not have worried. Porus, an honourable man, repaid Alexander's confidence with unswerving loyalty during the King's lifetime.

By now the King must have been aware, through long discussions with Ambhi, Porus, and other Indian dignitaries, that his original beliefs about the eastern stream of Ocean were in fact complete nonsense. Though Alexander's notions of world geography might be vague, he never failed to amass accurate intelligence about the countries through which he intended to pass. Yet our sources suggest that his first intuition of the truth only came when his troops were on the very verge of mutiny, just before they reached the Beas River (see above, p. 193). This is flatly incredible: it would have implied inefficiency of a sort that Alexander never tolerated for one moment. What seems far more likely is that he knew the truth very well – had, indeed, known it for some time – but kept it a close secret for fear of the effect it might have on his troops' already low morale. If he could coax them forward one river at a time, with Ocean a glittering goal always just over the next hill, he might yet attain his ends.

Alexander intended to rely for as long as he could on the substantial gap between his own true knowledge and any hearsay information which might filter through to the troops. He had the propaganda section minimise the scope and extent of his coming campaign. He also put out a rumour (which he could not himself have believed for one moment) that the Jhelum and the Chenab in some mysterious way formed the headwaters of the Nile, because crocodiles had been seen in them, and Egyptian beans grew along their banks. Why did he do this? The answer seems clear enough. Alexander knew his Herodotus; he may even have possessed a copy of Scylax' *Periplus*. His next project, after reducing India, was to explore the coasts of Arabia and the Persian Gulf. Ample supplies of fir, pine, cedar and other shipbuilding timber were available in the nearby mountains. Craterus had already been set to work on the construction of a vast fleet: so much was public knowledge. But to tell his troops just how long and hazardous a voyage they would be undertaking struck Alexander as highly inadvisable.

It was, indeed, a leakage of unwelcome topographical information which finally precipitated Alexander's show-down with his troops. He resumed his eastward march in early July, before the end of the monsoon – a great psychological blunder, but by now he seems to have been more than a little frayed himself. He crossed the Chenab and Ravi rivers, defeating some tribes and terrifying others into submission. One city, Sangala, was razed to the ground. Rain fell steadily from a grey sky: the air was steaming and humid. Alexander's veterans, moreover, were no longer the same eager youths who had set out from Pella eight years before. They had marched over 17,000 miles, and fought in every kind of battle and siege. Few can have come through this ordeal unscathed. Now, as they approached the rain-swollen Hyphasis [Beas], wild rumours began to circulate about the territory and people which lay ahead. Twelve days' march after the Beas they would come to a far greater river (presumably the Sutlej); and beyond this dwelt a fierce and warlike nation, with vast armies, chariots, and – worst of all – not less than 4000 fighting elephants.

Furthermore, the Beas appears to have formed the eastern frontier of Darius I's empire – a fact that would not be lost on any Macedonian. Up to this point Alexander could at least claim to be acting as Darius' successor, and recovering lost provinces that were his by right. The end, however remote, had always been in view. But once he crossed the Beas, there was no predictable limit to his ambitions, only a constantly receding horizon. What he intended now was (in the most literal sense) a march to the world's end. Small wonder that his veterans mutinied at this prospect; it is a remarkable tribute to the King's personal *charisma* that they had not done so long before.

Yet Alexander himself had few qualms. Between the stick of tough discipline and the carrot of rich plunder he had kept his army efficient and loyal for a decade: why should the formula not work once again? Mutinous talk was nothing new. He therefore halted his advance at the Beas, and gave the troops a holiday, with *carte blanche* to ravage and plunder the surrounding countryside. He could not offer them another Persepolis: this was the next best thing. Nothing could better demonstrate his failure to appreciate what he was up against. This time it was different: this time the usual bribes, threats and blandishments would no longer work. After the troops got back from their expedition, laden with wealth, he thought they would have changed their minds about going on. They had not. Exhorted to undertake further glorious exploits, they stood in sullen silence and refused to budge.

Having failed with the men, Alexander called a private meeting of his senior commanders. He was on very dangerous ground, since at this stage he needed his Macedonians more than they needed him – a fact which no doubt they realised. His address to this key group shows, all too clearly,

A gold medallion of Alexander found at Aboukir in Egypt.

what the main points of grievance were. The unknown, he assured his sceptical audience, always sounded worse than, in fact, it was. They should beware of exaggeration. The rivers were not so wide as rumour made out, the Indian warriors neither so numerous nor so valiant. As for elephants – they had beaten them once, they could beat them again. In any case, they were at last approaching journey's end. Soon, very soon, they would reach Ganges and the Eastern ocean. Why turn back when the goal lay so near? And if they *did* turn back, they risked losing all they had won.

There was no arguing with Alexander; in the last resort one could only agree to differ. Even that had its dangers. Nevertheless, after Alexander had several times invited comment, Coenus – old now, and perhaps already in the grip of his last illness – made a valiant attempt to get the truth through to him. The veterans, he reiterated, were worn out, done for, pushed beyond the last limits of human endurance. They wanted one thing only: to get home before it was too late. Alexander could mount other expeditions from Greece, with younger men. 'Sir,' Coenus said, 'if there is one thing above all others a successful man should know, it is *when to stop*.' Furious, Alexander dismissed the conference. Next day he summoned his officers once more, and tried another gambit. *He* was going on, he told them, whether they did or not – and so would many others. They were not necessary to his plans. If they wanted to return home, they could do so. 'And you may tell your people there,' he added, 'that you deserted your King in the midst of his enemies.' With that he retired to his tent, as he had done after the Cleitus affair, refusing to see anyone for the next two days.

It was pure bluff; and this time the bluff was called. Alexander's Macedonian officers, far from undergoing a change of heart – as the King confidently expected – kept up their angry, obstinate silence. Professional soldiers to a man, they were indispensable, and knew it. By the third day Alexander saw that there was going to be no tearful reconciliation. He therefore emerged from his self-imposed retreat, announced that he still intended to go on, and offered sacrifice 'in the hope of favourable omens for the crossing'. The omens, of course, were all against him – a convenient face-saving device. To climb down under pressure was unthinkable; to bow before the Divine Will indicated both prudence and piety. Twelve great commemorative altars, in honour of the twelve Olympian gods, were erected across the river. Then Alexander turned back towards the Jhelum.

When his decision to retreat was first made known, a laughing, tearful mob, hysterical with relief, thronged round his tent, calling down blessings on him for so generous a surrender. If Alexander ever felt like murdering the entire Macedonian officer corps with his own bare hands it was, surely, at this moment. He never got over his humiliation by the Beas, nor did he forgive those responsible for it. He was determined, by whatever means, to make the long homeward trek a hell on earth for them all; and in this aim he unquestionably succeeded.

A silver coin of Seleucus I (312–280 BC), Syria.

222

10　How many miles to Babylon?

above: Alexander as Heracles wearing a lion's-mane headdress, the paws tied around his neck.

A hunting scene is represented on this sarcophagus commissioned by King Abdalonymus of Sidon. Alexander figures in this and on the other parts of the sarcophagus (see page 259), but never as the central character.

Alexander's return march to the Jhelum began in autumn 326. While the army lay at the Chenab, a fresh embassy arrived from Abisares, with thirty elephants and other rare gifts. Once again the rajah of Kashmir failed to present himself in person. This time he pleaded illness as an excuse. (The illness many have been more than diplomatic, since a year later Abisares was dead.) Alexander, however, proved surprisingly lenient. He not only accepted the rajah's apologies, but confirmed him as governor of his own 'province'. In point of fact there was very little else he could do. To whip Abisares into line would call for another campaign, and the Macedonians were unlikely to relish the prospect of chasing elusive tribesmen up the Himalayas. Alexander's sudden loss of interest in northern India was largely due to circumstances beyond his control. To save time and trouble, all conquered territory as far as the Beas was simply made part of Porus' kingdom. Thus the Paurava monarch now found himself – paradoxically enough – more powerful than he had ever been before his defeat at the Jhelum.

Craterus, with remarkable efficiency, had Alexander's naval flotilla ready for him by the time he returned to the Jhelum. There were 80 *triakonters* (30-oar vessels), 200 undecked galleys, 800 service ships (horse-transports, grain-barges, lighters) and a multitude of rafts and smaller river-craft. Crews had been drafted from Phoenician, Cypriot, Carian and Egyptian volunteer units accompanying the expedition. The larger vessels were built on the spot, from timber cut in the Himalayas; the rest had been commandeered. Massive reinforcements – 30,000 infantry and about 6000 cavalry – had also arrived, from Thrace, Greece, and Babylon. The Babylonian contingent dispatched by Harpalus brought, in addition, badly-needed medical supplies, and 25,000 sets of new armour, all beautifully inlaid with silver and gold.

Despite the legendary wealth of the Indians, Alexander did not acquire much loot during this Eastern campaign. On the other hand his expenses (not least in bribes, bonuses and donations) were very heavy, and sometimes – as in the case of a 1000-talent gift to Ambhi – caused active ill-feeling. His daily mess-bill alone came to 10,000 drachmas: he never had less than sixty or seventy officers at dinner with him. Obviously, he could well afford this scale of living: Darius' treasures had made him the wealthiest potentate in

the known world. Yet by the end of his Indian campaign there are definite signs that he was hard-pressed for ready cash. By the time his flotilla entered the Indian Ocean, Alexander was once more (as in Macedonia) reduced to raising loans among his friends.

Wherever the Persian treasure might be, it was not coming through to India. Yet if Harpalus' 7200 men brought 25,000 suits of armour with them, they could just as easily have convoyed gold bullion. The inference seems clear enough: Harpalus had other, more personal, plans for its use. This ties in very well with the alarming rumours which now began to reach Alexander about his Imperial Treasurer's general conduct. At first Harpalus had done nothing more adventurous than make experiments in exotic gardening. But after a while this lame quinquagenarian discovered that money, in unlimited quantities, could buy a good deal more than hardy annuals, and brought over a glamorous Athenian courtesan on whom he threw away Alexander's gold with lavish generosity.

Harpalus seems to have been an affectionate, not to say uxorious patron: he never had more than one mistress at a time, and invariably became devoted to her. His next acquisition, Glycera, was set up as a princess in the

A stair-riser with Corinthian half-columns showing six 'donors'. The free style implies Western influence. Possibly second century AD.

226

palace at Tarsus. This might, just conceivably, have been the product of infatuation and nothing more. But in 327–6 the Tarsus mint began striking a series of Persian-type silver coins without reference to Alexander. Independent issues also appeared about the same time in Phoenicia and Cyprus. True or not, it was widely thought that Harpalus planned to revolt against the King. If Alexander never came back from the Far East – which to observers in Europe and Asia Minor seemed more likely than not – then Harpalus, with his immense financial reserves, could easily emerge as the most powerful man in the empire. He had been awarded honorary Athenian citizenship, in return for a gift of wheat which he sent to Athens during the grain famine of 330–326. Given Greek support, he could go on to dispose of Antipater. But if Alexander *did* come back, crowned with victory, then this embezzling (and possibly seditious) Imperial Treasurer would need all the friends he could raise. On either count, Athenian citizenship would not come amiss.

When these rumours first reached Alexander, he threw the messengers in jail; but a detailed report from the Chian historian Theopompus seems to have convinced him that some, at least, of the charges were true. Even so, there was little more he could do about Harpalus' activities until he got back to Babylon.

Before the fleet's departure down-river, Coenus sickened and died. Those who crossed Alexander's will seldom, whether by accident or design, outlived his displeasure for long. About the same time Porus was proclaimed King of all subjugated Indian territories – except, of course, for Taxila. But whereas Ambhi had to put up with a Macedonian 'resident' to keep a watchful eye on his activities, Porus (like the dynasts of Caria) ranked as an independent vassal prince, responsible directly to Alexander. This distinction indicates, with some clarity, the relative degree of trust which the King placed in each of them.

The flotilla set out from Jalalpur early in November 326. Nearchus of Crete had been appointed High Admiral, with a grand total of 1800 vessels under his command. At dawn on the day of departure some 8000 troops, including the Guards Brigade and the Companion Cavalry, began to file aboard. This, of course, was only a small portion of the whole expeditionary force. The rest were divided into three separate columns, under Craterus, Hephaestion, and Philip, the newly appointed satrap of Taxila. The Jhelum, here and as far as its confluence with the Chenab, was at least two and a half miles wide – space enough for over forty oared galleys to travel abreast. It must have been a highly impressive spectacle.

The fleet advanced at a very leisurely pace, no more than five miles a day, with frequent disembarkations. Craterus and Hephaestion went on ahead, Craterus advancing from the right bank, and Hephaestion – with the main body and 200 elephants – from the left: a sensible arrangement, considering the feud between them. Philip at first followed on with the baggage-train, but was afterwards sent east to march along the line of the Chenab, thus covering Hephaestion's left flank. Rapids and whirlpools at the confluence of the Jhelum and the Chenab gave the King a very rough passage. His light galleys in particular were tossed about like corks, quite out of control, oars snapping off as they swung broadside on to the turbulent current. At one point the royal flagship nearly floundered, and Alexander (who could not swim) only just managed to struggle to safety with the help of his friends. However, the flotilla got through in the end. Alexander now could – and did – claim that, like his hero Achilles, he had done battle with a river.

Once safely through to the broad waters of the Chenab, the fleet put ashore at a prearranged rendezvous, and the whole expeditionary force was once more mustered. So far Alexander had met only a little serious resistance; but now reports came in that two powerful tribes, the Malli [Malavas] and the Oxydracae [perhaps the Kshatriyas or Kshudrakas; a Hindu warrior caste] were mobilising in force to block his advance. They were said to have about 100,000 men under arms – not to mention 900 chariots. Alexander sent Nearchus and the fleet on in advance, to the meeting-point of the Chenab and the Ravi, divided his forces into three major assault-groups, and got ready to make a clean sweep of the Malavas before they could link up with their allies. At this point Alexander's veterans, realising that they were about to be pitched into yet another tough campaign (when all they had bargained for was an uneventful voyage), once again threatened to mutiny.

By a characteristic mixture of blarney, romantic rhetoric, and the most outrageous lies (Ocean lay so close they could almost smell the sea-breeze; the tribes facing them were 'womanlike') Alexander somehow talked them into going on. But though they cheered him, their morale was still perilously low – a fact which became all too clear during the tough campaign which followed. Alexander himself had lost none of his tactical flair (once again he scored a notable victory by marching fifty miles through waterless desert before dawn); but his men were near breaking-point. Like frightened and desperate troops the world over, they began to fight with savage, almost hysterical cruelty. Rapine and wholesale massacre were now commonplace. Resistance, stimulated by the Brahmin priestly caste, became correspondingly more desperate, and this in turn revealed the demoralised state of Alexander's hitherto invincible phalanx.

Twice they refused to mount the scaling-ladders during a siege, until the King himself led the way, and shamed them into following him. When he reached the top on the second occasion, he quickly cut down the defenders barring his way, and stood alone for a moment on the battlements – a perfect target for any archer. Then, with splendid but foolhardy bravado, he jumped down *inside* the citadel. There he stood, back against the wall, protected on one side by a large tree, and proceeded to take on all comers single-handed. After a moment he was joined by three other Macedonians: Leonnatus, Peucestas, his shield-bearer, and a highly decorated Guards officer named Abreas. These should have been the first of many – his gesture had had its desired effect – but such a crowd of soldiers now came swarming up the ladders that they collapsed into matchwood, leaving Alexander temporarily cut off.

While frantic Macedonian sappers battered their way through a postern-gate with mattocks and axes, the King and his three faithful aides held off a multitude. Abreas fell, shot in the face. Then a long Indian arrow drove clean through Alexander's corslet and breast, just above the lung. He dropped on one knee, half-fainting, but still had the strength to run his sword through another assailant before he collapsed altogether. Peucestas stood over the King as he lay there, covering him with the sacred shield of Ilium, hemmed in by eager attackers. But by now rescue was on the way. One assault-group scaled the wall on a series of improvised pitons. The postern-gate gave way, and a crowd of furious Macedonians charged through into the citadel, killing every man and woman and child they found there. Meanwhile Alexander was borne away on his shield to the royal pavilion; word went round that he was either dead or dying.

To extract the arrowhead proved a perilous operation. When it had finally been cut out, a major haemorrhage followed and Alexander lost consciousness.

For a week the King hung between life and death. No one believed he could survive, and a premature but circumstantial report of his death spread rapidly through the area. The Indians at once recovered confidence. In Alexander's advance base camp (now established at the junction of the Chenab and the Ravi) the news caused sheer consternation. His men could not imagine themselves under any other leader. No one else seemed qualified

Alexander as a Roman general, on a gold medallion from Aboukir.

to replace him. Now he was dead they would never get home again. 'Every difficulty seemed hopelessly insoluble without Alexander to get them through.' Nothing could more clearly demonstrate the personal and charismatic quality of the King's leadership – or its fundamental limitations. All he had built up depended on the awe and inspiration caused by his physical presence.

Almost the moment he recovered consciousness, the King wrote a public letter to the troops at headquarters, squashing the rumour of his death, and promising he would be with them as soon as he was fit to travel. But by now the men were in such a state that they flatly refused to credit what they heard. The letter, they said, was a forgery, something concocted by Alexander's officers as a device for boosting morale. When this was reported to the King, he knew that only his personal appearance could forestall a serious breakdown of discipline. His wound was still uncicatrised; but fit or not, he must move to base camp at once. He was carried on a litter to the Ravi; two vessels were lashed together, and his day bed set on a high platform between them where he could easily be seen from the river banks. Let the Indians learn that Alexander still lived, and lose their false hopes.

But he was still dreadfully weak; so weak, indeed, that his boat travelled some distance ahead of the others, 'in order that the quiet which he still needed . . . might not be interfered with by the beat of the oars'. When the boat put in to shore, a litter was waiting for him. He told his attendants to take it away and bring him his horse. With what iron exercise of will one can scarcely imagine, he got up, mounted, and slowly rode into camp in full sight of his troops. A sudden spontaneous storm of applause broke out, 'so loud that the river-banks and neighbouring glens re-echoed with the noise'. As he drew near his pavilion he dismounted, and walked the rest of the way. His veterans crowded around him, touching his arms and clothes with superstitious awe, as though to make sure he was not a ghost. Wreaths and flowers were showered on him. Then he passed out of sight into his tent – where, after this supreme effort, he probably at once lost consciousness. Even Alexander's extraordinary physique had its limitations, and there were signs that he never fully recovered from the effects of this appalling wound.

The King's friends took him seriously to task afterwards. He had no business, they said, to risk his life – and hazard the outcome of the entire expedition – by so gratuitous a display of heroics. Against their arguments Alexander might well have pointed out that, apart from anything else, his personal feat of valour had considerably shortened the campaign. The Malli were so shattered by the loss of their main stronghold, and the circumstances in which it had fallen, that they felt further resistance against this god-like figure was useless, and surrendered. At the same time numerous ambassadors arrived from the Oxydracae, who were so impressed by Alexander's campaign against the Malli that they made their own submission without striking a blow. If the King had deliberately set out to demonstrate just how indispensable he was, he could not have succeeded in a more striking fashion. From now on he was able to get away with almost anything, and showed an increasing inclination to do so.

The southward advance now continued, interspersed with minor campaigns. About February 325 Alexander's much enlarged flotilla emerged from the Chenab into the Indus. The confluence of these two great rivers marked the southern limit of Philip's satrapy. A frontier garrison-city, with dockyards, was built here, and new thirty-oared galleys laid down for the fleet. At the same time, to strengthen his communications with eastern Iran, Alexander replaced the unreliable Persian satrap of Paropamisus [Hindu Kush] by his own father-in-law, Oxyartes.

It took Alexander another five months to reach the head of the Indus delta. During that period he fought a series of bloody campaigns against various independent rajahs who blocked his advance, or rose in revolt once he had passed on. Again, the record of sheer slaughter is appalling. Diodorus does not exaggerate when he says that Alexander 'spread the terror of his name throughout the entire region', with fire, destruction, and wholesale enslavement. The ultra-fierce resistance he encountered was due in large part to holy-war propaganda spread by the Brahmin priests. As before, Alexander's only answer to a purely ideological opposition was sheer terrorism: many Brahmins who fell into his hands were hanged as a deterrent. Here the King misjudged his opponents. Resistance, far from being crushed, took on a new lease of life. Before 300 BC every Macedonian garrison in the Land of the Five Rivers had been wiped out.

Somewhere near modern Shikarpore Alexander divided his forces. Craterus, with Polyperchon as his second-in-command, was to take three battalions of the phalanx, the elephants, and all time-expired Macedonian veterans, and march overland into the province of Carmania (see map, p. 165). Here the fleet and the rest of the army would rendezvous with him, either at the mouth of the Euphrates, or at some nearer point along the Persian Gulf. The route Craterus was to follow ran through the Mulla Pass to Quetta and Kandahar, thus traversing the ancient satrapy of Arachosia. From here he was to march south-west, by Lake Seistan, the Kerman Desert, and the Jebal-Barez. Once again Alexander had been at some pains to keep him well away from Hephaestion – who, we may note, took over his post as Deputy Supreme Commander the moment he was gone.

The most interesting aspect of this move, however, is the detailed geographical knowledge it reveals on Alexander's part. Clearly he had the whole voyage of exploration planned out in advance, complete with rendezvous points. It is easy to forget the immensely valuable work which his intelligence section and surveyors and scientists were always doing in the background: mapping, measuring, collecting specimens, studying natural resources, sifting information of every type. But without their constant assistance, their reports on everything from salt-mines to desert routes, the expedition would have gone a great deal less smoothly.

With the appointment of Peithon as governor of Lower India to the sea, Alexander's campaign of subjugation was complete. Greek writers, bedazzled by the glamour of this exotic and unknown region, vastly exaggerated the importance of what was, in fact, little more than a large-scale raid. Alexander penetrated no further than West Pakistan, nor does his name once figure in the later Indian literary tradition. For a very brief period his representatives

ruled – in theory if not always in fact – over a region extending from Kashmir to Karachi. But their hold on the country remained precarious, and to the Indians themselves they were mere barbarian aggressors. No sooner had Alexander moved on than the destruction of his work began. Philip the satrap was killed by a group of mercenaries. Resistance gathered in the Punjab, under the leadership of a young Kshatriya commoner, Chandragupta. After Alexander's death Chandragupta was joined, ironically enough, by a Punjabi king named Parvataka, who is almost certainly Porus. Between them they conquered the empire which Alexander had dreamed of but never won. The Mauryan dynasty founded by Chandragupta held sway eastward to Bengal and the Ganges, southward as far as Mysore.

Nor did Alexander ever appreciate how fundamentally alien the Indian temperament was to anything he had hitherto encountered. When he first reached Taxila he was struck – like every visitor from the West – by the naked Jain ascetics and teachers, who became known in Greek as *gymnosophistae*, or 'naked philosophers'. Numerous stories, mostly apocryphal, are told about this confrontation of cultures. Alexander and his advisers, having the characteristic Greek taste for syncretic interpretations, seem to have convinced themselves that the *gymnosophistae* preached a local variant on Diogenes' Cynicism. Alexander persuaded one holy man to abandon his ascetic life and accompany his expedition. This person was written off by more high-principled sages as 'a slave to fleshly lusts' for choosing to serve any lesser master than God: he later burnt himself alive.

At Pattala, which Alexander reached in July 325, the Indus split into two main channels before reaching the sea. Alexander now left Hephaestion to fortify the citadel, and supervise the construction of docks and harbours, while he himself set out on a reconaissance voyage down the right-hand or

A silver tetradrachm of Ptolemy I (who succeeded Alexander in Egypt), struck *c*. 300 BC. The reverse shows the Ptolemaic eagle upon a thunderbolt. The aegis is thought significant as the symbol of divinity for a king who was also a pharaoh.

above: Another silver tetradrachm of Ptolemy as King of Egypt (305–283 BC), wearing diadem and aegis. Hook-nosed and prognathous, Ptolemy was a natural model for the new realistic portraiture now increasingly in vogue.

far right: An idealised marble bust of Ptolemy.

western arm. The south-west monsoon was blowing, and the fleet suffered considerable damage from storms. At one point, very near the sea, they had to run for shelter up a side channel, only to find themselves left high and dry by the tide – a phenomenon which, as Mediterranean sailors, they regarded at first with considerable alarm. The fleet finally found good anchorage off an island in the mouth of the estuary. They had reached Ocean at last.

Alexander's campaign of Eastern conquest could clearly go no further. Nevertheless, he had to display his authority over Ocean, however symbolic the gesture. He therefore sailed out to a second island, some twenty-five miles off-shore, where – again on instructions – he set up altars to Ocean and Tethys. After a brief exploratory cruise along the coast, he returned to his anchorage in the estuary. Here he sacrificed bulls to Poseidon for a safe voyage home, and set off back up-river. Though the eastern arm of the Indus would give his fleet another 200 miles to sail, it might, he hoped, prove somewhat less hazardous. In fact it gave him just what he was looking for. It was sheltered from monsoon winds. Its waters discharged into the Rann of Kutch, much of which at this period extended further inland, as a vast landlocked salt-water lake. Having reconnoitred the passage through to the sea, Alexander took his cavalry a three days' journey westward along the coast. Parties were left at various points to dig fresh-water wells. A harbour and dock were built by the salt lake, and provided with a garrison.

The King then returned to base, and began organising his projected expedition in detail. If the fleet was to sail right up the Red Sea into the Persian Gulf, it would need wells and supply-depots prepared for it at regular intervals. All reports agreed that the coast, for several hundred miles, was barren desert – a wind-scoured, dusty, red-rock wilderness, known today as the Makran. Alexander planned to march by this route, hugging the coast as far as possible, with the main body of the army and all non-combatants. As they went they would dig wells and lay down stacks of provisions. Nearchus was appointed admiral of the fleet.

Alexander's motives for undertaking this hazardous venture were somewhat mixed. He was genuinely concerned about the revictualling of the fleet. It would be dangerous to leave any unsubdued territory in the Iran-Baluchistan area: this meant reducing Gedrosia, the primitive satrapy bordered by the Makran. He also may well have been curious to find out whether a viable trade-route could be opened up between India and the Euphrates. All this seems reasonable enough. But Nearchus (who was in a better position than most to know the truth) recorded that Alexander, *although aware of the difficulties*, nevertheless conceived a burning desire, a *pothos*, to march by this route. According to tradition, both Queen Semiramis and Cyrus the Great had attempted the feat: the Queen – ominously – got through with twenty survivors, Cyrus with no more than seven. Once again Alexander was seized by the spirit of emulation: *ever to strive to be best*. It may also have occurred to him that his unwieldy host could do with a little trimming and pruning, especially among the non-combatants. This march would be a survival of the fittest.

Nearchus could not leave until the end of the monsoon, when the prevailing winds were due to veer round from the south-west and give him a following breeze – that is, in late September, at the earliest. Alexander and the army set out towards the end of August, well ahead of him. To begin with, all went as planned. A city, Rhambacia, was founded near modern Karachi. Apollophanes became satrap of the region, and Leonnatus also stayed behind, as military governor, with a considerable force at his disposal. Their instructions were to keep the natives docile and make preparations for the fleet's arrival.

Now Alexander moved on into Gedrosia, keeping as close to the shore as possible. To obtain provisions from the native tribes was virtually impossible. Nothing grew here except thorn and tamarisk and the occasional palm-tree. As they passed on into the Makran, the land became still more inhospitable. For a while Alexander kept advance parties digging wells; but presently he reached the mountains of the Talar-i-Bund, the Makran Coast Range, which come all the way down to the sea. Because of this he was forced to make a long detour inland, and it was now that the real suffering began. They ran desperately short of water, and often had to march anything from twenty-five to seventy-five miles between one brackish well and the next, for the most part at night. When they got there, the men were so maddened with thirst that they often plunged straight into the pool, armour and all. Many died from the effects of over-drinking after dehydration. Many more succumbed to heat stroke. In the end Alexander was forced to bivouac at least three or four miles from a water-point. Nevertheless, he contrived to preserve his prestige and popularity by sharing the men's worst hardships. Under a brazen sky the long column struggled forward, up and down the sides of soft, shifting sand-dunes, endlessly repeated like waves of the sea, where waggons sank to the axles, and boots filled with burning grit. Poisonous snakes lurked

A head of Alexander, found in Alexandria. It has been suggested that the somewhat idealised features are meant to indicate the King's deification.

in the herbage, poisonous plants were all around – prickly cucumbers that squirted a blinding juice, laurel-like shrubs which made pack-animals die foaming at the mouth. Too much water could be as dangerous as too little. One night the baggage-train and non-combatants were encamped in a dry wadi – something any Macedonian officer should have known better than to permit – when a sudden flash-storm broke in the hills. Down roared a great torrent of water through the darkness, carrying away tents, baggage (including the royal pavilion), almost all the women and children, and large numbers of the remaining transport animals. Many soldiers had narrow escapes from drowning, and survived with nothing but their weapons and what they stood up in.

The final catastrophe was a violent sandstorm which obliterated all landmarks, so that even the guides lost their bearings, and took a path which led further and further away from the coast. Alexander, realising what had happened, set off south with a small cavalry detachment, and eventually reached the sea. Here he and his men dug wells in the gravel – and to their delight struck pure fresh water. For a week the whole army marched along this coastal strip, always finding water when they dug for it. Then Alexander's guides picked up the road that led inland to Pura, the Gedrosian capital. Sixty days after first entering the Makran, that ragged column of gaunt, sun-blackened, weary men reached safety. Then Alexander sat down and counted his losses. He had started the march with about 85,000 persons, many of them non-combatants: of these not more than 25,000 now survived. His Companion Cavalry was reduced from 1700 to 1000. Horses, pack-mules, stores, equipment – all were lost.

Alexander had to find a scapegoat. His first, and most obvious, victim was the wretched Apollophanes, in whose satrapy the disaster had taken place. The King now sent a letter formally deposing him. This crossed with a dispatch from Leonnatus, who reported that local tribal levies had attacked his division, inflicted severe losses and then withdrawn. Among those killed was Apollophanes. Alexander, baulked of his prey, did what he could by converting this defeat into a propaganda victory, with Leonnatus destroying 6000 natives for the loss of fifteen cavalry and a few foot-soldiers. Troop morale was not yet up to digesting another defeat. A more cheerful dispatch arrived from Craterus, who had defeated two Persian nobles attempting a revolt, and was bringing them on to Alexander in chains. But the general news was far from encouraging. Rumours of treachery, inefficiency, and large-scale embezzlement came in from every side. Nothing, as yet, had been heard of the fleet. Many officials, confident that Alexander would never return from India, had set up as independent Oriental despots, and equipped themselves with powerful private armies. Here was a dangerous situation – and one which suddenly made Harpalus look far less like a figure of fun. Nor could it have arisen at a worse time. After the fearful casualties sustained in Gedrosia, Alexander's own prestige had lost much of its charismatic lustre: his epithet *aniketos* (invincible) now bore a large interrogation-mark after it.

After a short rest period at Pura, Alexander set out again: clearly there was no time to be lost. His immediate destination was Salmous [Gulashkird]

Roxane weeping over Alexander's bier, in an early fourteenth-century Persian miniature.

in Carmania, some way inland from the strait of Hormuz. Wisely, he relaxed discipline during this march. When the army entered Carmania it was welcomed by Astaspes, the Iranian satrap. Alexander already had a dossier on this man, who had allegedly been plotting treason during the expedition's absence in India. For the moment nothing was said: Alexander greeted Astaspes warmly, and confirmed him in his position. But by the time he reached Gulashkird, the King had collected more evidence. He had also felt the mood of sullen hostility in the province as a whole. Astaspes was abruptly put under arrest and then executed. Alexander's satrapal purge had begun.

In fact it might be said to have begun earlier: the satrap of Paropamisus [Hindu-Kush], whom he replaced by his father-in-law Oxyartes, was also afterwards executed for treason. Alexander's recent summons to the various satraps to meet him in Carmania with provisions and transport animals plainly had more than one purpose. As soon as the Ecbatana contingent arrived – that is, Cleander, Sitalces, and their two deputy commanders – they were arrested and condemned to death. Harpalus himself escaped capture: he knew better than to go anywhere near Alexander from now on. When the summons came, he fled to the coast, with a body of 6000 mercenaries, and some 5000 talents in silver. From here he sailed for Athens, hoping to cash in on his honorary citizenship. Harpalus' flight, coming after the execution of Cleander and Sitalces, removed any real fear of a *coup*. Alexander was playing a shaky hand with his usual cool flair and psychological insight. When he 'wrote to all his generals and satraps in Asia, ordering them, as soon as they had read his letter, to disband their mercenaries instantly' the order was obeyed without question.

On the other hand, only dire political necessity could have dictated it. There were quite enough unemployed mercenaries loose in Asia as it was, without adding to their number: the social effects of this policy were only too predictable. If they lacked a paymaster, they would turn to free-lance marauding for a livelihood. Soon all Asia was full of such wandering bands, and the moment the resistance movement began to develop again in Greece, they naturally made their way across the Aegean and joined it.

above: An elephant with bee (above) and anchor symbol (below) – the battle badge of the Seleucids – on the reverse of a Seleucus tetradrachm minted at Pergamum, *c.* 281/80 BC. The inscription reads BASILEOS SELEUKOU – 'issued by King Seleucus'; Seleucus ruled Babylon after the death of Alexander.

far left: Seleucus I, portrayed here on the obverse of one of his own tetradrachms, is wearing a helmet with a hide covering, equipped with a bull's horn and ear. Some regard the figure here portrayed as Alexander. The coin was minted at Persepolis, 300–290 BC.

A Roman bust of Seleucus, found in Herculaneum.

It was now December (325). Craterus arrived safely, with his troops and elephants; shortly afterwards word came that Nearchus had been seen in the vicinity. To begin with, Alexander could not credit this news, and actually arrested the provincial governor for spreading false rumours. Even when Nearchus appeared – in ragged garments, hair long and matted with brine – the King's first thought was that he and his five companions were the only survivors. Bitter distress at the presumed loss of the fleet eclipsed any pleasure he might have felt at his admiral's escape. But as soon as Nearchus revealed that the fleet had come through, and now lay at Hormuz undergoing a refit, Alexander's delight knew no bounds. He now made sacrifice to the gods, and held a great athletic and musical festival, in thanksgiving for the safe return of his fleet, and (according to Aristobulus) *'for his conquest of India and the escape of his army from Gedrosia'*. What the survivors made of this stunning if pious lie one can only surmise.

Before Alexander set out back for Persepolis, in January 324, he placed Hephaestion in charge of the baggage-train, the elephants, and the bulk of the army, and dispatched them by the long, easy coast road, where they would find plentiful supplies. He himself, with the Companion Cavalry and the light infantry, travelled overland. We may be tolerably certain that Craterus – no friend to Hephaestion – went with him. Nearchus, at his own request, had stayed with the fleet: their next rendezvous point was to be Susa.

After the Gedrosian disaster, a change for the worse seems to have taken place in Alexander. He became increasingly paranoid and suspicious, ready to believe any calumny against his officials, however unlikely its source. He would now punish even minor offences with exemplary sternness, on the grounds that an official who was guilty of minor irregularities might easily progress to more serious crimes. This line may have been dictated in part by the purge he was carrying out; but it hints at something more fundamental. There is a tendency nowadays to pooh-pooh the belief (universally held in antiquity) that Alexander's character had by this time undergone very considerable degeneration. The combined effects of unbroken victories, vast wealth, absolute power, continual heavy physical stress, and incipient alcoholism cannot be lightly set aside when reaching one's verdict. It was not political pressure alone which dictated the King's actions now, but his own increasingly dominant megalomania.

Towards the end of February Alexander reached Susa, where he made a lengthy halt. He was already full of plans for further campaigns of conquest, this time in the Western Mediterranean. North Africa, Spain, Carthage, Italy were all mentioned as possible targets. There was even a rumour that he intended to circumnavigate Africa. Nearchus arrived safely with the fleet, and the two men discussed this new project. The King sent orders for the construction of no less than 700 large new galleys at Thapsacus on the Euphrates. The Kings of Cyprus were commanded to supply this fleet with copper, hemp and sails.

It was at Susa that Alexander's satrapal purge finally ran its course. The governor of Susiana and his son were both put to death on the usual charges: maladministration, extortion, failure to deliver supplies to the army in Gedrosia. All organised opposition in Asia was now effectively crushed, and

overleaf: An aerial view of ancient Susa: to the left, the Kerkha River, in antiquity the Choaspes. The mound was occupied from prehistoric times. Darius took up his residence here in 521 BC, and carried out extensive building projects. Destroyed by Xerxes, spared by Alexander, today Susa is nothing but a mass of crumbling ruins.

Alexander felt free to proceed with his systematic policy of Orientalisation. Despite some ingenious special pleading by modern scholars, it is safe to say that this did *not* imply any ideological belief in racial fusion or the brotherhood of man: its ends were far more immediate and practical. It was restricted to the higher branches of government service and the army (in particular the officer corps); its two main objects were to integrate Persian generals and colonels into the command structure, and to create a joint Perso-Macedonian administrative class. Indeed, it could be plausibly argued that Alexander's ultimate aim was to discard his Macedonian cadres altogether. After the heavy losses sustained in India and the Makran, Alexander reduced the number of Companion Cavalry divisions from eight to four, and then added a fifth, based on the Royal Squadron. For the first time, Iranians were not only brigaded with these units at squadron level, but fully integrated. Some privileged Persians were actually admitted to the Royal Squadron, and issued with Macedonian arms.

To make matters worse, the 30,000 Iranian youths whom Alexander had sent to be given a Macedonian military training (see above, p. 201) now reappeared at Susa, having completed their long and arduous course. Alexander was loud in their praises. He not only called them his 'Successors' (which was bad enough) but made it clear that if necessary they could be used as a 'counter-balance to the Macedonian phalanx'. It is hardly surprising, then, that their presence caused deep alarm and resentment among Alexander's veterans, who with a mixture of scorn and envy nicknamed them 'the young war-dancers'. To a very large extent their fears were well-grounded. Babylon had long since replaced Pella as the centre of Alexander's universe; he cared little more about what happened in Greece, now, than he would about any other province on the periphery of his vast empire.

His high-handed, not to say dictatorial, efforts to enforce top-level integration reached a climax with the famous Susa mass-marriages, where between eighty and a hundred high Macedonian officers took Persian or Median brides. Alexander himself took *two* wives at this ceremony, the daughters respectively of Darius and of Artaxerxes Ochus. If he was going to strengthen his claim on the Achaemenid throne, he might as well make a thorough job of it – even if this meant being saddled with no less than three regnant Queens. Hephaestion he also married to a daughter of Darius – ostensibly because he wanted their children as his own nephews and nieces. But Hephaestion's rivals would not be slow to see another, more ominous, explanation for this royal favour.

Already the office of Chiliarch, or Grand Vizier, had been revived for him. He had recently taken over as sole commandant of the Companion Cavalry, and was now, beyond any doubt, the second man in the empire, the King's most likely successor. None of this increased his popularity. Nor did the marriages themselves have the effect which Alexander hoped. They had been made will-nilly, at the King's express command, and almost all of them were repudiated soon after his death. To the Macedonians they symbolised Alexander's Oriental despotism at its very worst. His idea of creating 'a new ruling class of mixed blood, which would be free of all national allegiance or tradition', proved an utter failure.

His troops now thoroughly distrusted him, and he was reduced to pacifying them by means of wholesale bribery. Most of the men were heavily in debt to the traders, merchants, horse-copers and brothel-keepers who accompanied the expedition. Now that Alexander once more had access to ample funds he decided it was high time these debts were cleared off. To win favour, he announced that he would settle them himself. He therefore called for a detailed schedule, with names, so that payment could be made at once. This piece of munificence cost him no less than 20,000 talents and did little to improve relations between him and his men.

A far more urgent problem, and one largely created by Alexander's own policies, was that of the countless unemployed Greek mercenaries still at large. From a merely social menace (which was bad enough) they looked like becoming a serious political and military threat. The King had already taken steps to ease this problem. He enrolled all the mercenaries he could in his own army, and, as we have seen, planted numerous garrison-colonies throughout the Far East. But such measures by no means accounted for them all. Some, in any case, loathed Alexander and all he stood for so much that they refused to serve under him whatever the inducement. What brought the crisis to a head, of course, was the King's emergency decree ordering the satraps to dissolve their private armies. This at once threw a vast body of well-trained, ruthless toughs out of work, and made them

A larger-than-lifesize head of Alexander, probably of the early third century BC.

243

available on the international market. Moreover, when Alexander began his purge of imperial administrators, quite a few Persian satraps and commanders seized what funds they could and fled to Taenarum, the anti-Macedonian recruiting centre in southern Laconia.

This conjunction was too good an opportunity to ignore, and an Athenian general, Leosthenes – probably with the connivance of his government – started running an underground ferry-service for mercenaries from Asia Minor to the Peloponnese. Here was a potentially explosive situation indeed. The mercenaries had found a centre, an organisation, and leaders who could pay them – Harpalus among others, who now reached Taenarum with his 5000 talents still intact. The 3000 rebel settlers from Bactria also made their way back to Greece about this time. Unless Alexander took firm action, fast, he looked like having a major crisis on his hands. As a first step he now drafted a proclamation, addressed directly to the exiles themselves. It read as follows: 'King Alexander to the exiles from the Greek cities. We have not been the cause of your exile, but, save for those of you who are under a curse [i.e. for sacrilege or murder; Alexander also made an exception in the case of the Thebans] we shall be the cause of your return to your own native cities. We have written to Antipater about this to the end that if any cities are not willing to restore you, he may constrain them.'

In other words, the King was preparing, with great finesse, to ditch his Greek quislings (who were expendable): to shift the blame for the exiles' plight, by implication, on to Antipater (who was not expendable yet, but soon would be); and to collect some easy popular credit by reversing the previous Macedonian party line and supporting democrats for a change. In March the final draft was read out to Alexander's assembled troops. The King wanted an official announcement made at the Olympic Games that summer, and his special envoy Nicanor – Aristotle's adopted son – left on this mission soon afterwards. With him he took a second decree: Alexander now required that the cities of the League should publicly acknowledge him as a god.

That this was a mere political device is unlikely in the extreme: in fact the *practical* advantages that Alexander could derive from his own deification were virtually nil. It would inevitably antagonise the Macedonians (a prospect which by now he must have regarded with some equanimity), and Persian opinion was bound to consider it sheer blasphemy. Sophisticated Greeks would ridicule the King's pretensions with mocking epigrams. Perhaps the best (certainly the most ironic) comment was to come from Damis the Spartan. When the question of divine honours was under debate, he said: 'Since Alexander desires to be a god, let him be a god.'

Yet whatever his divinisation meant to anyone else, it is plain that Alexander himself took it very seriously indeed. Year by year, with that growing isolation that is the penalty of an unbroken ascent to absolute power, Alexander's control over his own latent megalomania had grown progressively weaker. What finally broke it were the psychological shocks inflicted by the mutiny on the Beas and the nightmare of the Gedrosian desert. 'He took refuge from the insecurity of power in the greater exercise of power: like a god intervening in the affairs of mortals, he would order the

right: Alexander on horseback: a detail from the so-called 'Alexander sarcophagus' now in Istanbul. It was commissioned by King Abdalonymus of Sidon, who had obtained his throne through Alexander's good offices, when the Macedonian army entered Sidon *en route* for Tyre.

Overleaf
left: Alexander bending over the corpse of Darius, in a Persian miniature of *c.* 1525. Darius was not, in fact, killed in battle, but myth preferred the more heroic version.
right: Iskander the Two-Horned (Alexander) defeating the Russian champion: a nice instance, in this Persian miniature, of how myth tended to accumulate round the King's personality in later ages.

Macedonian and Persian warriors in combat, on the 'Alexander sarcophagus'. It is generally believed that the Macedonian represents Alexander's *alter ego* Hephaestion.

fate of princes and of nations.' He became a god when he ceased wholly to trust his powers as a man, taking the divine shield of invincibility to combat his inner fear of failure. He was formidable still: but he had come very near the end of the road.

In Spring 324 Alexander left Susa. Hephaestion, with the bulk of the infantry, was dispatched west to the Tigris, by the overland route. The King himself sailed down the River Eulaeus, cruised along the coast until he reached the Tigris estuary, and then made his way upstream to Hephaestion's camp. From here he continued as far as Opis, the highest navigable point on the river, some 200 miles north of Babylon. At Opis, the King assembled his Macedonian troops, and announced the imminent demobilisation 'of all men unfit through age or disablement for further service'. He promised them lavish bonuses and severance pay, enough to make them the envy of their fellow-countrymen when they returned home (not to mention a walking advertisement for future recruits). His words produced a near-riot. Those he proposed to relase shouted that it was an insult to wear men out with long service and then throw them on the scrap-heap. The younger time-expired veterans demanded their own discharge. They had served as long, fought as hard; why discriminate between them? They were scared that he no longer needed them, that they would become a tiny isolated minority in a virtually all-Persian army, that he had the whip-hand at last, and knew it. Their worst fear (and with good reason) was that 'he would establish the permanent seat of his kingdom in Asia', that they would not see home again for years, perhaps never. In the end they threatened to walk out on him *en masse*.

right: A Boeotian helmet found in the River Tigris, possibly left by one of Alexander's soldiers.

In a blinding fury Alexander sprang down from the dais, accompanied by his officers of the guard, and strode through the ranks pointing out the chief trouble-makers. Thirteen men were arrested, and dragged off to summary execution. A horrified silence fell. Then the King (with that psychological flair which never deserted him in a crisis) went straight back to the platform, where he began a cuttingly contemptuous speech by listing all the benefits and favours the Macedonian army had received from *his father Philip*. 'Yet', Alexander said, 'these services are small compared with my own' – which he then proceeded to enumerate in full. He reproached his men bitterly for their disloyalty and cowardice. Then came the final thrust. 'You all wish to leave me,' he cried. 'Go, then! Out of my sight!' With that he swept off to his private quarters, leaving the assembled troops silent and dumbfounded.

As usual on such occasions, Alexander shut himself up *incommunicado*, and waited. Crowds of veterans stood about hopelessly outside his pavilion. He refused to see them. On the third day he let it be known that he was using the 'Successors' to form new Persian units on the lines of the old Macedonian *corps d'élite* – a Persian Royal Squadron and Companion Cavalry, a Persian Guards Brigade. At the same time he summoned the cream of the Iranian fighting nobility, and appointed them to all brigade commands previously held by Macedonians. These high dignitaries were also, in Achaemenid fashion, termed the King's 'kinsmen', and entitled to exchange the kiss of friendship with him. When the troops learnt what was happening, their resistance broke down altogether. They all rushed to Alexander's pavilion, offering to surrender both the instigators of the mutiny and 'those who had led the cry against the King'. They refused to disperse until Alexander dealt with them: it was a kind of sit-down strike in reverse.

Having now got them in a suitably contrite mood, Alexander emerged from seclusion prepared to be magnanimous. At the sight of all these battle-scarred old toughs crying their eyes out he shed tears himself – probably from sheer relief. One elderly, grizzled cavalry officer, who acted as spokesman, said their main grievance was Alexander's having made Persians his kinsmen. 'But I regard you *all* as my kinsmen,' the King exclaimed. Afterwards they all picked up their arms (thrown down at the doors in token of supplication) and marched back to camp, bawling the victory paean at the tops of their voices; though one might have thought that if anyone had a right to sing that particular song just then it was Alexander himself.

Nevertheless, the Macedonians were still by far his best troops, and he had no hesitation in flattering them with a grandiose public gesture once he had gained his point. Another vast banquet now took place, to celebrate a double reconciliation: between Alexander and his veterans, between Persians and Macedonians. By addressing the mutineers as 'kinsmen' the King had raised them, socially speaking, to the level of any Persian noble. He emphasised their privileged position at the banquet itself, where they had the seats of honour beside him and drank from the royal mixing-bowl.

As soon as the celebrations were over, Alexander went ahead with his demobilisation scheme – but on a far more massive scale than he had originally planned. No less than 11,000 veterans were discharged, a total which

The head of the young Heracles appears on the obverse of this silver tetradrachm of Alexander, minted at Sidon *c.* 317–316 BC.

far right: The reverse shows Zeus seated, with eagle and sceptre, and the inscription 'Alexander'.

suggests that most of the younger time-expired men went with them. The terms of discharge were extremely generous. Active-service pay was to be continued to cover the period spent travelling home. Over and above this, each man received a severance bonus of one talent. Alexander promised that the sons born to the veterans' native wives would receive, *gratis*, a good Macedonian-style education – 'with particular attention to their military training'. When they were grown up, he added, somewhat vaguely, he would bring them back to Macedonia. In fact, from these boys – there were about 10,000 of them – he meant to create 'a royal army of mixed blood and no fixed domicile'.

As commander of the discharged veterans on their long homeward march, Alexander chose Craterus, with Polyperchon as his second-in-command. But this apparently routine appointment was merely a prelude to the most coveted post in the empire. When Craterus reached Macedonia, he was 'to assume control of Macedonia, Thrace and Thessaly, and assure the freedom of Greece'. In other words, he would supersede Antipater as Regent, or rather, now, as Viceroy. Antipater himself received orders to hand over his command, raise fresh drafts of Macedonians as replacements for those lately discharged, and bring them out to Babylon.

Antipater had known for a long time now that the next blow might well be aimed at him. The executions of Callisthenes, Philotas, Parmenio, and his own son-in-law, Alexander of Lyncestis, had shown only too clearly which way the wind was blowing. Alexander also seems to have convinced himself that Antipater – the one really powerful Old Guard noble left – was plotting to seize his throne. It must have very soon become apparent to Antipater that, on top of everything else, he was to be made the scapegoat for Alexander's repressive government in Greece – though in fact he had done no more than carry out the King's orders. His replacement by Craterus would be publicised as the dawn of a new democratic era, an argument to which the return of perhaps 40,000 democratic exiles would lend some plausibility.

On the other hand, if Antipater obeyed the royal summons to Babylon, he was a dead man, and knew it. Since he enjoyed considerable popularity in Macedonia, and (rather more important) had the whole Home Army behind him, he could afford to temporise. Calculating that Alexander, for the moment at any rate, had no more desire for an open trial of strength than he did, Antipater sent out his son Cassander to begin negotiations with the King, and sat tight.

What were Antipater's chances in the event of a straight show-down? He was well-known (and well-liked) in Macedonia, whereas Alexander had been abroad for ten years. His troops were efficient, loyal, and *fresh*; Alexander's were worn out after endless campaigns, had been largely replaced by Orientals (whom they detested), and had underlined their attitude by staging two full-scale mutinies. Antipater had every reason for confidence. Meanwhile he began, very discreetly, to look round for potential supporters among the Greek states. There were two powers – Athens and Aetolia – that strongly opposed the Exiles' Decree, because its enforcement would involve them in territorial losses. Antipater negotiated a secret alliance with the Aetolians, and almost certainly approached Athens as well: with her vast fleet and impregnable naval arsenals, the violet-crowned city would be indispensable to any commander organising the defence of Greece.

It was now, early in July 324, that Harpalus appeared on the scene again, a political hot potato with a genius for mistiming his intrigues. If he offered his cash and troops to Antipater (as he must surely have done when he heard of the Viceroy's dismissal) they were doubtless refused with more haste than politeness. As a revolutionary Harpalus showed himself peculiarly inept. No one else could have gone peddling open revolt to men who were pinning their hopes on secret diplomacy. With bland cheerfulness, he now descended on Piraeus, followed by his entire private army – apparently in the naïve expectation of receiving a hero's welcome. Instead, he found the harbour closed against him. By the middle of the month, however, he was back again. This time, more tactfully, he presented himself as a suppliant, with only three ships – and 700 talents in cash. Once inside the city, he very soon collected massive support for his projected revolt.

At this point, in rapid succession, envoys arrived from Antipater, Alexander, and Olympias, each firmly demanding Harpalus' extradition. Argument raged as to whether Harpalus should or should not be surrendered – and if so, to whom. In the end Demosthenes devised a formula to stall everybody and leave the situation open. Harpalus himself was taken into what amounted to protective custody, and held under guard. His money was turned over to a special commission (which included Demosthenes) and stored for safe-keeping on the Acropolis. This move drew bitter recriminations from the war-party. Hypereides even complained that by arresting Harpalus they had thrown away the chance of a satrapal revolt. But at least Harpalus was still alive, and not in Alexander's hands.

Demosthenes now left for Olympia, where the Exiles' and Deification Decrees were proclaimed about the beginning of August. As an official Athenian delegate, he was empowered to negotiate with Nicanor, Alexander's representative, on any matters arising from the decrees which affected Athens. Apart from territorial problems (in particular the status of Samos, where Athens had settlers) the future of Harpalus must surely have come up during these talks. Whatever agreements the two men made were, for obvious reasons,

Zeus holding the eagle, with a coin-sheaf symbol below, on the reverse of a tetradrachm of Ptolemy I.

kept secret. But Alexander (somewhat grudgingly, it is true) *did* leave the Athenians in possession of Samos; so there was probably a *quid pro quo* involved, and the most obvious would be the surrender of Harpalus. If Demosthenes in fact struck such a bargain, he clearly did not intend to honour his side of it. No sooner was he back in Athens than Harpalus – with the connivance of persons officially unknown – contrived to escape.

This, of course, triggered off a major political scandal, which hardly diminished when it became known that of the original 700 talents, only half had found their way to the strong-room on the Acropolis. Demosthenes was thought to have pocketed no less than fifty talents himself. Charges and countercharges, involving most of the best-known public figures in Athens, were hurled to and fro with angry abandon. A commission was set up to investigate the affair, but six months later its members had still not published their findings.

The debate at Athens – on the motion that Alexander should be recognised as a thirteenth god, like Philip – was a lively affair. Demades, proposing (an act which cost him a ten-talent fine when Alexander was safely dead), uttered one shrewd word of warning to the opposition. While they were concentrating on the heavens, he told them, they might well lose the earth – meaning Samos. The hint was taken. Even Demosthenes, a convinced opponent of deification on principle, now gave Demades his grudging support. 'All right,' he growled, 'make him the son of Zeus – and of Poseidon too, if that's what he wants.' The motion was carried.

The death of Hephaestion

To escape the torrid heat of the plains, Alexander moved on east from Opis to Ecbatana, the Great King's traditional summer retreat. Here, as soon as all urgent business had been settled, he staged a lavish and protracted festival in honour of Dionysus, with athletics, music, and 3000 Greek artistes specially brought over to provide entertainment. Every evening there would be an epic drinking-party. After one of these, Hephaestion (whose capacity for alcohol seems at least to have equalled Alexander's) collapsed and was put to bed with a high fever. His physician prescribed a strict plain diet, and for a week Hephaestion followed it obediently. Then he began to feel better. Early one morning, as soon as the doctor's back was turned, he got up, wolfed a whole boiled chicken, drank about half a gallon of chilled wine, and – not surprisingly – became very ill indeed. Alexander, warned that he had taken a turn for the worse, came hurrying back from the stadium, where he was watching the boys' athletics. When he reached his friend's bedside, Hephaestion was already dead.

The King's *alter ego* has not gone down to posterity as a very sympathetic figure. Tall, handsome, spoilt, spiteful, overbearing, and fundamentally stupid, he was a competent enough regimental officer, but quite incapable of supporting great authority. His most redeeming quality was his constant personal devotion to Alexander. To someone who asserted that Craterus showed him equal loyalty, the King replied: 'Craterus loves the King; Hephaestion loves me for myself.'

The violence and extravagance of the King's grief went beyond all normal bounds. For a day and a night he lay on the body, weeping: no one could comfort him. General mourning was ordered throughout the East. Alexander cut his hair in token of mourning, as Achilles did for Patroclus, and even had the manes and tails of his horses docked. Hephaestion's physician was crucified, and the temple of Asclepius in Ecbatana razed to the ground. The body was embalmed, and sent on ahead to Babylon, with a royal escort commanded by Perdiccas. A funeral of the magnificence that Alexander had in mind would take time to prepare. It was finally celebrated in the early spring of 323, and every province of the empire contributed to its cost.

After Hephaestion's death, no official appointment was ever made to the vacant command of the Companion Cavalry: it was still known as 'Hephaestion's Division'. Many of the Companions – led by Eumenes – tactfully dedicated themselves and their arms to the dead man. Just what sort of future the King had had in mind for his lost favourite we can only surmise. But one fact is worth noting. During the month after Hephaestion's death, Roxane became pregnant; and the son she subsequently bore was Alexander's sole legitimate heir.

After his providential escape from Athens, Harpalus returned to the Peloponnese, collected his squadron, and sailed for Crete – that home of all

below: This figure, from the 'Alexander sarcophagus' at Sidon, is generally identified as Hephaestion.

lost causes – where he was promptly assassinated. The murderer was a Macedonian agent, acting in collusion with Harpalus' second-in-command. Alexander, it would seem, had paid off yet another score. He would have been less than human had he let his defaulting Treasurer go scot-free.

Demosthenes probably figured in the dossier that Philoxenus (now Governor of Cilicia) acquired on all Harpalus' private contacts. At all events, in March 323 an Athenian grand jury found the great orator guilty of accepting bribes, and fined him fifty talents. He could not pay, and was imprisoned. Later, however, he escaped – like Harpalus, with the connivance of his guards – and got away to Aegina, where he remained until Alexander's death.

A whirlwind expedition

A Hellenistic king-list from Babylon, of 175 BC (the time of Alexander III). The obverse, shown here, is inscribed in Babylonian, beginning with the name of Alexander the Great; it continues with the names of the Hellenistic kings of Mesopotamia up to the time of uninterrupted Arsacid rule.

The best panacea for grief is work; and there was only one kind of work that Alexander knew. In the winter of 324–3, when his misery had subsided into mere moody aggressiveness, he launched a whirlwind campaign – his last, as it turned out – against the Cossaeans. These were mountain tribesmen dwelling south-west of Ecbatana. It took him about five weeks to exterminate them; this he called 'an offering to the shade of Hephaestion'. All the time his mind was full of plans for new conquests and adventures. Before leaving Ecbatana he sent a reconnaissance expedition off to the Caspian Sea, complete with carpenters and shipwrights. They were to cut timber in the great Hyrcanian forest, and build a fleet of Greek-style warships – ostensibly for a voyage of exploration, but in fact, no doubt, as a preliminary to that long-deferred campaign against the Scythians.

The whole army now set out for Babylon. They were met on the road by the Chaldean seers, who warned the King that a great disaster would befall him if he entered Babylon. However, they added, he would escape this danger if he undertook to restore Bel-Marduk's ziggurat and temple. In any case he should avoid entering the city from the eastern side (i.e. facing the setting sun). Here was a splendid piece of effrontery. Alexander had, in fact, ordered work to begin on this vast undertaking at the time of his first visit, seven years before (see above, p. 162). Expenses were to be met from temple funds – the usual procedure in such cases. These had been going straight into the priests' pockets for a century and more, and once the project got started, a profitable source of income would dry up overnight. As a result, of course, almost nothing had been done. Now the priests were belatedly attempting to scare Alexander into footing the bill himself. The remarkable thing is that he played safe and followed their advice. While the bulk of the army marched into Babylon, Alexander himself pitched camp a safe distance outside.

Philosophical rationalists like Anaxarchus soon talked him into a more sceptical attitude, and he made up his mind to ignore the Chaldeans' warning. Yet even now he still tried (though without success) to find a way into Babylon through the swamps and marshes lying west of the river. Several appalling omens followed his final entry: Alexander's opinion of Greek philosophers dropped to zero. However, he had other distractions. Ambassadors arrived daily, from every corner of the Mediterranean world: some in search of profitable alliances, some defending themselves against accusations, all bearing official tributes and the statutory gold crowns or wreaths. One country which sent no delegation to Babylon was Arabia: ample excuse for a punitive expedition. Even Arrian is prompted to comment that the real motive was simply 'Alexander's insatiable thirst for extending his possessions'. Ships sent out to reconnoitre the Arabian coastline now came back with glowing reports of the country's size and prosperity. Phoenician galleys were dismantled, carried across country on pack-animals, and reassembled on the Euphrates. A vast harbour-basin was dug at Babylon, large enough to accommodate a thousand vessels.

While his naval preparations went forward, Alexander busied himself with the celebration of Hephaestion's funeral. This pious task once discharged, he lost no time in getting outside the city limits once more. Boarding a flotilla of small boats, he and his friends sailed down to inspect the marshy river reaches of the Euphrates, with its canals and dykes and flood-gates. He also wanted to examine the navigational facilities for his Arabian fleet, which included two vast Phoenician quinqueremes.

By entering Babylon and then quickly leaving again before any disaster could befall him, the King felt he had finally disproved the Chaldeans' prophecy. But as the boats pushed their way through those stinking overgrown, malaria-haunted swamps, an incident took place which caused both him and the soothsayers considerable uneasiness. As he sat at the tiller of his boat, a stray gust of wind blew off the sun-hat he was wearing, with its royal blue-and-white ribbon. The ribbon fluttered away, and caught in the reeds

Marsh country by the Euphrates: scene of Alexander's last (and perhaps fatal) boat-trip.

right: The Ishtar Gate at Babylon (reconstruction).

by an ancient royal tomb: all the old kings of Assyria were buried here among the marshes. This was a grim enough portent for anyone. But the sailor who swam across and rescued the ribbon all unwittingly made matters worse by putting it on his own head to avoid getting it wet. Alexander gave him a talent as reward for his kindness, and then a sound flogging for *lèse majesté*. Some accounts say he actually had the wretched man beheaded, 'in obedience to the prophecy which warned him not to leave untouched the head which had worn the diadem'.

When the King returned to Babylon he found Peucestas there, with a force of 20,000 Iranians from Persia. Philoxenus had also arrived, bringing a Carian contingent; so had Menander from Lydia. The Arabian invasion force was beginning to take shape. Alexander now carried his integration policy one step further. He rebrigaded the infantry battalions of the phalanx, using four Macedonians – as section-corporal and file-leaders – to twelve Persians. While he was organising the reallocation of men to their new units, he left his parade-ground dais for a moment, with his aides, to get a drink. During his absence an escaped Babylonian prisoner mounted the dais, donned the King's royal cloak and diadem, and seated himself on the throne. When interrogated under torture as to his motives, he would only say that the god had put the idea into his head. Alexander suspected some kind of nationalist plot; and the incident is so curiously reminiscent of the Rite of the Mock King in the Babylonian *Akitu* (New Year) Festival, due at this time, that he may even have been right.

Our sources are unanimous in reporting a number of such ominous portents shortly before Alexander's death. These are worth more consideration

257

than they normally get. It is most often taken for granted that they were manufactured after the event. But in this case they are just as likely to have been manufactured *before* the event, by those most interested in getting Alexander out of the way. They would certainly suggest that the King's death was due to natural or divine causes, rather than to human agency. The best prophet – to adapt Euripides – is he who knows what will happen in advance.

More embassies now arrived, this time from Greece, and their delegates behaved in Alexander's presence 'as if their coming were a ritual in honour of a god'. With them came Cassander, to negotiate with the King on his father's behalf, and perhaps (if Alexander proved impervious to reason, or showed alarming signs of mental instability) to arrange for his discreet removal. He got off to a bad start by bursting into nervous laughter when he saw a Persian prostrate himself before the royal throne. At this Alexander jumped up in a paroxysm of rage, seized Cassander by the hair with both hands, and beat his head against the wall. Years afterwards, when he was himself King of Macedonia, Cassander still trembled and shuddered uncontrollably at the mere sight of Alexander's portrait; and the hatred engendered during that visit to Babylon lasted until his dying day.

The fleet's training programme was now in full swing, but Alexander, despite the prospect of a new campaign, was sunk deep in *accidie*, and drinking so heavily as to cause his Greek doctor serious concern. He was, he admitted on one occasion, 'at an utter loss to know what he should do during the rest of his life'. On this the Roman emperor Augustus (himself no mean empire-builder) made a comment that many historians have since echoed. He felt astonishment, he said, 'that Alexander did not regard it as a greater task to set in order the empire which he had won than to win it'. But for Alexander conquest and *areté* were all; the dull but essential business of administration held no charms for him. The chaos he had left behind him in the East, even the threat of civil war at home, could not distract him from the lure of Arabia.

But the dream, this time, was to remain unfulfilled. On the evening of 29 May Alexander held a banquet for his admiral Nearchus. The usual deep drinking took place. After dinner the King wanted to go to bed, but his Thessalian friend Medius was giving a late party, and persuaded him to attend it. Here, after further carousing – in commemoration of Heracles' death – the King was given a large cup of unmixed wine, which he drained straight down, and instantly 'shrieked aloud as if smitten by a violent blow'. He was carried back to his quarters and put to bed. Next day he had a high fever. Despite this he got up, bathed, had a siesta, and once more wined and dined with Medius. That night his fever was so intense that he slept in the bathing-house for the sake of coolness.

The following morning, 31 May, he went back to his bedroom, and spent the day playing dice. By the night of 1 June he was in the bathing-house again, and here, on the morning of the 2nd, he discussed the projected Arabian voyage with Nearchus and other senior officers. He was now in constant and increasing fever. By the evening of 3 June it became plain that he was very seriously ill. Nevertheless, he had himself carried out next morning to perform the daily sacrifice, and to hold a briefing for his officers.

A bronze coin of Cassander, minted *c.* 300 BC. The obverse shows Heracles, and the reverse a horseman.

On 5 June he was forced to recognise the gravity of his illness, and ordered all high officials to remain within call of his bedside. By the evening of 6 June he was almost speechless, and gave his ring to Perdiccas, as senior officer, so that routine administration would continue to function smoothly. A rumour spread through the camp that he was already dead. His Macedonian troops crowded round the palace, threatening to break down the doors if they were not let in to see him. Finally a second entrance was knocked in his bedroom wall, and an endless file of veterans passed slowly through to take their leave of him. Sometimes he would painfully raise his head a little: more often he could do no more than move his eyes in token of greeting and recognition.

During the night of 9–10 June a group of his officers kept vigil on his behalf in the nearby temple of 'Sarapis' – probably in fact that of Bel-Marduk. But when they asked the god if it would help Alexander to be moved into the shrine, the oracular response came that it would be better for him if he stayed where he was. At this the King's friends, gathered round his bedside, asked him – it was, after all, a vital question – to whom he bequeathed his kingdom. Weakly Alexander whispered: 'To the strongest'. His last all-too-prophetic words were: 'I foresee a great funeral contest over me.' Early in the morning of 10 June 323 BC, his eyes closed for ever.

There is much circumstantial evidence (and some direct testimony) which suggests that neither Alexander nor Hephaestion died of natural causes. Our ancient sources all record a tradition that Alexander was poisoned: that Aristotle prepared the drug, that Antipater's son Cassander

immediately below: A lion-hunt frieze on the Sidon sarcophagus. King Abdalonymus, who commissioned the sarcophagus, is here shown holding the centre of the stage, with Alexander apparently coming to his aid.

bottom: A battle between Greeks and Persians is represented in this frieze on the Sidon sarcophagus. Hephaestion takes the central role.

brought it to Babylon, and that it was administered to the King, in unmixed wine, by his cupbearer Iolaus – another of Antipater's sons. If on the other hand the King was not poisoned, the chances are that he was suffering from either raging pleurisy or, more probably, malaria (the latter picked up during his boat-trip through the marshes). In either case advanced alcoholism, combined with the terrible wound he sustained in India, had finally lowered even his iron resistance to a point where he could no longer hope to survive.

Few men – and fewer women – lamented Alexander's passing. In Greece and Asia alike he was regarded as a tyrannous aggressor. For 20,000 miles he carried his trail of rapine, slaughter, and subjugation; he imposed his will, but little else. When he moved on, rebellion flared up behind him; and when he died, the empire he had carved out at once split apart into anarchic chaos. The forty years that followed saw an indescribably savage and bloody struggle between his surviving marshals. When Cassander liquidated Roxane and her thirteen-year-old son (310), Alexander's direct line became extinct.

The King may have demanded deification in his own lifetime, but he got mythification after he was dead. While his physical remains, hijacked by Ptolemy to Alexandria, lay on view in a glass coffin, his legend took root and flourished. By the time world-conquest came into fashion again, with Augustus, Alexander was already a giant, a demigod, a superhuman figure of romance. Iskander the Two-Horned was no less strange a mediaeval metamorphosis than Virgil the Magician. Round that elusive and charismatic personality myth still crystallises today: he has even been credited with those lofty if impracticable ideals embodied in the League of Nations.

I have tried, insofar as the evidence would allow it, to strip away the accreted myth, and discover the historical Alexander of flesh and blood – no easy task. His true genius was as a field-commander: perhaps, taken all in all, the most incomparable general the world has ever seen. His business was war and conquest. It is idle to palliate this central truth, to pretend that he dreamed, in some mysterious fashion, of wading through rivers of blood and violence to achieve the Brotherhood of Man. He spent his life, with legendary success, in the pursuit of personal glory; and until very recent times this was regarded as a wholly laudable aim.

'Is it not passing brave to be a king, and ride in triumph through Persepolis?'

A bronze statuette of Alexander from Rheims. This Roman work, probably of the Flavian period (AD 69–96), emphasises the god-like aspect of Alexander. *Far left:* A gold medallion of Alexander, found at Aboukir in Egypt, and probably struck in 242/3 AD to celebrate the 'Olympian' Games held at Beroea. *Immediately below:* A deified head of Alexander wearing the ram's horn and elephant-scalp, on a tetradrachm of Ptolemy I.

Sources of Information

BIBLIOGRAPHY I: ANCIENT EVIDENCE

Key to Abbreviations

AClass: Acta Classica

ANSMusN: American Numismatic Society
Museum Notes

BCH: Bulletin de Correspondance Helléni-
que (Paris, de Boccard)

BMusB: Bulletin of the Museum of Fine Arts
in Boston

BVAB: Bulletin van de Vereeniging tot
Bevordering der Kennis van de Antieke
Beschaving (Leiden, Brill)

CPh: Classical Philology (Chicago, University of Chicago Press)

CQ: Classical Quarterly (Oxford University
Press)

CW: Classical World (Newark, N.J., Rutgers
State University)

DA: Dissertation Abstracts. A Guide to
Dissertations and Monographs available
in Microfilm (Ann Arbor, Michigan)

F and F: Forschungen und Forschritte
(Berlin, Akademie-Verlag)

G and R: Greece and Rome

HSPh: Harvard Studies in Classical Philology
(Cambridge, Mass., Harvard University
Press)

Hermes: Hermes. Zeitschrift für klassische
Philologie (Wiesbaden, Steiner)

Historia: Historia. Revue d'histoire ancienne
(Wiesbaden, Steiner)

JBerlM: Jahrbuch der Berliner Museen

JHS: Journal of Hellenic Studies

JNG: Jahrbuch für Numismatik und Geld-
geschichte (Kallmünz, Lassleben)

Klio: Klio. Beiträge zur alten Geschichte
(Berlin, Akademie-Verlag)

MDAI(A): Mitteilungen des Deutschen
Archaologischen Instituts (Athen. Abt.)

MDAI(R): Mitteilungen des Deutschen
Archaologischen Instituts (Röm. Abt.)

MP: Griffith, *Main Problems* (Heffer)

n.s.: new series

PACA: Proceedings of the African Classical
Association

PCPhS: Proceedings of the Cambridge
Philological Society

Phoenix: The Phoenix. The Journal of the
Classical Association of Canada (University of Toronto Press)

RA: Revue archéologique (Paris, Presses
Universitaires)

RFIC: Rivista di filologia e di Istruzione
Classica (Turin, Loescher-Chiantore)

SE: Studi Etruschi (Florence, Olschki)

TAPhA: Transactions and Proceedings of
the American Philological Association
(Cleveland, Ohio, Press of Case Western
Reserve University)

(a) *Literary*

Since this book is designed for the general reader, I have wherever possible listed the appropriate parallel-translation Loeb edition for each author: it should not be supposed that I invariably regard this as the best edition available, or indeed the best translation. If a better translation is known to me, and easily available, I list it. Minor writers not listed can be found in Jacoby or Robinson (see below s.v. MISCELLANEOUS). L = Loeb.

AELIAN Claudius Aelianus (*c*. AD 170–235). Roman-domiciled epitomist. *Varia Historia*, ed. R.Hercher (Teubner) 1864. No English translation available.

AESCHINES (?390–?330 BC). Athenian orator and politician. *Works* ed. and tr. C.D. Adams. London 1919(L).

ARISTOTLE (384–322 BC). Philosopher and scientist. *Politics* ed. and tr. H.Rackham, London 1932 (L). *Eudemian Ethics* ed. and

tr. E.Rackham, London 1935 (L).

ARRIAN Flavius Arrianus (second century AD). A Greek from Bithynia, who governed Cappadocia under Hadrian, saw military action during the Alan invasion of 134, and studied under Epictetus. His *History of Alexander*, based largely on Ptolemy and Aristobulus, is still the soundest study of Alexander (though by no means so sound as romantic enthusiasts sometimes like to pretend: he is a master of artful omission). *History of Alexander and Indica*, ed. and tr. E.I.Robson (L). 2 vols., London 1929–33 (both text and translation are highly erratic). *Arrian's Life of Alexander the Great*, tr. Aubrey de Selincourt, London (Penguin Classics) 1958 (an excellent version, but at present, most regrettably, out of print).

ATHENAEUS of Naucratis in Egypt (*flor. c.* 200 AD). His one surviving work, *The Deipnosophists*, ed. and tr. C.B.Gulick, 7 vols., London 1927–41 (L), is chiefly

261

valuable for the innumerable fragments it preserves from fifth and fourth century BC authors, playwrights in particular, whose work is otherwise lost. Relevant fragments collected by Jacoby and Robinson (see below s.v. MISCELLANEOUS).

CTESIAS of Cnidos (late fifth century BC). Greek physician at the Achaemenid court in Persia: wrote works on Persia and India. J.Gilmore, *Fragments of the Persika of Ctesias*, London 1888; R.Henry, *Ctesias: La Perse, L'Inde, les Sommaires de Photius*, Brussels, Office de Publicité S.C. 1947.

DIOGENES LAERTIUS (? early third century AD). Biographical epitomist. *Lives of Eminent Philosophers*, ed. and tr. R.D.Hicks, London 1925 (L).

DEMADES, DEINARCHUS, HYPERIDES, LYCURGUS Statesmen and orators in Athens in the time of Philip and Alexander. Their surviving speeches and fragments are collected in *Minor Attic Orators*, Vol. II, ed. and tr. J.O.Burtt, London 1954 (L).

DEMOSTHENES (384–322 BC) of Paeania in Attica, Athenian orator and politician. *Olynthiacs, Philippics, &c.* ed. and tr. J.H. Vince, London 1930. *De Corona* and *De Falsa Legatione*, ed. and tr. C.A. and J.H. Vince, London 1926 (L).

DIODORUS SICULUS (first century BC) a Sicilian from Agyrium, who wrote a *Universal History*, much of it preserved, in forty books. This is the earliest connected account of Alexander's reign which we possess: Diodorus devotes the whole of Book XVII to the period 336–323. The sources he uses are still a matter of fierce scholarly debate; despite his chronological confusion and scissors-and-paste methods he often presents extremely valuable material. Books XVII and XVIII form Vols. VIII and IX of the Loeb edition, edited respectively by C.B.Welles (Vol. VIII, 1963: a brilliant piece of scholarship) and R.M.Geer (Vol. IX, 1947).

HERODOTUS (*c.* 490–*c.* 430 BC) of Halicarnassus. *The Histories*, ed. and tr. A.D.Godley, 4 vols., London 1920–25 (L); tr. A.de Selincourt, London (Penguin Classics) 1954.

HESYCHIUS (? fifth century AD) of Alexandria, lexicographer. Ed. M.Schmidt, Jena 1858–68. Kurt Latte's superb new edition (Hauniae, Munksgaard: Vol. I, 1953: Vol. II, 1966) had reached the letter O at the time of his death.

ISOCRATES (436–338 BC): Athenian pamphleteer, rhetorician and orator. *Works* ed. and tr. G.Norlin and LaRue Van Hook. London 1928–45 (L).

JULIUS VALERIUS (? third–fourth century AD). Wrote a Latin version of the Alexander-Romance by Pseudo-Callisthenes. Ed. B.Kuebler, Leipzig 1888. No English translation available.

JUSTIN (? third century AD). Marcus Junianus Justinus, epitomiser; made a digest of Trogus Pompeius' *Historiae Philippicae*, written during the reign of Augustus. *Abrégé des Histoires Philippiques de Trogue Pompée*, ed. and tr. E. and L.T.Chambry, 2 vols., Paris 1936. No English translation available.

MISCELLANEOUS W.W.Boer (ed.), *Epistola Alexandri ad Aristotelem*, The Hague, 1953. F.Jacoby (ed.), *Die Fragmente der grieschischen Historiker* (FGrHist) Pt. II (Zeitgeschichte) B, pp. 618–828 (Alexandergeschichte) with Commentary (pp. 403–502, Nos. 117–53), Berlin 1929. C.A.Robinson (ed.), *The History of Alexander the Great* Vol. I (Brown University Studies XVI) Providence R.I. (1953) translates all the fragments in Jacoby, including those of Callisthenes, Nearchus, Chares of Mytilene, Ptolemy, Cleitarchus, and others).

PAUSANIAS (second century AD). Travel-writer and geographer, best known for his *Description of Greece*: tr. and ed. W.H.S. Jones, H.A.Ormerod, R.E.Wycherley, 5 vols., London 1918–35 (L).

PLINY Gaius Plinius Secundus (23/4–79 AD), military officer and polymath, whose scientific curiosity led to his death during the eruption of Vesuvius which destroyed Pompeii. *Natural History*, ed. and tr. H. Rackham, W.H.S.Jones, 10 vols., London 1938–62 (L).

PLUTARCH of Chaeronea (*c.* 46–120 AD). Biographer, dilettante scholar, Delphic priest; procurator of Achaea under Hadrian. His *Life* of Alexander is based on a number of authors now known only from fragments, including Callisthenes, Aristobulus, Chares and Onesicritus: tr. and ed. B.Perrin, *Plutarch's Lives* Vol. VII, London 1919 (L). See also his *Lives* of Demosthenes (*ibid.*) and Phocion and Eumenes (Vol. VIII). Plutarch wrote two early essays on Alexander, *On the Fortune or the Virtue of Alexander, Moral.* 326D–345B (Loeb *Moralia* Vol. IV, tr. and ed. F.C. Babbitt, London 1936), and there are numerous other references scattered through the *Moralia* (see especially 179D–181F, 219E, 221A9, 522A, 557B, 781A–B, 804B, 970D, 1043D). For a first-class discussion and commentary see now J.R. Hamilton's edition of the Alexander *Life* (Oxford 1968).

POLYAENUS (*Flor. c.* 150 AD). A Macedonian rhetorician and excerptor, now remembered only for his volume of tactical anecdotes, *Strategemeta* (ed. J. Melber, Leipzig 1887). There is no English translation available.

POLYBIUS (?203–?120 BC). Greek statesman and historian; later moved to Rome under the patronage of the Scipionic Circle. His main value for this period is his detailed criticism (20.17–22) of Callisthenes as a military historian, especially as regards Issus. *The Histories*, ed. and tr. W.R. Paton, London 1925 (L).

PSEUDO-CALLISTHENES Name given to the unknown author of the so-called 'Alexander-Romance', extant in many versions (including three Greek ones) of which the earliest is perhaps late second century AD, though probably based on a romance in circulation not long after Alexander's death. Text: W. Kroll, *Historia Alexandri Magni*, second edition, Berlin 1958; tr. E.H. Haight, *The Life of Alexander of Macedon*, New York 1955. See also P.H. Thomas, *Incerti Auctoris Epitoma rerum gestarum Alexandri Magni cum libro de morte testamentoque Alexandri*, Leipzig (Teubner) 1960.

QUINTUS CURTIUS (? first century AD). His *History of Alexander* (ed. and tr. J.C. Rolfe, 2 vols., London 1946, (L)) lacks Books I and II, and has gaps between Books V and VI and in Book X. As a source Curtius' stock has risen somewhat in the last few years: he is frequently uncritical and given to overblown rhetoric, but careful analysis reveals highly valuable material.

STRABO (64/3 BC–AD 21+). A Greek from Amaseia in Pontus, who spent long periods of his life at Rome and in Egypt. His *Geography*, ed. and tr. H.L. Jones, 8 vols., London 1917–32 (L), is a vast storehouse of useful facts and anecdotes, historical as well as geographical, concerning every area through which Alexander passed.

SUIDAS Not a personal name, but the title of a lexicon ('The Suda' = 'Fortress' or 'Stronghold') compiled in its present form about the tenth century AD, and mostly based on other digests and epitomes. Yet much material in it derives, ultimately, from first-class sources now lost.

VALERIUS MAXIMUS (first century AD). Rhetorician and excerptor: his *Factorum ac dictorum memorabilium libri IX* (ed. C. Kempf, Leipzig, Teubner, 1888) was dedicated to Tiberius, and though entirely uncritical, contains one or two illuminating anecdotes.

(b) *Epigraphic*

Inscriptions from Philip's and Alexander's reign of historical significance are collected, with a full commentary, by M.N. Tod in *Greek Historical Inscriptions*: Vol. II, From 403 to 323 BC, Oxford 1948.

(c) *Numismatic*

AULOCK, H. von: 'Die Prägung des Balakros in Kilikien', JNG 14 (1964) 79–82.

BABELON, J. Le Portrait dans l'antiquité d'après les monnaies. Paris 1942.

BELLINGER, A.R. Essays on the Coinage of Alexander the Great (Numismatic Studies 11) New York 1963.

HILL, G.F. 'Alexander the Great and the Persian lion-gryphon', JHS 43 (1923) 156–161.

KLEINER, G. Alexanders Reichsmünzen (Abhandlungen der deutschen Akademie der Wissenschaften zu Berlin, Klasse für Sprachen, Literatur und Kunst, Akademie-Verlag No. 5) Berlin, 1949.

KRAAY, C.M. *Greek Coins*, London 1967.

NEWELL, E.T. *The dated Alexander coinage of Sidon and Ake*, Oxford University Press 1916. *Myriandros kat' Isson*, New York 1920. *Tarsos under Alexander*, New York 1919.

NOE, S.P. 'The Corinth Hoard of 1938', ANSMusN 10 (1962) 9–41.

SELTMAN, C. *Greek Coins*, second edition, London 1955.

(d) *Iconographic and miscellaneous*

ANDREAE, B. *Das Alexandermosaik* (*Opus nobile* XIV). Bremen 1959.

BANDINELLI, G. 'Cassandro di Macedonia nella Vita plutarchea di Alessandro Magno', RFIC 93 (1965) 150–64. 'Un ignorato gruppo statuario di Alessandro e Bucefalo', SE 18 (1944) 29–43, with plates V–VII.

BERNOULLI, J.J. *Die erhaltenen Darstellungen Alexanders des Grossen; Ein Nachtrag zur griechischen Ikonographie*. Munich 1905.

BIEBER, M. *Alexander the Great in Greek and Roman Art*. Chicago 1964.

BIJVANCK, A.W. 'La bataille d'Alexandre', BVAB 30 (1955) 28–34.

DAUX, G. 'Chroniques des Fouilles en 1961', BCH 86 (1962) 805–13. 'Chroniques des Fouilles en 1957', BCH 82 (1958) 761–5 with figs, 14–16.

DELLA CORTE, M. 'L'educazione di Alessandro Magno nell'enciclopedia Aristotelica in un trittico megalografico di Pompei del II stile', MDAI(R) 57 (1942) 31–77.

DEL MEDICO, H.E. 'A propos du trésor de Panaguriste: un portrait d'Alexandre par Lysippe', Persica 3 (1967/8) 37–67, plates ii–iv, figs. 8–15.

GEBAUER, K. Alexanderbildnis und Alexandertypus. MDAI(R) (1938/9) 1–106.

JOHNSON, F.P. *Lysippos*. Durham, N. Carolina. 1927.

JONGKEES, J.H. 'A portrait of Alexander the Great', BVAB 29 (1954) 32–3.

LUNSINGH-SCHEURLEER, R.A. 'Alexander in faience', *ibid.* 40 (1965) 80–3.

MINGAZZINI, P. 'Una copia dell'Alex. Keraunophoros di Apelle', JBerlM 3 (1961) 7–17.

NEWELL, E.T. *Royal Greek Portrait Coins*, New York 1937.

PFISTER, F. 'Alexander der Grosse in der bildenden Kunst', F. und F. 35 (1961) 330–4, 375–9.

PICARD, C. 'Le mosaïste grec Gnôsis et les nouvelles chasses de Pella', RA 1 (1963) 205–9.

RICHTER, G.M.A. *The Portraits of the Greeks*. 3 vols., London, Phaidon 1965.

ROBERTSON, M. 'The Boscoreale figure-paintings', JHS 45 (1955) 58–67, plates XI–XIII.

RUMPF, A. 'Zum Alexander-Mosaik', MDAI(A) 77 (1962) 229–41.

SCHREIBER, T. *Studien über das Bildniss Alexanders des Grossen*. Leipzig 1903.

SJÖQVIST, E. 'Alexander-Heracles. A preliminary note', BMusB (Boston) 51 (1953) 30–3, figs. 1–5.

SUHR, E.G. *Sculptured Portraits of Greek Statesmen, with a special study of Alexander the Great*. Baltimore 1931.

UJFALVÝ, C.de *Le Type Physique d'Alexandre le Grand*. Paris 1902.

BIBLIOGRAPHY II: MODERN STUDIES

This bibliography does not claim to be exhaustive (the literature on Alexander is so vast that to list it all would fill a fair-sized volume); nor does it represent all I have read in the field. I only include here items I have found of special use or interest – often through differing radically from the views which they express. Even in the world of scholarship Alexander still has a striking tendency to raise the emotional temperature of discussion. The problems he poses are perennial and fundamental; that is why no interpretation of his life, aims, and achievements can ever claim definitive status. The enigma remains.

ANDREOTTI, R. 'Per un critica dell'ideologia di Alessandro Magno', Historia 5 (1956) 257–302.

ATKINSON, J.E. 'Primary Sources and the Alexanderreich', AClass (Cape Town, Balkema) 6 (1963) 125–37.

BADIAN, E. 'Agis III', Hermes 95 (1967) 170–92.
'The Administration of the Empire', G&R 12 (1965) 166–82.
'Alexander the Great and the Creation of an Empire', History Today 8 (1958) 369–76, 494–502.
'Alexander the Great and the Greeks of Asia', *Ancient Societies and Institutions: Studies presented to Victor Ehrenberg on his 75th birthday* (Oxford, Basil Blackwell 1966) 37–69.
'Alexander the Great and the Loneliness of Power', Journal of the Australian Universities Language Association 17 (1962) 80–91. Reprinted in *Studies in Greek and Roman History* (Oxford 1964) 192–205.
'Alexander the Great and the Unity of Mankind', Historia 7 (1958) 425–44. Reprinted in Griffith (MP) q.v., pp. 287–306.
'Ancient Alexandria', *Studies in Greek and Roman History*. pp. 179–91.
'The death of Parmenio', TAPhA 91 (1960) 324–38.
'The death of Philip II', Phoenix 17 (1963) 244–50.
'The first flight of Harpalus', Historia 9 (1960) 245–6.
'Harpalus', JHS 81 (1961) 16–43.
'A King's Notebooks', HSPh 72 (1967) 183–204.
'Orientals in Alexander's army', JHS 85 (1965) 160–1.

BALSDON, J.P.V.D. 'The "Divinity" of Alexander the Great', Historia 1 (1950) 383–8.

BERVE, H. *Das Alexanderreich auf prosopographischer Grundlage*. 2 vols., Munich 1926.

BRUNT, P.A. 'The Aims of Alexander', G and R 12 (1965) 205–15.
'Alexander's Macedonian Cavalry', JHS 83 (1963) 27–46.
'Persian accounts of Alexander's campaigns', CQ 12 (1962) 141–55.

BURN, A.R. *Alexander the Great and the Hellenistic World*, second revised edition. New York 1962.
'The generalship of Alexander', G and R 12 (1965) 140–54.
'Notes on Alexander's campaigns, 332–330 B.C.', JHS 72 (1952) 81–91.

CLOCHÉ, P. *Alexandre le Grand*. Neuchatel, 1953.

Histoire de la Macédoine jusqu'à l'avènement d'Alexandre le Grand (336 av. J.-C.). Paris 1960.

Un fondateur d'empire: Philippe II, Roi de Macédoine (383/2–336/5 avant J.-C.), St-Etienne, 1955.

CULICAN, W. *The Medes and Persians.* London, Thames and Hudson 1965.

DROYSEN, J.G. *Geschichte Alexanders des Grossen.* 1833. Rev. ed. (H.Berve) 1931.

EDDY, S.K. *The King is Dead. Studies in the Near Eastern resistance to Hellenism, 334–331 B.C.* Lincoln University, Nebraska 1961.

EHRENBERG, V. *Alexander and the Greeks.* Tr. R. Fraenkel van Velsen. Oxford 1938. Ch. II, 'Pothos', reprinted in MP pp. 73–83.
Alexander und Aegypten. Leipzig 1926.

FREDERICKSMEYER, E.A. 'Alexander, Midas, and the oracle at Gordium', CPh 56 (1961) 160–8.
'The Religion of Alexander the Great. Dissertation of the University of Wisconsin 1958.' Résumé DA 19 (1959) 1747.

FULLER, J.F.C. *The Generalship of Alexander the Great.* London, Eyre and Spottiswoode 1958.

GHIRSHMAN, R. *Perse: Proto-iraniens, Mèdes, Achéménides.* Paris, Gallimard 1963. (Tr. S.Gilbert and J.Emmons, London 1964).

GRIFFITH, G.T. 'Alexander and Antipater in 323 B.C.', PACA 8 (1965) 12–17.
'Alexander's generalship at Gaugamela', JHS 67 (1947) 77–89.
'Alexander the Great and an Experiment in Government', PCPhS 10 (1964) 23–39.
'The Macedonian Background', G and R 12 (1965) 125–39.
'*Makedonika.* Notes on the Macedonians of Philip and Alexander', PCPhS n.s. 4 (1956/7) 3–10.
The mercenaries of the Hellenistic World. Cambridge 1935.
'A Note on the Hipparchies of Alexander', JHS 83 (1963) 68–74.
(Ed.) *Alexander the Great: the Main Problems.* Cambridge 1966.
'The Letter of Darius at Arrian 2.14', PCPhS 194 (n.s. 14) (1968) 33–48.

HAMILTON, J.R. 'Alexander's early life', G and R 12 (1965) 117–24.
'Alexander and his so-called father', CQ n.s. 3 (1953) 151–7. Reprinted in MP pp. 235–42.
'The cavalry battle at the Hydaspes', JHS 76 (1956) 26–31.
Plutarch: Alexander. A Commentary. Oxford, Clarendon Press 1968.
'Cleitarchus and Aristobulus', Historia 10 (1961) 448–58.
'Three passages in Arrian', CQ n.s. 5 (1955) 217–21.

HAMMOND, N.G.L. 'The Two Battles of Chaeronea (338 B.C. and 86 B.C.)' Klio 31 (1938) 186–218.

JONES, T.B. 'Alexander and the Winter of 330–329 B.C.', CW 28 (1935) 124–5.

MARSDEN, E.W. *The Campaign of Gaugamela.* Liverpool University Press 1964.

MERLAN, P. 'Isocrates, Aristotle, and Alexander the Great', Historia 3 (1954) 60–81.

MILNS, R.D. 'Alexander's pursuit of Darius through Iran', Historia 15 (1966) 256.
'Philip II and the Hypaspists', Historia 16 (1967) 509–12.
Alexander the Great. London, Robert Hale 1968.

MOMIGLIANO, A. *Filippo il Macedone.* Florence 1934.

NARAIN, A.K. 'Alexander and India', G and R 12 (1965) 155–65.

OLMSTEAD, A.T. *A History of the Persian Empire.* Chicago 1948.

PEARSON, L. 'The Diaries and Letters of Alexander the Great', Historia 3 (1955) 429–55. Reprinted in MP pp. 1–28.
The Lost Histories of Alexander the Great (Philological Monographs 20). New York 1960.

ROBINSON, C.A. *The Ephemerides of Alexander's Expedition.* Providence (Brown University) 1932.

SAMUEL, A.E. 'Alexander's Royal Journals', Historia 14 (1965) 1–12.

SCHACHERMEYR, F. *Alexander der Grosse: Ingenium und Macht.* Vienna 1949.

SCHMIDT, E.F. *Persepolis.* 2 vols. Chicago 1953, 1957.

STEIN, A. *On Alexander's Track to the Indus.* London 1929.

STRASBURGER, H. 'Alexanders Zug durch die gedrosische Wüste', Hermes 80 (1952) 456–93.

TARN, W.W. *Alexander the Great.* 2 vols, Cambridge University Press 1948.

TODD, R. 'W.W.Tarn and the Alexander Ideal', *The Historian* 27 (1964) 48–55.

WELLES, C.B. 'Alexander's historical accomplishment', G and R 12 (1965) 216–28.
'The discovery of Sarapis and the foundation of Alexandria', Historia 11 (1962) 271–98.

WILCKEN, U. *Alexander the Great.* Tr. G.C. Richards. New edition with introduction, notes and bibliography by E.N.Borza, New York, W.W.Norton & Co. Inc. 1967.

WOODCOCK, G. *The Greeks in India.* London, Faber and Faber 1966.

WUEST, F.R. *Philipp II von Makedonien und Griechland in den Jahren von 346 bis 338.* Munich 1938.

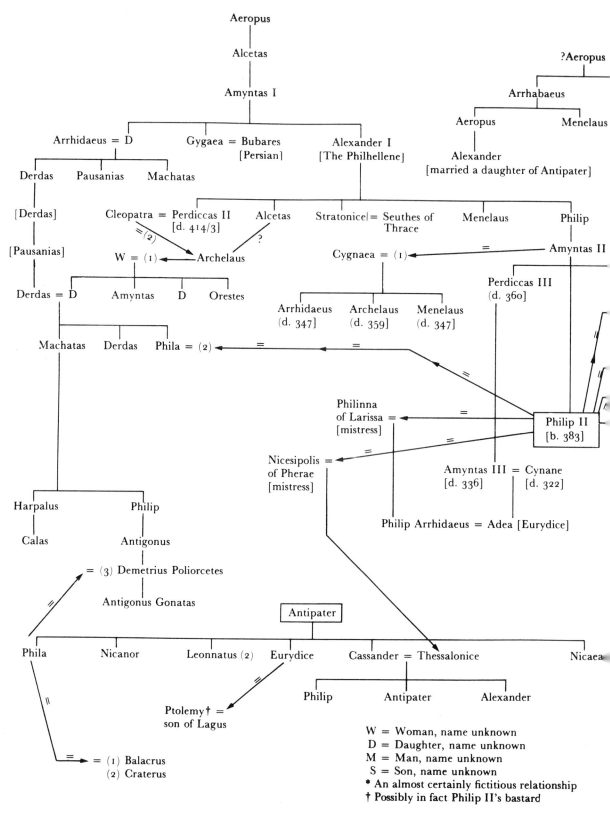

Aeropus

Alcetas

Amyntas I

?Aeropus

Arrhabaeus

Aeropus   Menelaus

Arrhidaeus = D   Gygaea = Bubares   Alexander I
[Persian]   [The Philhellene]

Alexander
[married a daughter of Antipater]

Derdas   Pausanias   Machatas

[Derdas]   Cleopatra = Perdiccas II   Alcetas   Stratonice = Seuthes of   Menelaus   Philip
[d. 414/3]   Thrace

[Pausanias]   = (2)   Cygnaea = (1)   =   Amyntas II
              W = (1) ← Archelaus   ?

Derdas = D   Amyntas   D   Orestes   Arrhidaeus   Archelaus   Menelaus   Perdiccas III
                                          (d. 347]   (d. 359]   (d. 347]   (d. 360]

Machatas   Derdas   Phila = (2) ←   =   ←   =

Harpalus   Philip   Philinna
                              of Larissa =   =   Philip II
Calas   Antigonus   [mistress]   [b. 383]

= (3) Demetrius Poliorcetes   Nicesipolis =   =
                              of Pherae   Amyntas III = Cynane
Antigonus Gonatas   [mistress]   [d. 336]   [d. 322]

                              Antipater   Philip Arrhidaeus = Adea [Eurydice]

Phila   Nicanor   Leonnatus (2) Eurydice   Cassander = Thessalonice   Nicaea

                              Philip   Antipater   Alexander
Ptolemy† =
son of Lagus

= (1) Balacrus   W = Woman, name unknown
(2) Craterus   D = Daughter, name unknown
                    M = Man, name unknown
                    S = Son, name unknown
                    * An almost certainly fictitious relationship
                    † Possibly in fact Philip II's bastard

266

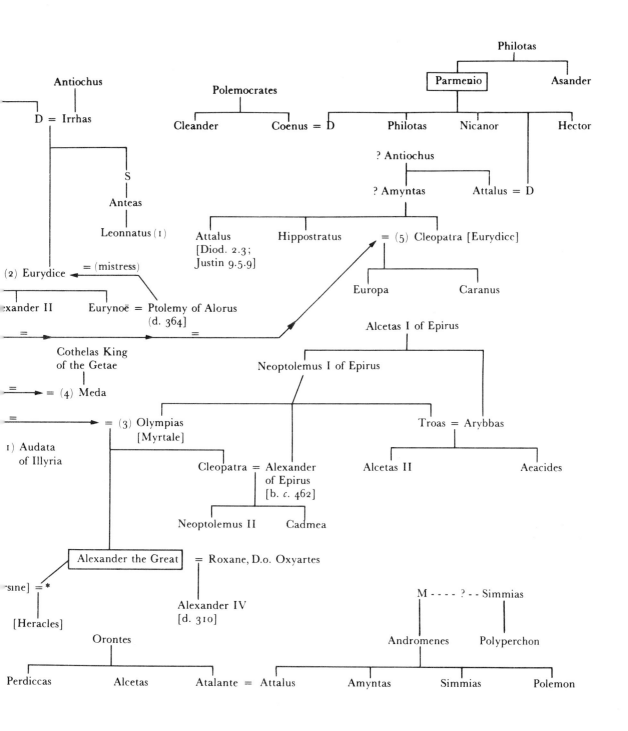

THE ARGEAD ROYAL HOUSE OF MACEDONIA
AND RELATED FAMILIES, FIFTH TO
FOURTH CENTURIES BC

Index

Audata, 28
Augustus (Emperor), 54, 258, 260
Autaratians, 77, 78
Autophradates, 117–18
Axius (Vardar), R., 20
Azimilk, King, 142

Babylon, Babylonians, 118, 121, 131, 153,
    154, 162–9, 170, 173, 182, 225, 238, 242,
    251, 254, 255, 256, 257, 260
Bactria, Bactrians, 97, 115, 156, 159, 161,
    169, 181, 182–3, 186, 191, 195, 196, 197,
    199, 201, 204, 214, 244
Bagoas (1), 54, 65
Bagoas (2), 185
Bardylis, King of Illyria, 26, 28
Beas (Hyphasis) R., 221, 225, 244
Bel-Marduk, 162, 255, 259
Bessus, 159–60, 161, 182–3, 184–5, 186,
    191, 195, 196, 204
Black Sea, 45, 76
Boeotia, 49, 50, 52, 82
Bokhara, 187, 196
Bosporus, 45
Brahmins, 219, 229, 231
Bucephalas, 32, 35–7, 40, 214, 219, 220
Byblos, 134, 138, 144
Byzantium, 45, 47, 49, 76

Callisthenes, 91, 114, 152, 169, 203, 251
Cambyses, 143, 144
Cappadocia, 117, 118
Caranus, 66, 71, 82
Caria, 25, 104, 225, 228, 257
Carmania, 231, 238
Carthage, Carthaginians, 135–6, 140, 142,
    239
Cassander, 2, 252, 258, 260
Caspian, 181–3, 185, 255
Castabala, 122
Celaenae, 104, 115, 134
Cephisus, R., 49
Chaeronea, 49–51, 52, 53, 56, 62
Chaldaeans, 255–6
Chandragupta, 208, 232
Charidemus, 85, 118
Chenab, R. 220, 221, 225, 228, 229, 231
Chios, 64, 152, 227
Cilicia, Cilician Gates, 111, 114, 118, 120,
    121, 122, 133, 134, 143, 255
Cleander, 111, 182, 188, 238
Cleitus (the Black), 34, 98, 188, 198–9, 222
Cleitus (the White), 214
Cleitus (s.o. Bardylis, q.v.), 77–8, 81
Cleopatra (niece of Attalus), 56, 61–2, 63,
    64, 68, 71, 82
Cleopatra (d.o. Philip II), 65
Climax, Mt., 114
Coenus, 111, 182, 196, 197, 200, 208, 214,
    215, 222, 228
Companion Cavalry, 78, 98, 159–60, 187,
    188, 196, 199, 202, 213, 228, 237, 239,
    242, 250, 254

Corinth, Corinthians, 36, 55, 56, 63, 74–5
Cossaeans, 255
Craterus, 20, 172, 186, 187, 196, 197, 205,
    213, 214, 221, 225, 228, 231, 237, 239,
    251, 253
Crenides, 29, 40
Crete, 152–3, 228, 254–5
Cunaxa, 153–4
Curtius, Q., 187, 198, 205
Cydnus, R., 121
Cyme (Aeolis), 72
Cynane, 28, 71
Cyprus, 138–9, 142, 153, 225, 227, 239
Cyropolis, 196
Cyrus (the Great), 170, 173, 195, 234
Cyrus (the Younger), 153–4

Dahae, 195, 200
Damascus, 30, 134
Danube, R., 76, 77, 170, 192
Dardanelles (Hellespont), 45, 49, 64, 65,
    86, 91, 92, 94, 109, 116, 133, 152
Darius I (The Great), 55, 203, 221, 239
Darius III (Codomannus), 15, 64, 65, 81, 91,
    99, 101, 109, 114, 116, 117–18, 121, 122,
    123–9, 131–3, 134–5, 140, 142–3, 144,
    152, 153, 154, 155–61, 162, 171, 173–4,
    182–4, 185, 186, 195, 199, 221, 225, 242,
    244
Dascylium, 94
Datames, 118
Delphi, 50, 53, 55, 56, 64, 75, 150
Demades, 85, 253
Demaratus of Corinth, 36–7, 98, 171
Demetrius (Bodyguard), 213
Demosthenes (orator), 32, 45, 47, 49, 72,
    74, 81, 85, 252–3, 255
Didyma, 151, 152
Diodorus Siculus, 54, 82, 96, 98, 231
Diogenes (the Cynic), 75, 232
Dionysus, 13, 28, 205, 253
Dium, 32, 35, 99
Drangiana (Seistan), 184
Drapsaca, 191

Ecbatana, 161, 171, 174, 181, 182, 187,
    195, 238, 253, 254, 255
Egypt, Egyptians, 32, 134, 144, 149, 152,
    219, 220, 221, 225, 232, 233
Elaeum, 92
Elatea, 49
Elimiotis, 20, 28
Elis, 115
Epaminondas, 23–4, 25, 26
Ephesus, 64, 65, 99, 101, 102, 103, 104, 151
Ephialtes, 110–11
Epirus, 20, 28, 64, 65–6
Erythrae, 64
Esagila, 162, 166, 255
Eumenes (of Cardia), 90, 254
Euphrates, R., 131, 153, 154, 155, 159,
    165, 231, 234, 239, 256–7
Euripides, 199, 258

Eurydice, 23, 53

Gaugamela (Tell Gomel), 2, 26, 124, 154, 155–61, 162, 171, 187, 219
Gaza, 35, 143, 144, 173
Gedrosia, 234–7, 239, 244
Getae, 77
Glaucias, 77–8, 81
Glycera, 226–7
Gordium, 104, 111, 115, 116, 117, 134, 150
Granicus (R., and battle), 2, 26, 32, 34, 94–9, 101, 104, 116, 124, 152, 156, 198
Guards Brigade (Hypaspists), 51, 77, 89, 182, 196, 202, 214, 215, 219, 228, 250
Gymnosophistae, 219, 232

Haemus R., 51
Haliacmon (Vistritza) R., 20
Halicarnassus (Bodrum), 25, 104, 109–11, 116
Halys, R., 133, 142
Haranpur, 208, 213, 214
Harpalus, 121, 169, 182, 225, 226–7, 228, 237, 238, 244, 252–3, 254–5
Hecataeus, 72, 74
Hecatompylus, 182, 185
Hegelochus, 116
Hellenic League, 55–6, 63, 73, 74–5, 82, 84, 85, 89, 99, 104, 109, 114, 159, 181, 244
Hephaestion, 186, 188, 196, 203, 204, 205, 206, 207, 214, 228, 231, 232, 239, 249, 253–4, 255, 256, 259
Heracles, 20, 21, 23, 34, 37, 80, 92, 135, 140, 144, 156, 159, 198, 206, 225, 251, 258
Hermeias, 38
Hermus, R., 115
Herodotus, 203, 221
Hindu Kush, 159, 187, 191, 192, 203, 204, 231, 238
Homer, 40, 98, 149
Hyrcania, 181, 184, 185, 255

Ilium, 92, 94, 96, 229
Illyria, Illyrians, 19, 21, 23, 26, 28, 32, 50, 64, 66, 76, 77–8, 81
India, Indians, 77, 122, 201, 203–4, 220, 221, 225, 226, 228–31, 234, 237, 239
Indus, R., 203, 204, 205, 207, 208, 231
Ionia, 64, 94, 101, 115, 138
Iphicrates, 23
Isocrates, 37, 47, 133
Issus, 2, 26, 122, 123–9, 133, 134, 144, 156, 160

Jalalpur, 213, 228
Jaxartes, R., 195, 196
Jhelum (Hydaspes), R., 204, 207, 208, 213–19, 220, 222, 225, 228

Kabul, 191, 195, 204

Kandahar, 191, 192
Kashmir, 208, 225, 231
Khawak Pass, 191
Khyber Pass, 204, 205
Kushan Pass, 204

Lade, 104
Lamia, 82
Lampsacus, 94
Langarus, 77, 78
Lanice, 34
Leonidas (Alexander's tutor), 35, 38
Leonnatus (Bodyguard), 68, 199, 229, 234, 237
Leosthenes, 244
Lycia, 111, 114, 117, 138, 196
Lycurgus, 55, 85
Lydia, 94, 101, 143, 196, 257
Lyginus, R., 77
Lyncestis, 20, 22, 23, 25, 26, 251
Lysimachus (Bodyguard), 75, 199
Lysippus (artist), 26, 32, 80, 175

Maeander, R., 104, 115
Magi, 173
Malli, 228, 230
Maracanda (Samarkand), 34, 195–6, 197
Marathus, 133
Margiane, 196, 201
Margus (Murghab) R., 186, 191
Marsyas, R., 115
Massaga, 205
Massagetae, 195, 196–7, 200
Mausolus (of Caria), 25, 109, 111
Mazaces, 144
Mazaeus, 153, 154, 155, 159–60, 162–5, 166, 169, 182
Medes, Media, 97, 176, 195, 198, 242
Medius, 258
Melkart, 135–6, 142
Memnon of Rhodes, 32, 94, 97, 98, 99, 101, 109, 110–11, 116, 117, 118, 133, 196
Memphis, 144, 151
Menander, 257
Menapis, 32
Mercenaries, 32, 49, 50–1, 64, 99, 104, 110–11, 116, 121, 129, 131, 152, 161, 182–3, 232, 238, 243
Methone, 32, 36, 72
Midas, 116; Gardens of, 20, 38, 45
Mieza, 39
Milesians, Miletus, 101, 103, 104, 109, 151
Mithridates, 98
Mithrines, 101
Molossians, 20, 28
Myriandrus, 122
Mysia, 101
Mytilene, 38, 117

Nabarzanes, 129, 182–3, 184, 185
Naucratis, 149
Naupactus, 49